DESTINY'S SPEAR

FROM HITLER'S OBSESSION TO PATTON'S POSSESSION

RODNEY E WALKER

Copyright © 2022 Rodney E Walker.

All rights reserved. No part of this book may be reproduced, stored, or transmitted by any means—whether auditory, graphic, mechanical, or electronic—without written permission of both publisher and author, except in the case of brief excerpts used in critical articles and reviews. Unauthorized reproduction of any part of this work is illegal and is punishable by law.

ISBN: 979-8-88640-133-2 (sc)
ISBN: 979-8-88640-134-9 (hc)
ISBN: 979-8-88640-135-6 (e)

Because of the dynamic nature of the Internet, any web addresses or links contained in this book may have changed since publication and may no longer be valid. The views expressed in this work are solely those of the author and do not necessarily reflect the views of the publisher, and the publisher hereby disclaims any responsibility for them.

One Galleria Blvd., Suite 1900, Metairie, LA 70001
1-888-421-2397

CONTENTS

Dedication vii
Introduction ix

1. Destiny and Defiance (Hitler defines his destiny as a possessor of the Longinus and its historical power) 1
2. Religion and Philosophy (Hitler debates worldview with notable twentieth century Jewish philosopher in his youth) 11
3. What is a Jew? (Hitler takes stand to define his destiny and inquires about differences in races) 19
4. Patton (George Patton reveals his knowledge of the spear and his own metaphysical beliefs) 26
5. Homeless Artis (Hitler is homeless and struggles to become an artist in Vienna) 35
6. Anti-Semitic (Hitler takes note of Jewish community in Austria and has feelings of alienation) 39
7. The Occult (Hitler Joins the Thule Society, whose doctrines teach the supremacy of the Aryan race) 44
8. WWI & Reincarnation (Patton directs battles on the fields of France, feeling that he's been there in another life) 53
9. The Harlem Hellfighters (Segregated African American soldiers are allowed to fight with the French and exceed all expectations) 60
10. Corporal Hitler (Hitler enlists as a corporal in WWI and miraculously evades direct enemy fire using mystical powers) 72
11. Victory for Hellfighters (The Harlem Hellfighters overcome German soldiers and battle racial prejudice in their own camp) 77

12. Wounded in Hospital (Wounded Hellfighters must remain at a French hospital and not integrate with white American wounded) 83
13. Patton and Hitler Get It (Patton and Hitler both get wounded in battle. Patton refl ects on déjà-vu experience, while Hitler becomes bitter over the lack of German nationalism) 89
14. The Longinus (African American Christian Hellfighter soldier at French hospital comes to learn about the Longinus through Nurse Sophia) 98
15. Patton and Marshal Ney (After WWI, Patton returns to base camp to research historic figure, Marshal Ney. He believes himself to have once been Marshal Ney)....................106
16. Postwar Germany (Hitler attends beer hall after the war and rouses citizens to join a Workers' Party, which later becomes the Nazi party)...112
17. Pearl Harbor, Hawaii (Patton is sent on a mission to work with intelligence in Hawaii because of Japanese expansion in Asia) 122
18. The List (Patton creates list of Japanese suspects who might be spies for Japan. One fisherman, Hirata, is a prime suspect, in touch with a Japanese secret sub).................126
19. The Other List (Hitler obtains list of subversives, who burn down the Reichstag building, and seizes the opportunity to become Chancellor of Germany) 137
20. The Hakoah Club (A Jewish Sports Club in Austria becomes subject to controversy as the Austrian Nazi Party prepares for Hitler's annexation of the country).............142
21. The Anchluss (Hitler unites Austria and Germany in a friendly invasion and finally takes possession of the Longinus) ...153

22. The Invasion (Hitler invades most of Europe in recordbreaking speed, and Patton understands that the Longinus has afforded his success)... 157
23. Hirata (Fisherman Hirata is tricked by Japanese navy to reveal secrets of Pearl Harbor, allowing them to plan an attack on Battleship Row) 162
24. Pearl Harbor (Pearl Harbor is attacked, officially ushering the US into world war. Patton is anxious).................. 169
25. Plans of Action (The US armed forces map out battle strategies in every theater. Patton's invasion of North Africa is first—Operation Torch, designed to light the way)... 178
26. Operation Torch (Patton leads first shore invasion of North Africa with intention to invade Casablanca. Hitler's invasion of Russia is unsuccessful. Plots develop to assassinate Hitler on Russian Front) 182
27. Captain Horn (Patton meets a German-born soldier in his army who offers help in locating the Longinus in Germany)... 193
28. Casablanca Spared (Patton is victorious in North Africa without having to invade Casablanca, thanks to the prayers of Sophia, who worked with the Hellfighters in World War I).. 204
29. Patton and Montgomery (Patton and British Field Marshal Montgomery team up to drive Nazi General Rommel out of North Africa)... 210
30. An Inquisition (Captain Horn is commissioned to interrogate military prisoners in North Africa. He is emotionally reunited with old acquaintances)......................... 215
31. The Suspension (Patton and Montgomery are paired up to invade Sicily, but Patton is suspended from duty after slapping an army sergeant) 220

32. Operation Fortitude (While relieved from duty, Patton is advised to lay low to keep the Nazis guessing about him. He is part of an operation designed to confuse the Nazis as to the whereabouts of an anticipated invasion. Though not involved in D-Day, he delivers his famous speech)............226
33. The Crescendo (The Allies invade Normandy, and Rommel is part of another plot to assassinate Hitler)..............234
34. Patton's Return (Patton is returned to duty after D-Day and pushes his troops through southern France in pursuit of Nazi strongholds. Captain Horn is with him to interrogate prisoners and learns more about locating the Longinus)..240
35. The Last Attempt (Hitler is distressed by his war on two fronts and calls Tiger tanks to entrap the 101st division in the Battle of the Bulge. Patton commissions an army chaplain to distribute a Christmas prayer, which becomes a rallying cry to change the direction of the war)...................247
36. In the Fatherland (Patton takes his army to aggressively fight the Nazis on their own soil but has orders not to invade Berlin after comments about invading Moscow too)....254
37. Camps and Castles (Patton and Eisenhower accidentally come across a Nazi death camp while Captain Horn and his task force make their way into Nuremburg in search of the Longinus) 259
38. The Longinus (The Longinus is discovered in an underground chamber, Hitler commits suicide, and the Longinus is sent to Patton on a cargo plane)..........................267
39. Longinus Lost (Patton takes possession of the spear and has it transported to General MacArthur to bring the war to a close in Asia. The transport plane crashes, leaving the Longinus lost in the mountain ranges of North Korea. The spear is picked up by a wandering group of Chinese nationals) 274

DEDICATION

To my dad, Donald Leon Walker. Thank you for being an early inspiration behind my ever-wondering mind. You were only a child during that Great Generation, but I often wondered how the world appeared through your young eyes. You told me stories about your school report on Hitler and how Italian prisoners of war were being held at the local schoolhouse. You told me how you went to the airfield in Sioux City to greet the sailors, soldiers, and airmen as they returned home on leave—and you saluted each respective group by singing their military theme songs as you waved. Thanks, Dad. My own children's history will now be richer. You worked hard and kept us, your children, together. Enjoy your eternal reunion in heaven!

I want to thank my wife for her patience and diligence as a proofreader and for helping to change the course of this story for the better. I would like to thank my children for always being a ready and willing audience.

INTRODUCTION

The single-most defining moment for the birth of a civilized Europe, and indeed the development of the Western Hemisphere, took place on a Roman cross in fulfillment of an ancient prophetic promise. For centuries, Europe's growing pains could not be disassociated with its religious beginnings as the struggle for church expansion straddled a threshold between spiritual empowerment and political power. These two Western agents of expansion, spiritual empowerment and political power, have historically surrounded a controversial item used in the fulfillment of that great prophetic promise. It is the Longinus spear (known as the Spear of Destiny) used in the crucifixion of Jesus Christ.

Destiny's Spear is a true story about the Longinus, Adolf Hitler, and the last twentieth century battleground where world powers rose up against Nazi agents of expansion and conquest. It is a novel chronicling the actual lives of Adolf Hitler and General George Patton as their destinies are changed in pursuit of the Roman spear. Biographical records, personal letters, and historical events are woven together, creating an awesome tapestry of factual events dramatized in fictional dialogue.

Evidence of the historic power behind the Longinus dates back to the great Crusades, as well as the reign of Charlemagne of France, and Attila the Hun. However, now, with the world at war, both Hitler and Patton live out their own mystic convictions about the transmigration of souls and the power behind the Longinus

The story begins with the historic event of Hitler visiting the famous Hofburg museum in Vienna, Austria, where he had epileptical visions of grandeur and power while gazing upon the Longinus. This true life-changing event is paralleled by George Patton's opportunistic push for total victory during World War II when he personally commits himself to shooting Hitler "like a snake" to save Europe from his megalomaniacal plans.

As Hitler learns how to harness powers of darkness by joining a racist cult, his political ambitions draw him closer to a circle of like-minded Germans who support his aberrant worldview of dominance and racial superiority. Without much resistance, he eventually invades Austria, seizes the spear, and effectively ushers in a world war.

General George Patton, a mastermind in strategic tank offensives, loves the history of the Longinus and believes himself to be the reincarnation of Marshal Ney, who saved Europe from Napoleon's wrath by hiding the Longinus from him. However, he learns how the power of prayer is not only effective for battle, but can help blaze a trail of unstoppable victories against the enemy.

Once the spear is captured by Patton's army, Hitler actually commits suicide in accordance with the prophecy that tragedy will befall whosoever loses its possession. Though Supreme Allied Commander Eisenhower orders Patton to return the item to the Austrian museum, Patton has a counterfeit spear fabricated and keeps the original to help General MacArthur bring the war to an end in Asia.

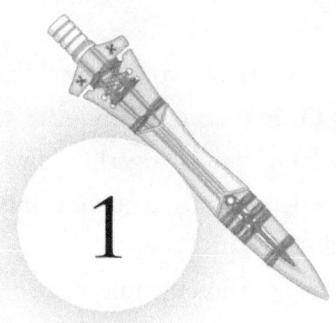

1

DESTINY AND DEFIANCE

It was cold and overcast, and no Austrian was really expecting such weather that day. Austria during this time of year always offered a rude introduction to winter—a foretaste of bitter cold made tolerable only by warm beer and schnitzel. Traffic slowed and people recommenced their routine domestic habits, which kept them cheerfully preoccupied indoors.

It was 1898, and Austria was still reeling from the economic boom of the *Grunderzeit* era, a time of heightened industrialization that socialites had taken advantage of by making modest private investments. Only envious neighbors, such as Hungary and Germany, held reservations against Austria's good fortune. From their perspective, it created a slight imbalance of political power in their common region.

Hungary was Austria's eastern neighbor, and both countries struggled to maintain a united foreign policy. Though the threat of a spreading Ottoman Empire from Turkey strengthened their bonds, the two regions were becoming very different internally. Austria and its western neighbor, Germany, shared a similar heritage, but they had their differences as well.

German visitors who crossed into Austria during this time were delighted with its culture and new flamboyancy. They marveled at both the architecture and the majestic Alps. When mingling with the

Austrians, many Germans would say, "I'm mostly German, but my grandfather was a true Austrian," and then they would cock their heads back, clap their large hands together, and release a forceful, throaty laugh, which, ironically, only true Germans did, to the annoyance of the more refined Austrians.

Now only the occasional mule-drawn carts could be seen at the main boulevards, though some would brave the capricious climate of this season for a profit. Vendors with fresh produce and homemade canned fruits sometimes waited until the last day of fall to sell their stashed-away treasures for a higher price just before the cold season. On a moderately cold day, one could smell the baked dough of fresh pretzels wafting around the center of town.

Schools started arranging winter events in the community. There was the Oktoberfest, which afforded both the Austrian poor and the bourgeois an opportunity to fraternize and forget their prejudices and class-consciousness. They would pretend not to notice any local accents as they sang the *"Ja Ja"* song, arms interlocked, beer mugs raised.

They played several different types of beer games to induce inebriation. There were pouring games, which penalized maladroit contenders who spilled—their penalty was to engulf half a mug of frothy black ale on demand, and then try again. Then there were drinking games. Those who could skillfully roll a Corona coin from off the tip of their nose and direct its bounce from the table into a beer mug won whole pitchers of homemade distilled barley. Successful contenders could do anything they wanted with it, including dumping it on the heads of giggling *frauleins* who dared to watch up close. After sobering up, these hooligans would later apologize and gallantly ask the young women out for a date.

The only noticeable absence at these events was that of the seemingly ubiquitous Jew. The prejudices toward them were real, though largely unspoken at this time. For the most part, the Austrians simply tried to avoid dealing with the overtly religious ones.

Vienna was Austria's mecca of culture, banking, and worldly foundations, some established by the royal family. The Jewish community there was always teeming with hustle, bustle, talk, and trade. Many were secularized and blended in well with the fair-skinned Austrians—and then there were the orthodox, living at the edge of town, and who refused to blend in. They were from a large Jewish enclave in Russia that had been forced out. They were honored to be seen as different, and they were smug in their ways.

Many fine *kinderslaughtern* schools were nicely placed in an area called Lambach, a suburban region about sixty miles from Vienna. By rail it might take one hour and a half to get there, and students enjoyed group field trips for the change of scenery. Not many of them had traveled beyond the confines of their towns and were awestruck with Austria's landscape of captivating and picturesque villages, blue, glassy streams, and towering mountain ranges.

The pride of every school in the country centered on visiting the famous Hofburg museum in Vienna. Students wore their bicolored uniforms as a badge of honor. They would line up perfectly at the front steps, standing erect as if ready to enter battle. Girls were adorned in smart, prissy but formal-looking skirts. Those from upper-class families might wear the state flower tucked indiscreetly through their golden hair about one inch above the right ear; a small *Edelweiss* would turn even the plainest looking *fraulein* into a princess. Those who wore them would preemptively smile and say *danke* to onlookers whom they presumed would compliment their appearance—even before the onlooker had time to think about saying anything.

Passersby always appreciated the students' display of trained corporate discipline as they stood impeccably aligned, waiting for the teachers' whistle toot. One toot meant stop, listen, and erase any expression of emotion from your face. Two toots meant march. Three toots meant you were in serious violation of a scholastic rule, and you had better prepare for the ensuing measure of discipline. Even the private parochial schools used this system.

This particular day was unlike any other, however. The pupils at the Franciscan Abbey, a school housed in an eleventh century monastery in

Lambach village, had waited all summer to attend the famous museum. The headmaster, a monk, had announced the trip at the close of the summer session.

Attending the museum was a hallmark event in any student's experience. For many, it was an initiation to Austrian history, culture, and national pride. Many parents waited for their children to return with meaningful souvenirs that they would discuss at dinner. There were Neanderthal artifacts, canvass artwork from the Impressionists and Van Dyke, as well as biblical artifacts. In Austria, Martin Luther's fifteenth century crusade against idolatry had been passively ignored. Idols and icons were always legitimized under the premise of collecting appreciable religious artwork.

Father Eisenbraun always looked forward to this school trip to see the latest exhibitions. He was unlike any other priest at the abbey. Though often stern, he was a kind man and loved to teach religious history. He had a huge forehead, and the structure of his jaw framed his face in such a way that it made it appear to have been chiseled after the visage of a Greek god. He stood at six feet seven inches and had sandy brown hair, which he kept neatly combed back and parted on the left side. Among the clergymen, he was the only one who proudly wore a simple mustache that was only about as wide as his nose. He never let it grow to the edges of his mouth, and no one ever understood why, as this was neither the style among clergymen nor laymen.

He not only appreciated religious history, but also adored the very history of the abbey. The stately structure had been well preserved for nearly eight hundred years, and now was partly functioning as a modest Catholic school. It had a bold impact on the community, as many of the local priests and nuns had been educated there. The abbey kept its traditional religious sign of the equilateral cross (which later became known as the swastika) on both the worship hall and study areas. This cross was accepted as a sign of good luck, and during this period of heightened cultural appreciation was held with considerable esteem as a symbol of religious heritage.

Father Eisenbraun taught both those in the religious school and those placed in secular classes; to him, there was no difference. He dared to engage his classes in discussions about the infamous Crusades and other more embarrassing events in the history of the Catholic Church.

"These events were not about the love of God, but the political works of men," he would say grimly. Often, young girls in his class would wait patiently for him to finish his tangents, but the young boys were filled with wonder, a sense of adventure, and boldness. Massive crusading armies of knightly warriors sweeping across Europe to battle the infidels had contemporary implications for the Ottoman Turks, and every boy knew it.

Father Eisenbraun conducted mass every Wednesday and was more than suggestive in keeping the tradition of fasting from meat on Fridays. "We eat fish on Fridays because of its symbolic importance to our faith and its natural benefits to our brain," he would say. "Remember, our Lord also ate broiled fish with his disciples after the resurrection."

If there were ever a student whom Father Eisenbraun could easily ignite while storytelling, it was Adolphus. His nickname was "Dolphie." He had small, steely blue eyes like his father, and was unlike the other boys in several noticeable ways. Rather than spending time after school playing with a makeshift ball in the streets, Adolphus arranged groups of athletically challenged runts like himself (due to his diminished stature) to play cowboys and Indians. Every now and then, he could recruit an impressively larger boy to join in and role-play. The larger, more popular boys were always the cowboys, and they always won. Dolphie played these games tirelessly, despite enduring a lung problem.

Dolphie attended only secular classes at the abbey and by now had abandoned even the slightest interest in religion, though his parents were Catholic. Some of the boys would tease him because of his last name, Hitler, which could be interpreted as meaning hidder or to hide away, thus they would mockingly suggest that he study religion to prepare for his future as a monk hidden from society. Though at one time he wanted to be an abbot, now the very notion struck him as absurd. He no longer dedicated any time to thinking about his future, as it often produced a headache.

A brisk but brief rainfall had abruptly ended. The sun began to appear and whitewash the stone buildings of Vienna. Though chilly, the air was mountain-crisp and clean, and the students were relieved that they wouldn't have to stand in the rain before the museum opened.

The piercing shrill of one whistle toot sounded, and the standing students went on alert. Another toot came, and its echo bounced off the stone buildings in the town square. Father Eisenbraun was not very impressed by the clamorous way in which they disembarked from the train. He thus waited until they were perfectly still before he blew the double toot to march them through the large golden framed doors of the Hofburg museum.

While the students were approaching the doorway, they were reminded to remain silent and keep traffic flowing until they reached the first exhibit. They would all gather there to hear the guide's brief presentation, and then proceed to the next one.

They went in one by one, each boy removing his school cap with the precision of a military facing movement as each stepped through the doorway.

The inside of the museum was beautiful. It was an enormous hall filled with different types of displays. Some were protected behind glass, and others were roped off, restricting visitors from coming within six feet.

"*Achtung, achtung*, you will all gather here now," the tour guide directed. "Do not block the walkway. You may draw close to this exhibit." The tour guide was a tall, pale, thin man who bore a resemblance to some of the stiff pale characters in the fifteenth century paintings. "This is the work of the Austrian artist Jacob Seisenegger. It was done in the fifteenth century. Notice how the earth and sky in this image are divided into thirds...." The guide went on delving into the history of the piece, dissecting the artist's every technique and exploring his expressed and unexpressed intentions. Many of the students were engaged because they had seen this particular piece in a school art book. Others didn't care for it.

After reviewing about seven other famous paintings, the guide announced, "Now good pupils, we are going to pass through the works and relics of religious history, and I understand that this is the group from the Franciscan Abbey, is it not?" Some of the children dared to silently nod in the affirmative.

"Good," he said. "Let's walk this way. Remember, don't block the middle aisle. We're going to gather around that glass box at the end of this hallway."

This particular hallway felt different to the students. There was a hushed feel in the air, and Father Eisenbraun attributed it to a sense of holiness because they were in the religious area. An audible mumbled word or two could be heard among them as they all slowly drew near the next exhibit. It was encased in a lit glass box, which gave the item inside a special glow. They had heard how the British king's crown jewels were kept in such a box in London and thought perhaps that this must be a relic from Austria's royal family. But it wasn't.

A sense of excitation grew in Father Eisenbraun. Adolphus happened to be walking beside him when he said in a whisper, "This next historical piece is probably the most valuable in the whole museum. Just to look upon it is a privilege that brings me joy and sorrow because, well..." He suddenly stopped himself, remembering where he was. Adolphus however was engaged, and his steely eyes locked upon the glass box. He didn't blink for nineteen seconds. He didn't understand what was happening to him, but there was something about it that shook his very being. The only other time that young Hitler had been shaken like this was when he was caught by the school headmaster for rebelliously tearing up his achievement certificate and using the remnant pieces as toilet paper. He was visibly shaken then. But now he was shaken internally.

The tour guide stood alongside of the case. He was partly illuminated by the light shining through the glass, or—as it appeared—by the item in the glass box. He cleared his throat and began in a posh Viennese accent, "This is the Roman spear that pierced the side of Jesus Christ. Look at its sleekness in the midsection. These spears were only kept by a particular legion of Roman soldiers. In fact, it's sometimes referred to as the 'Longinus,' named after its Roman owner." Adolphus blinked twice and was entranced again. "This spear was used during the Crusades and always brought victory. It was then used by Charlemagne against the Muslim invaders and brought him true victory. Paradoxically, it may be used for either great good or great evil for whoever possesses it."

(Hitler would later be quoted concerning the experience: *"I stood there quietly gazing upon it for several minutes, quite oblivious to the scene around me. It seemed to carry some hidden inner meaning which evaded me, a meaning which I felt I inwardly knew yet could not bring to consciousness. I felt as though I myself had held it before in some earlier century of history. That I myself had once claimed it as my talisman of power and held the destiny of the world in my hands…" Adolf Hitler,* The Spear of Destiny)

Forgetting where he was, young Hitler interjected, "How could it be used for both?"

"Dolphie!" Father Eisenbraun barked. "You were all told to save your questions for the end of the tour. I'm sorry, sir."

"Not at all," replied the tour guide. "It's a valid question, which has merit for an immediate answer. How could something regarded as holy be effective for both great good and evil for its possessor? I can only suggest this. It has been used for both great good and evil. In the Bible you will find that crucifying Jesus was God's way of offering a perfect sacrifice for the salvation of man, uh, if he puts his faith in this way."

Father Eisenbraun interrupted. "Good sir, are you elucidating from the doctrinal teachings of Martin Luther?"

"No, not at all," the guide responded, attempting to avoid a religious discussion about Catholic doctrine. "I'm merely quoting from the Bible. And we have Guttenberg Bibles on display in the next wing for all of you to peruse. Now then, in response to the question, we all can understand how this act of sacrifice may be considered to be good, and the spear was used to prove that Jesus was dead—that God's sacrifice was completed. Others suggest that because this object came into contact with his holy blood, it carries a type of uh, special power, if you will. Nonetheless, these are considered to be good things. Now you may also read how this man was innocent, traded in for money, and became subject to a death by torture at the hands of man. This injustice at the hands of men was a great evil on their part, my children. And we know how Judas, the traitor, even committed suicide after realizing this fact. So there you have it. The spear was initially used for both good and evil. We refer to it now as the "Spear of Destiny."

Wonderful! Though slightly confusing to Dolphie's secular mind, it somehow made sense, and it was wonderful. He understood and appreciated such concepts and had been pondering his own destiny since attending the abbey. There had been heated conversations with his father on the subject, which now made him conscientious about his future.

His father, Alois Hitler, had a short temper that was sometimes attributed to his habit of consuming alcohol; whisky was his preference. He became predictably unpredictable, and little Adolphus had become so used to it that he began to internalize some of the same brute characteristics.

"I couldn't bear to sit behind a desk and twiddle my hands all day, Poppie," he would say.

"So what are you thinking of doing?" his father asked. "You have no special skills. I'm providing well for your mother. You all are going to good schools, and we have a roof over our heads. Civil service jobs and the military will always be strong employers."

"Yes, yes, I know, Poppie, but you must understand I am different."

"You are different, as fools are different from the wise. Yes, we've known about your differences since you were born. You were born smaller than usual, and so now you think you have to prove…"

"That's not what I mean," Dolphie said. "I would do a million other things before thinking of civil service."

"Yes, such as?"

"Such as canvass artwork. Mother likes it, and artwork is far more noble than groveling around trying to please empty-minded bureaucrats who have nothing better to do but try to impress one another with their petty rules."

Alois Hitler was a customs inspector who had pride in what he had achieved and was not sheepish about demonstrating it. Despite having little education, he had been promoted to a high level in the civil service and truly wanted his sons to experience the same measure of success. However, after his eldest son ran away, and the very youngest died from the measles, Adolphus had to bear the pressure of making a name for himself for the family's sake. Being subject to disrespect and shouting was too much for him to take from any family member; so he reached over, grabbed Adolphus by the collar, and shook him like a captured rabbit. Then, in his usual method of discipline, he proceeded to slap his face using the front and back sides of his rheumatic hands. He never intended to ball his fists, but the arthritis caused them to curve naturally. Enraged, he shrieked as he struck the boy, "You will apply for civil service—(slap)! You will give up your foolish notions—(slap)!—You will start listening to me—(slap)! He then shoved the petrified child into a worn-out chair, not noticing once again how the child's bold expression of cold defiance remained, particularly in his eyes.

Internally, Adolphus was becoming a cauldron of implacable anger toward his father, who rarely showed any compassion or sympathy. The relationship was further complicated by the disharmony with his half-brothers, who would steal from him.

Now, however, he felt liberated in not having to commit any time to worrying about them. He had a destiny that they couldn't understand. He had a meaning that they wouldn't comprehend. He had a future that no one could stop, and it was all embodied in the 'Spear of Destiny'. It would somehow become his spear. It would forge his destiny.

The train ride back to Lambach was a blur of green and gray colors with intermittent visions of field battles and a radiant spearhead that glistened in the sun. In the mind of Adolphus, certain events were now destined to come. His only question was how to initiate a chain of events that could start the ball rolling.

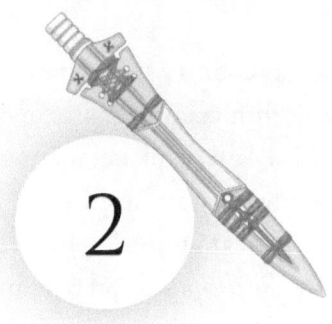

2

RELIGION AND PHILOSOPHY

....

He was churning inside like a bucket of buttermilk, and he understood why. He did not possess the slightest faith in any Christian claims and had to reconcile this fact with his destiny. He had learned to respect the religion of his parents. He had learned to respect his religious school. He learned to appreciate Austria's history, even its religious past. He tolerated these things as a dutiful son tolerates being burdened with responsibility, yet he now possessed something truly spiritual; it felt more religious than dead Catholic masses droned in Latin. He thrived on a spiritual destiny that was completely his own, but how could this be when it was so closely attached to an historic religious 'savior' whom his history teacher lectured about at the abbey?

It was 1899 and Alois Hitler decided to move his family once again, this time to the industrial city of Linz for the sake of Adolphus. The monastery had afforded him nice opportunities to learn to sing, understand history, and excel at other courses in the humanities, but young Adolphus still failed to demonstrate any aptitude or inkling in a technical field, which would pave the way for a cushy civil service position in the *Bunderstrate*. Alois wouldn't entertain any discussions of destiny. The future required technical skills, and the upper Austrian city of Linz was the country's vanguard of technical advancement. The famous seventeenth century mathematician Johannes Kepler had developed the "third law of planetary motion" there, and the local Johannes Kepler University attracted visiting lecturers from all around Europe. It was Alois' dream for Adolphus to attend there, so he decided to enroll him in the *Realschule* to prepare his destiny.

The *Realschule* in Linz was a clean, officious building. These types of schools extended the education of enrollees by allowing them to advance in the sciences, math, or technical fields. There was something almost sterile about them. Every classroom had the feel of a laboratory. Adolphus' classes were all-male, and many of the students came from notable Austrian families. There was Gustav Rudolph, who was supposedly related to the family of the late Wolfgang Amadeus Mozart's wife. There was also little Arnold, who was a third cousin, twice removed, of Sigmund Freud. And then there was Ludwig Wittgenstein, a simple looking boy who really was as aloof as Adolphus, who yet would later become one of the greatest philosophers of the twentieth century.

Ludwig came from a very privileged family of highly musical and intellectual overachievers. They dwelled in a luxurious home known in the community as the *Palais Wittgenstein*. Musicians, such as Johannes Brahms, would frequently visit their home to give Wittgenstein's sister piano lessons after having a social chat with their father, a wealthy steel businessman. There was talk around school that he was a little genius. He had been homeschooled up to his present age of fifteen and enjoyed toying with mathematical concepts and music composition simply to pass the time. He was truly brilliant, but he struggled in social circles. He insisted that his schoolmates refer to him as *Herr* Wittgenstein suggesting that he was somehow above them all; they secretly sneered at him for this.

Despite a slight difference in age, Hitler and Wittgenstein were in one class together. It was advanced geometry, and there were only nine registered students in total. The two boys sat adjacent to each other in parallel rows.

Professor Eichmann had taught geometry for seven years at the *Realschule* in Linz. He appeared diminutive, but he was the average height of his adolescent students, which meant that he was able to speak to them eye to eye. None of the boys liked this because Professor Eichmann had the habit of breathing heavily in discussions, and his breath often carried a foul odor. As with all of the staff, however, the students had the utmost respect for him.

One afternoon, Professor Eichmann swaggered into the classroom carrying his attention wand. He tapped it on the podium three times, as was the custom among the instructors, and began in his regular pontificating tone. "You will now finish your lesson in *Deductive Systems and Completeness*. Monday I lectured about Gödel's theory of logical axioms, non-logical axioms, and the rules of inference. By way of review, Hansel, briefly explain to the class what the desirable property of any deductive system is. "Hansel was a stocky sixteen-year-old who wanted to work with his uncle as an engineer. He had the build of a wrestler; his arms resembled the overstuffed sausages that hung in the neighborhood butcher shop. He was popular among the smaller boys, but had no trace of any aptitude for mathematics or logical reasoning. He was also known for his sometimes-annoying habit of laughing when facing pressure, and he started to squirm before he rose from his seat to answer the question.

Attempting to suppress a grin, he said, "Herr Eichmann, would… would you pl…please repeat the, uh, the question, please?"

"Are you not hearing so well these days, Hansel?"

"No, sir…I mean, yes, ha ha. I mean, I just didn't hear the last part of the question, sir."

"Sit down, boy," Eichmann said sternly. "Who can address the class and explain, with appropriate composure, Gödel's theory regarding desirable properties of a deductive system?"

"Professor Eichmann?"

"Ludwig Wittgenstein, yes?"

"May I attempt to answer the question?"

"Indeed you may."

"Thank you."

The expression on Hansel's face was one of relief and self-disappointment as Ludwig slowly rose to his feet to face his instructor. Ludwig became oblivious to his anxious classmates because he was accustomed to thinking through the roles of mathematical logic alone in his room. He toyed with imponderable questions of philosophy and morality as a type of hobby, and this was simply another occasion for him to continue a dialogue that had begun in his mind when his family suffered the tragic loss of his brother.

"The desirable property of any deductive system is that it be complete," he said. "This allows for logical consequences and absolute truths to be understood. Without completeness, everything becomes relative, and truth becomes obscured."

"Hmmm," said the professor. "Please continue. What do you mean by everything becomes relative?"

"Well, sir, without absolute truths, there can never be a consistent method of measuring anything, because everything becomes subject to the eye of the beholder."

"Yes, but isn't that how we arrive at truth? If something isn't true to the beholder, then it is absolutely untrue to him. Even in Gödel's theory, truth can be proven from a given set of axioms that the individual can ascertain."

"Yes, sir, but where do these axioms come from? Who made them? If the individual is left to find truth alone from his self-made collection of axioms, then everyone will have his own set of truths, which will most assuredly contradict everyone else's. Therefore, truth must come from outside of the individual's experience and not be limited to personal subjection. Truth must come from perfection, someone or something unbiased, unchanging, without any flaws, or else it becomes a simple natural matter of opinion."

"This appears to disqualify all of mankind, doesn't it?"

"Yes, sir, this is where mathematical logic enters a realm of religious philosophy, suggesting that only a creator of man can represent absolute truth and set certain axioms before us to help us ascertain truths."

The frown on Dolphie's face was beginning to become a deep sinking scowl. Though he was a pensive thinker, too, he didn't agree with his classmate's assessment of arriving at truth. He had his own understanding of how to arrive at truth and could no longer contain himself.

"Professor?"

"Yes, Adolph Hitler?"

"Yes, I'd like to contribute if I may, please."

Professor Eichmann was reluctant to allow Dolphie to speak as he was already weary of where this discussion was going. Dolphie, to him, was a misfit with only a few redeeming drawing skills, who was always behind in his work, and too easily distracted to be able to think constructively. Nonetheless, he was pleased with his sudden urge of taking initiative and allowed him to speak.

"What would you like to add, young man?"

"What is wrong with having contradictory truths? Doesn't the history of the world tell us that this must be so? The Darwin theory says that the strongest will prevail, and in my opinion, they should prevail. Anyone holding onto his own fragile set of truths, whatever they may be, should be forced to accept the stronger set of truths or else risk extinction because the strongest may achieve the divine right to rule. No one ever dares to ask the victor what truths he believes in. Why can't…"

"Thank you," said the professor. "You may sit down." Adolph was not quite finished and wanted to stress another point in his argument. He reluctantly sat and then sprang up back to his feet.

"Professor Eichmann, why can't…"

"That will be enough, Adolph. Sit down!"

There was a stillness in the room for a few seconds; the only audible sound came from outside of the window as the commuter cable trains came to a screeching halt. The class was never given to open debates, but all nine of the students were ready to weigh in on the discussion.

Dolphie had introduced an element of social order derived from a topic of mathematical logic, and Professor Eichmann was not interested in providing a platform for this type of discussion. Up to this point, Dolphie's reputation was that of a scatterbrained, immature misfit from a rustic village who happened to have a few drawing skills. Now he was seen as something a little different.

The outside stone steps of the *Realschule* building were a common gathering place for the young men before departing for home via the commuter train. Though they were cold, hard, and uncomfortable to sit on, they were conveniently out of the way of any foot traffic, which allowed for huddled discussions. It was Friday, and most of them bragged about their weekend plans. A few of them were still chatting about Professor Eichmann's controversial exchange involving Ludwig and Dolphie. Another commuter train arrived, so they slowly began to pick themselves from off the steps and head for the train stop.

Ludwig was sitting apart from all of the others on the opposite side of the steps, reading a musical score sheet that he kept bound between his leather book straps. He was in no hurry to go home and considered waiting for a later train a worthy sacrifice in order to avoid having to board with such a loud group. He listened to the bungling sounds of his classmates as they shuffled, slid, and stammered down the steps onto the train platform. He smirked at their clumsiness.

When the crowd dissipated, Dolphie appeared from around a stone pillar and began to walk toward Ludwig. He, too, usually waited a while after school before leaving for home. Dolphie, however, had to walk over an hour alone to arrive at his family's apartment. He was ashamed of not being able to afford the trains, and usually waited for everyone else to leave in order to keep it a secret.

The two boys looked intently at each other, each expecting the other to start a conversation. But Dolphie could see by Ludwig's tense composure that he was not interested in continuing a debate over the social ramifications of mathematical logic. Since they both were holding reading material, Dolphie figured it would be safe to broach a conversation from that standpoint.

"Hello, what a committed student you are, still reading Gödel's theories on a Friday after school.

"This is a composition by Johannes Brahms," said Ludwig. "He comes to our home sometimes, and my father knows him well."

Pretending to be interested, Dolphie offered, "My mother once said something about this man, and I told her I preferred Wagner. Didn't Brahms conduct an orchestra at last summer's music festival?"

"Yes, he arranged for our family to have special seats."

"I see, you must play an instrument, too, then. And I'd bet that your father named you after Beethoven."

"I play the clarinet, and I'm not named after Beethoven. What do you do?"

"I draw. I'm going to be an artist."

"May I see some of your work there?"

"This isn't any work of mine, my friend. This is a comic book"

"A what?"

"A storybook about western America. It's terrific, and a German author from Linz wrote it. I was going to ask you if you wanted to play cowboys and Indians with us next Friday after school. You would make a good Indian."

"Thank you, but I'm too busy with my studies for that sort of thing. You say an Austrian writes these things?"

"You haven't heard of Karl May? He's an important man. Maybe your father lunches with him, too, but you just don't recognize him."

"The only thing we know about America is that they have savage Indians and black people from Africa running around trying to get everyone to treat them like Europeans rather than servants."

"Yes, my father says they had a national war not long ago, and the head chancellor was murdered in a theatre. The Indians, I think, are still fighting the cowboys, but, well, never mind about that now, just think about playing with us next Friday. I can put you in the Indian group and..."

"I said I'm too busy for that. And I don't like violent games. I don't like the thought of violence. Don't you know about my brother?"

"I've never heard of your brother."

"You're probably the only one in our class who doesn't know, so I might as well tell you. I had a brother who committed suicide with a pistol. Every time we hear guns or canons at the parades, my mother and sister start acting strangely."

"Suicide? That's too bad; he will burn in hell for that."

"How can you say that? You don't know that!"

"That's what the priest says in my father's church. I think he would know. It's Friday, just ask the priest at the Linz cathedral about it after the Friday service."

"Cathedral? Fridays are special for my family; I don't eat and have to go home shortly after school."

"What type of Catholic tradition is this? My parents at least eat fish on Fridays?"

"I'm not Catholic. My grandfather was a Jew, so we celebrate the *Shabbat* on Fridays."

"What's a *chavvot*, and what is a Jew? Can one be Austrian and a Jew at the same time?"

"Can one be Austrian and write fictional fantasies about American Indians? Listen, I have to leave now. I'm already late for Shabbat—uh, it's a kind of celebration. I'm sorry I can't play your cowboy game, and you are as wrong as you can be about my brother—no matter what your priest says. I must be going, Dolphie."

"Well, have a good *chavvot*. And maybe my mother can pray your brother's soul into purgatory. See you on Monday."

3

WHAT IS A JEW?

Walking home had become so routine that Dolphie often took different streets to keep his sense of adventure alive. He couldn't understand Ludwig's lack of interest in playing cowboys and Indians, but accepted that he must have been a very sheltered child. He passed the town hall, the greengrocer store, the barbershop, and the firehouse before turning down the street where his family dwelt. There was something about walking up the front steps, which always sobered his mind up, driving away any impulse to play cowboys and Indians or read comics. Deep down he knew that he should prepare himself to explain to his father what he had or should have learned that day.

The front door closed gently. Dolphie walked in, and an overwhelming aroma of baked bread and fried fish met him before he could set his comic book down.

"Momma? Momma?"

"Dolphie? Is that you?" Mrs. Hitler was a shamefaced modest woman who tried very hard to present herself as a cultured wife and mother. For her husband's and children's sake, she took up an interest in classical music, experimented with cooking expensive delicacies, and kept the apartment as clean as possible. Though one could clearly see through her natural mannerisms that she had a peasant upbringing, Mrs. Hitler had a heart of gold, and Dolphie loved her very much.

"Hi, momma! And where is everybody?"

"I sent your sister to the store for some dough, and your father won't be home until very late today. How was school?"

"It was fine, momma. Where's Poppie?" he said, relieved that his father wasn't there to chastise him for his tardiness.

"There was a train accident near the German border, and your father has to go inspect it."

"What is there to inspect about a train accident? Won't they need doctors to tend to the injured?"

"Yes, of course, but the train was carrying three cars of commercial merchandise, and it all spilled out when the train jumped the tracks. You know your father's work requires him to inspect all merchandise that comes over the border."

"You mean that Poppie has to go all the way to the border to sift through spilled trash to clear it for customs?"

"It's an important job, Dolphie, and you must respect that!"

"Momma, you know I could never do what he does. He keeps insisting that I take up an interest in the civil service, but I will never, never be able to spend my time like he does—sifting through trash to take inventories. You understand me, don't you?"

"Dolphie, you are as strong-willed as your father, and you will be able to do anything you put your mind to. I've seen your talents."

"Momma, I'm much more interested in canvas art than anything else right now. The *realchule* classes are interesting, but I want to go to art school. Why can't Poppie respect that?"

"Give it time, son. Give it time. Now go wash your hands for dinner."

Dolphie went to his room. The materials that lay sprawled across his bed were a constant reminder of his double life; there was his unfinished math homework lying alongside his comic books, personal drawings, and war novels. Since finding one of his father's war magazines over the Franco Prussian war, Dolphie had taken a deeper interest in war and history—and the cowboy comic magazine "Old Shatterhand" provided him with an appreciation for western battle strategies. It seemed that anything but preparing for a governmental job with the civil service captured his imagination now.

His sister returned from the greengrocer and knocked at the door, reminding him that dinner was prepared. "Dolphie, Dolphie, come to the table," she said.

"I heard you and I'm coming," he responded as he made his way to the door.

As was the custom at the Hitler household, Dolphie remained standing until his mother took her seat. She said a brief prayer, and they sat down to dine. Though it was just the three of them at the kitchen table, Dolphie wasn't as aware of his father's absence as he had been at other times. His mind was full of questions, and sometimes it was easier asking his mother. They spoke as they passed the baked fish.

"Momma, what is a Jew?" Dolphie asked in between bites. Trying not to appear too uncomfortable at the question, she responded, "A Jew? What brings this question up, my darling?"

"There's a boy at school who says he's a Jew and can't eat on Fridays. He doesn't even eat fish like we do."

Klara Hitler felt a sudden rush of heat rise to her face. She was noticeably turning pink by this time. She remembered having this type of discussion with her husband before. Then she was abruptly interrupted and directed to never bring it up again. It was a type of family skeleton that revolved around Alois Hitler's mother, who had worked as a maid for a Jewish family. One day, while under the influence of five pints of beer, Alois's uncles said that the eldest son in the Jewish family had grown fond of his mother and incessantly began to make passes to lure her into his bedroom. As stable jobs during these times were difficult to obtain, the senior Mrs. Hitler never protested to the son himself, but complained about it in the privacy of her own home. According to rumors, it wasn't long after this time when she became pregnant with Alois.

"Well, Dolphie, they are a type of religious group of people with very different traditions."

"My friend Eva says that she and her mother met one in Vienna at the grocery after school. She said she was a nice girl," said his sister.

"Why yes, they are lovely people. They are just, different."

"Can any Austrian become Jewish?" Dolphie inquired. "No, darling, I think they are born into this faith," said Momma.

"Then it is both a religion and a race at the same time."

"Perhaps, your fish is getting cold, Dolphie."

Dolphie sat and pondered while chewing his last piece of fish. He sat and gazed into his plate, uninterested in continuing any conversation, despite the fact that both parents had emphasized dinner conversation as a way of reinforcing social graces. But Dolphie was always indifferent to learning the social graces that his mother and sister Paula thought to be so particularly important. If he couldn't feel free to speak his own mind without worrying what someone thought, he'd rather not speak at all.

Alois and Klara Hitler, however, had meant these dinner times to be therapeutic for Dolphie. Since the age of thirteen, he started to become less communicative with his parents and more unpredictable in aggressive behavior. There was the time, when playing cowboys and Indians, that he insisted upon organizing a mock hanging for the captured Indians. He went so far as to tie a hangman's noose around his friend Heinrick's neck before the two started to exchange punches. The six boys went home wondering how the brawl ever got started. Then there was the time when the neighbor's dog gave birth to six Golden Labrador puppies. Paula had caught Dolphie torturing one of them by dangling it high in the air by the ears to see when it would start to whimper. Each time it began to whimper, Paula noticed that Dolphie would start to shake it violently until the yelps were so loud that its mother would start to howl and whimper from across the yard.

Paula broke the silence. "Momma, if I finish my chores, could I visit Helena this evening?"

"I'm afraid not. I was talking to Helena's mother just this afternoon, and I think they're preparing to visit Vienna this weekend. I don't think a visit today would be a good idea."

"What are they going to do there?" Dolphie offered, attempting not to be too antisocial at the dinner table.

"I think they plan to visit their grandmother, and then all of them are going to the museum this weekend," said Klara.

Immediately, Dolphie's mind raced back a few years to his fateful visit. He still tenaciously kept the experience hidden within his soul—tucked away for safe keeping until he could assume the role of an heir to its prophetic claims. The Spear of Destiny was an ever-living memory, and he longed simply to return to Vienna and see it again. Not a single day passed without his being reminded of something that had happened on the day of his visit to the museum.

The following years in Dolphie's life were seen as relatively uneventful by his family and friends. Though he had learned to feign an interest in his work at *realschule* to pacify his father, there was a silent storm building inside of him; every now and then the thunder in his soul would sound and the lightening in his eyes would flash. Then his violent temper tantrums would subside. Still, his father often resorted to physically pounding him into submission, sometimes with a bullwhip, until the rage in both of them subsided. Now and then, however, he would pound too hard, and the only thing that would restrain Alois from beating his son to near unconsciousness was the desperate cries and pleas from Klara and Paula.

It plagued the family, and it seemed as if the violence would continue forever. Then, on an overcast autumn morning, as gleaners in the fields prepared to load up their mule-hitched carts and local schools began to prepare social events for the Oktoberfest, Alois died. He had made his habitual stop at the local bar and ordered a glass of wine when his bad lung ruptured, causing him to collapse even before being served. There, at the same table he had frequented for years, surrounded by familiar faces that had grown old with him, his body finally surrendered to his habit of overindulgence. It was sudden, but had been anticipated for a long time; there had been embarrassing signs of his approaching demise—the deep incessant coughs, the dizzy spells, and the gut-wrenching pain just under his breastbone became as frequent as a woman's third trimester labor pains. When summoned, Dolphie couldn't bear to see his father's lifeless body on a stretcher. He cried uncontrollably.

The day of Alois' funeral was bittersweet to many. The local newspaper printed, "The harsh words that fell from his lips could not belie the warm heart that beat under his rough exterior." Many would stroke their beards and shake their heads affirming that, "Yes, he was a good man." Paradoxically, many others were consumed with both a terrible sense of grief, and yet relief that he could no longer make a spectacle of himself or his poor children.

The funeral was well attended by friends, neighbors, and colleagues, and there was a light drizzle of rain outside, which effectively hushed them into silence as the priest carried out his religious duties. Dolphie didn't dare look up. He kept his eyes cast upon the stained coffin decorated with *Edelweiss* flowers now enveloping his father's body. His eyes welled up again with tears, and he began to think about eternal things. He wondered if his father would go straight to heaven or have to be prayed out of purgatory. Deep down, he knew that the senior Hitler had the best of intentions for him and the family. And yet, how could such an overpowering brute be fit for anyplace but the infernal house of the wicked? The brutal beatings, the implacable rages, and the instigations of violence in drunkenness were still living impressions he had for this now-dead man. It didn't make much sense, and he visualized how that freshly lacquered coffin would later sink into the earth after the burial until it reached the pit of the damned. *(Later, Dolphie would return to his hometown as the dictator of the Third Reich and order tank divisions to obliterate it to remove any trace of family remains.)*

An organist played the "*Introit - Requiem Aeternam,*" the traditional hymn that asks for eternal rest. The priest wore black vestments, signifying mourning, and the traditional Latin chants were solemn and magnificent.

"Dominus, Christus Sanctus," the priest began in Latin. Since the untimely death of Dolphie's younger brother, family funerals were hauntingly disturbing.

They were overbearingly religious, ceremonially formal, and awkwardly surreal.

Though numb with grief, Dolphie nonetheless felt liberated to pursue his long-awaited dreams of becoming an artist.

His father had left enough inheritance to support his family, and Dolphie would have enough to vagabond his way around Vienna and find a practical way of starting a living as an artist. His father's death had allowed him to reach a crossroads. Now, undaunted by the uncertainty of his success in an unfamiliar setting, he kissed his mother goodbye and assured her he would return soon after establishing himself in what he wanted to do. Biting her lip with grief, she packed his favorite food in a basket, washed his nearly worn out clothes, prayed for him, and let him go.

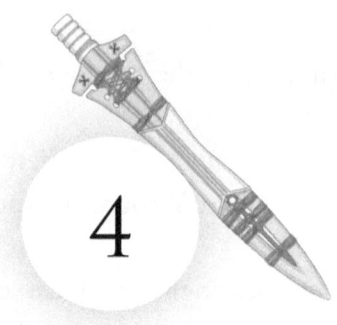

4

PATTON

Approaching life's crossroads would begin a chapter of another young man's journey. It was around 1904-1905, but in a faraway place known as the mother of all US presidents. It was a place of new beginnings. Early European settlers had landed there to find new political and spiritual freedoms. It was also the kind of place that inspired stories like the ones found in the "Old Shatterhand" comic book series that Dolphie would continue to read through his adulthood. Though the winters were frosty and rigid, and the summers humid and sweltering, the powder blue skies, lush velvet green plains, and Blue Ridge Mountains made it one of the happiest places on the eastern shores of the United States. Several geographical spots were hallowed ground; one-third of all domestic battles took place there, where soldiers either died in large company formation or standing alone. Their blood enriched the soil and yielded a spirit that spawned transparent patriotism.

Life there was simple, structured, neighborly, and dignified—the perfect environment to nurture future heads of state or military leaders. Several notable military academies were the pride of Virginia and most, if not all of them, boasted a heritage that predated the Civil War. Young men would travel from as far as the West Coast to launch their auspicious commissioned careers for the sake of God, country, and family.

However, one such young man, a Californian, would arrive and rapidly gain the reputation for being "too military." It would seem that his destiny had been set that way—his birthday prophetically happened to fall on what would later be Armistice Day, November 11th. At the time, he had neither studied Greek nor German and knew only a little French and Latin. Moreover, he was dyslexic, which may have accounted for his poor spelling. His father had attended the prestigious Virginia Military Institute, and as a dutiful and loving son, it only made perfect sense for him to follow in his father's footsteps and give himself to continuing a long family heritage of heroic military movers and shakers—something he had dreamed about since childhood.

Georgie Patton had also soberly reached a crossroads in his life—either a rugged regimented road to manhood and family honor, or a faded fate of mediocrity and diminished family honor. He would choose the rugged road, and it would suit him very well. No one now could imagine that "Georgie Patton," whose black and white child portrait portrayed him in girlish golden locks, would become such a brash in-your-face military academy cadet. But he hit the ground running, and when he didn't run, he swaggered.

Though it was his first time outside the golden state of California, the loving, reaffirming words that his father spoke on the day of his departure quieted his anxious spirit. His father's words were always both reassuring and challenging, and George never ever wanted to disappoint him.

His class of new cadets contained nearly one hundred and fifty not-so-confident and sometimes timid men from all across the country. They were traditionally referred to as "rats," which was designed to humiliate and strip them of any personal pride. They were to embrace a new image and a new sense of pride from the academy, which theoretically would then form their character. George Patton, however, always carried himself with the air of an upperclassman. He was rigid and rigorous.

Even when commanded to stand at ease in close formation, George stood rigidly. He didn't smile much anymore, even during free time, as he attempted to perfect the gritty expression of an invincible soldier.

He talked about aspiring to be Chief of Staff for the Army, and sometimes the upperclassmen felt uncomfortable with ambitious freshman cadets. From time to time, they even conspired to harass and haze such ones into a subordinate spirit. On one such occasion, George was approached by a senior cadet who had twice earned "cadet of the month." He was a tall, lanky southerner from Georgia and didn't really take well to non-southern cadets. When he stood at attention, his profile was remarkable. His broad square shoulders and robust chest made him the poster boy of the academy, and most freshmen admired him as they would an all-star baseball pitcher.

"Cadet Patton," he said.

"Yes, sir."

"Why do you insist on wearing your dress uniform during non-duty hours? Don't you know that this could spoil the morale of your fellow cadets? We all need to see each other dressed down from time to time, and I'm tired of looking at you like that."

"Sir," Patton responded, "my uniform is now a part of who I am at my very core. To wear it during non-duty hours is to remind myself, and others, I would hope, that I find it honorable, as I freely choose to wear it without being ordered or expected to. I should think that this would inspire my fellow cadets to realize that we're not dressing up in costumes during duty hours to role play, but we should be becoming what these uniforms represent."

"Why do you always try to outdo everyone, cadet?"

"Sir, I'm committed to giving my best. I am compelled inwardly to this end. I do this without malice, but in the healthy spirit of honor and competition."

"Very well, cadet. Carry on, but I think you might start to see things differently after a while."

"Thank you, sir, and I hope not."

These were the kind of conversations that George had gotten used to. It wasn't so much that he always tried to outdo his fellow cadets—though he was very competitive—but his natural ways simply seemed to require more self-discipline, more self-sacrifice, and more self-efficacy. He would later be quoted as saying, "There is only one type of discipline, perfect discipline."

The barrack quarters were modest but well furnished for the cadet student. Each room accommodated three men, on the premise that there should always be a tiebreaker lest any disputes occur. They were provided with a bed, dresser, mirror, and a rack upon which they hung their Government Issue rifles and sabers. Secretly, it always delighted George to see the rack of weapons on the side of the room. It made him feel like a knight whose trusted armor was always at his disposal. He shined his saber twice a day—once in the morning so that it would shimmer all day long, and again at night so that it might still be shimmering in the morning.

Frank and Eudell were his *commerades de chambers*. Though they were both from different states, each of them came from a military family.

Frank, from Washington State, was short, quiet, and well determined. He was the son of a preacher and endeavored to serve his country both as an army medic and as a conscientious objector. To Frank, both roles were equally important because they were the perfect complement. His was the character of a tender kind of warrior—though nonetheless a warrior. Despite his socially accommodating and even-toned speaking habits, at times he would ruthlessly debate why no one had the singular right to take the life of another. He would emphasize his position, quoting biblical scriptures and standing square-shouldered like a puritan schoolmaster. Frank was also an intellectual over-achiever, which struck a stark contrast to George's rugged exterior. This caused some discomfort for both of them, but the two admired one another's qualities.

Eudell was from Rocky Mount, Tennessee. He was a southern gentleman whose grandfather had fought alongside General Walker during the Civil War. If Eudell had been born a dog, he would have been a Labrador Retriever—faithful, playful, even-tempered, and sportive. He loved to show the scar on the back of his neck where his best buddy had tried to remove a tick with a lit match. The imprint resembled a four-leaf clover, which inspired his schoolmates to call him "Lucky." Eudell was usually the pick of the squads when it came to sorting out teams for athletic competitions.

It was a week before the annual freshman assembly when each new rat cadet had to recite the academy's traditional policy against hazing. The idea of this event made George nervous, and he tried to hide it. He was never comfortable making public presentations; sometimes he stammered or would use the wrong word. Often times, he would simply say something brash, even vulgar, to shock his listeners. But George's resolve to any weakness was usually the same: drill, drill hard, and then drill more. He would stand in front of the mirror and drill until he got it down to a science. One Sunday afternoon, he got dressed in his formal attire and started at it.

"Honorable faculty, staff, and fellow cadets, it is my noble duty to partake in this historic tradition by coming before you now in order to elucidate my, my, uh, d ----n!"

"Brother Rat?"

"What is it, Frank?" Patton said, annoyed with himself.

"Perhaps you're working too hard at it now. Give yourself a little R and R and attack it later, and I'm sure you'll have no problems."

"That's not the way I work. Drilling leads to perfection. You know that."

"Yes, we all agree, but it's the way you drill. You're too tense. If you keep drilling that way, you'll be bound to boggle it up at the assembly."

"D ---- d, and who in heaven made you the barrack commander of drill..."

"And there's another thing I've wanted to talk to you about, brother. All of this cursing that you're starting to do is dishonorable to the academy. You know what the manual says. But for the last two weeks, you've been swearing and cursing and...."

"Okay, okay, brother rats," said Eudell. "Listen, Georgie, I mean, Cadet George, Cadet Frank has a point. We've all been under a strain this week, but your language is becoming a little, uh, unsavory, if you will, and the rat manual directly addresses it."

"Let me ask you brother rats something," said George. "What type of language do you think you're gonna hear once we've been graduated and go on active duty? You can be a preacher boy officer or a first-class scrub, but you're gonna hear the blunt realities of raw communication no matter where you go in this man's army, and there ain't gonna be no tea parties after no Sunday service."

"Hey, I resent that, cadet. He's just verbally attacked me! I may be the son of a preacher, but I haven't begun to do any preaching to you because I'd first have to scrub your filthy mouth out with…."

"Cadets, that's enough," said Eudell. "We'll all do penalty tours for a month if they hear us talking like this, see?" he said placing his hands on both of their shoulders. "Now listen, the two of ya. Neither one of us is gonna make it without buddy care. George, why don't you let Frank give you a few pointers on your presentation? I don't know why, maybe it's because his dad's a preacher, but he's got this way of talking, which I think can help you. And Frank, I'm sure George can help you lose a little of that gut if you sit down and listen to how he self-trains. All I'm saying is this: Let's get through this initiation week without getting into each other's hair."

Both Cadets Frank and George felt ashamed. They knew that at all costs a good cadet does everything possible to preserve the morale of his buddies, but they had let envy jade their relationship. Cadet George, endeavoring to restore honor, initiated the attempt to make amends. Standing erect and shamefaced, he said, "Brother Rat, it was wrong of me to disregard your sensitivities, which are well supported by our manual. I'm sorry, and please pardon my foul language."

"That's okay, George. I know I'm a little oversensitive when it comes to things like cursing because of my preacher dad. Sometimes, I just feel like I need to be more like him, and he doesn't tolerate rough talk, if you know what I mean. Don't let it get to ya."

All three young men sat down to recline on their cots. This breakthrough experience of settling their first dispute somehow made them more comfortable with each other and willing to talk about themselves. They were emotionally relieved and ready to learn more from one another.

Cadet George continued, "My folks are like that, too, but you know my dad wasn't no preacher."

"Yeah, I know. I was thinking about your dad when I was passing the old courtyard yesterday. Weren't his barracks on the wing that they plan to renovate now?"

"That's right, and when he was a freshman here, they were just building it. They started during cadre week."

"George," Eudell asked, "did you grow up in the church like Frank?"

"I got my religion at a young age because my mother is a very spiritual woman," George said. "Don't get me wrong, my dad is like the priest of our house, like the Bible says, but I learned something special from my mother that I'm not sure a lot of people understand.'

Patton now was beginning to regret this conversation because he was exposing thoughts that were too personal to risk exposing. He had introduced a topic that he knew he would have to explain, and he could tell by the expressions on Frank and Eudell's faces that they expected him to go on.

He braved the risk of humiliation and continued, asking, "Brother cadets, have you ever heard of soul wandering?"

"Yeah, I think I have," said Cadet Eudell. "That's when you're in purgatory and someone has to pray you out. The Catholics teach that. You Catholic, George?"

"No, that's not what I mean. What I'm talking about is what they call the transmigration of souls. Brothers, I believe that I've lived in other lifetimes, and I'm destined for great things."

"Wait, wait a minute now." Cadet Frank was following very closely and had anticipated that George would say something heretical. "You know what the Bible says, right? It's appointed for man to die once, and after this, the judgment, but you're talking about being reincarnated. I don't think..."

"Now, you're not going to get into this preaching mode again," George replied. "I know what the Bible says, but I'm telling you that I just know I've lived during the time of Christ, and other times as well."

The silence was deafening. Frank and Eudell looked at each other. They were both seriously thinking the same thing: *Will they have to report this to the commandant's office and suggest that their roommate is psychotic?*

"George, if you lived during the time of Christ, what did you do? Were you a Jew or a Gentile?" asked Frank.

Cadet George began to do something that his roommates had rarely seen him do. He began to grin. It was a smug self-contented type of grin, which made them feel as if he had led them into a cleverly calculated trap. He then swaggered over to his desk, opened the drawer and produced a sheet of lined paper. He was still grinning as his eyes fell upon the opening stanza. It became an opportune time to practice public speaking and enlighten his roommates on his writing skills.

He cleared his throat as if addressing an assembly of men.

Then he started:

I have sinned and I have suffered,
Played the hero and the knave;
Fought for belly, shame, or country,
And for each have found a grave.

I cannot name my battles
For the visions are not clear,
Yet, I see the twisted faces
And I feel the rending spear.

Perhaps I stabbed our Savior
In His sacred helpless side.
Yet, I've called His name in blessing
When after times I died.

Cadets Frank and Eudell were now sitting upright on their cots. They were surprised about two things: They couldn't believe that anyone with such a rough exterior could produce and arrange such thoughtful words into a poem. However, they were also surprised that he would dare to identify with the soldier that pierced the side of Christ with a spear.

"It ain't finished yet, but I'm working on it," said George. "I know it sounds crazy, brothers, but I do think that I have a certain sense about these things."

"But the crucifixion of Christ, George?"

"Oh, I just took a little poetic liberty about that. I can't say that I was the d ----- d Roman soldier who threw that spear, which is why I wrote that "perhaps" I stabbed the Savior. Did you hear that? "Perhaps." But half of the things that we read about the Roman army in our strategy class I already knew somehow. And I've never studied the Romans 'til now.

"Cadet George, do me a favor and don't tell anyone about this. This sense that you have—don't even mention the subject of reincarnation."

"Brother Rat, I don't intend to tell anyone, and I didn't intend for you two to tell anyone."

"All right, this conversation won't go beyond these old walls," said Frank. "Say, do you know what spear you were talking about in that poem?"

"Of course, it's the Longinus, named after the Roman soldier. It was used in the Crusades. Charlemagne won forty-seven battles with it, and Napoleon went looking for it, but it had been smuggled away. It always assured victory."

"Very good, brother rat," said Frank, impressed. "But do you know where it is now?"

"Well, of course! The Swiss got hold of it through the Catholic Church."

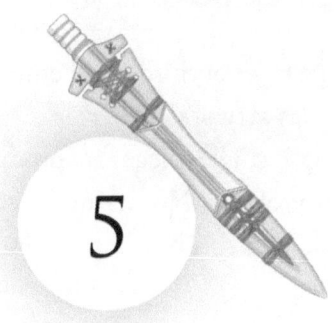

5

HOMELESS ARTIS

He slowly became alert and aware of his deplorable surroundings. He strained to fall back into slumber, cringing at the thought of facing another day at the run-down shelter for homeless vagabonds. The musty, torn wool blanket that shrouded his face was still damp with three days' worth of tears, saliva, and mucous. But he kept it close because it had become a familiar companion in this sad environment. He was oblivious to its moldy stench as he breathed it in.

Fortunately, there was always the familiar aroma of cabbage soup in the morning, which lifted his spirits and reminded him of home. But since the untimely death of his mother, Dolphie felt he had been cut off from the world. He was orphaned. He was told that she died of breast cancer, but he knew that she had never truly recovered from his father's death and probably truly died of a broken heart. In any case, Dolphie was now a prodigal who could never return home.

The events of the preceding four months had created a roller coaster ride of rebounding high hopes, disappointments, and disillusionments, which centered on his rejection from enrollment at the prestigious Vienna Art institute. He had worked hard at creating different color hues, following the rules of thirds, and employing every learned artistic technique for canvas artwork.

However, every single piece he produced lacked one essential element—a quality of life. No matter how much he tried, there was no life in his work, and this had become increasingly evident since the death of his mother.

The mumbling voices around him were always an annoyance. There were always men who stumbled around his cot on their way to the community shower, slamming their fists against the walls in protest of the lack of heated water and poor water pressure. Others were expressively sensitive to the chilled water once it made contact with their infectious bedbug bites. Then there were the sometimes-gregarious sounds of women on the other side of the walls. The men and women were supposed to sleep in separate quarters, but everyone knew that this was a side of Vienna where true gentlemen were unseen and womanizers frequented. It had the feel of a circus carnival community where the bizarre and perverted were commonplace.

Yet, he imagined how his mother might have enjoyed working here. There was a staff of workers and volunteers that oddly seemed out of place. Like his mother, they were simple and peasant-like, but they had hearts of gold. They smiled when there really wasn't anything to smile about. They sang and hummed tunes to themselves as they busied about cleaning and serving some of the most unappreciative people he had ever seen. They were a religious group dedicated to saving the souls of men, and they shared Bible lessons in group gatherings three times a day.

They reminded him of Father Eisenbraun, the Spear of Destiny, and some of the workers in the Hofberg museum. But there was no time to think about that now. In his mind, Dolphie pushed away the once cherished thoughts that he had about his destiny of taking the world by storm as an artist. He decided finally to pick himself out of bed and eat a free breakfast of cabbage soup and fresh biscuits.

By this time, the bathroom was relatively free from the throngs of dirty men who had been boozing all night. He shuffled along the tile floor without picking up his feet. The floor was usually cold, which always helped the men rouse out of their slumber. In front of the bathroom sink, he stared at the shiny brass plate over the basin, which functioned as a mirror. He peered at his unshaven reflection, but didn't recognize himself anymore. Somehow he had grown seven years older in the past month.

His only plan, which had become a structured routine by now, was to eat and walk himself to the courtyard to possibly sell hand-painted postcards and artwork. Perhaps someone would take an interest in his work. Perhaps someone would notice his talent and commission him to do enough work to defray the cost of an apartment on the nice side of town where better prospects were.

He entered the kitchen.

"*Guten tag.* Did you enjoy your sleep, sir?"

Dolphie didn't make eye contact with the cheerful *fraulein*, though her voice was pleasant to listen to. He had become self-conscious and ashamed of his state of homelessness, despite his insistence that all true artists begin this way.

He answered in his usual monotone. "Y-Yes, and thank you very much. Is there any black coffee left?"

"We've just finished making the third and final pot. I'll place a cup on your tray."

Her name was Leisele, and she volunteered in the kitchen. She was a sweet girl who had large eyes and thick dark hair. For most of the descent men, she was a breath of fresh air among the other frowsy women who lodged there as virtual prostitutes.

"I see you have your usual art supplies. You must be headed toward the courtyard again."

"Uh-huh."

"Did you know that there was another plaza about two blocks away from where you usually go, which has more people and better scenery? There aren't as many flowers and trees, but a lot of artists sell postcards of the shops and museum.

"Shops and a museum? Wo-would that be the Hofberg museum?"

"Why yes! So you've seen it. I'm sure an artist like you can get a lot of business there. There's always a group of tourists who stand around all afternoon. It's a much nicer side of town, even though some businesses are beginning to have trouble."

"I've been there, *fraulein*, and there isn't any plaza around that area."

"Oh, but there's a wonderful plaza there! It must have been completed about two years ago. There are new shops and markets there, too!"

"Then how could some businesses be in trouble if more tourists are coming through and everything is better there?"

"Some businesses are closing for some reason. I guess bigger businesses are becoming more popular. One of the men who sleeps in your room lost his business on that side of town. He blames the Jews. I don't really understand it, but my father says that even the mayor wants the Jews to leave the area—something about the way they do business, I guess. I feel sorry for them. They've created more jobs, they don't bother anyone, and yet they've had such difficult times."

"Which way did you say the plaza was?"

"Just turn left when you leave the front door and walk straight ahead. If you don't want to take the commuter tram, you'll have to pass through two alleyways. You won't be able to miss the plaza because you'll notice a lot of people walking around there. Remember, our doors won't open tonight until seven-thirty because it's cleaning night tonight, but I'm sure there will be a bed available for you."

"Seven thirty, y-yes. Thank you."

Dolphie finished his breakfast, rose from his chair, and made his way out of the shelter without looking back.

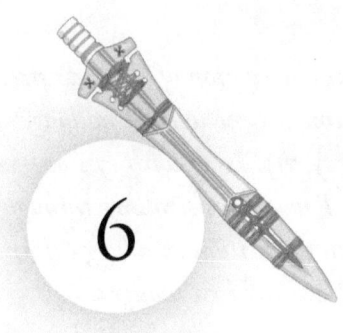

6

ANTI-SEMITIC

....

The Hofberg museum felt farther away than it actually was because it forced him to return to where his dreams had all begun years ago. He shuffled along the streets with his supplies tucked underneath his arm. A commuter train went by, which made him think of the school trip he had taken with the children from the abbey.

Shuffling through an alley, he could see a view of the main boulevard just ahead of him. The environment had changed slightly. The stone buildings were the same, but there were more shops and more people in this area of Vienna now. Life seemed to be moving at a faster pace. He leaned against a corner wall to take it all in. There were children being affectionately dragged along by their mothers, storeowners with souvenirs hanging from their storefronts, and young lovers who were so bold as to actually hold hands in public. Then there were the people in black who appeared to pepper the boulevard as they walked briskly. Bearded men with long curly locks wearing long black caftan coats, accompanied by scarfed women carrying funny loaves of bread, made him feel as if he were in another country. The Jewish community had grown significantly.

Later, in *Mein Kampf,* Hitler would write:

"... the visual observation of Vienna's streets had rendered invaluable services. There came a time when I no longer as before wandered blindly through the mighty city. Now with eyes opened I looked at people as well as buildings. As I was once strolling through the inner city, I suddenly happened upon an apparition in a long caftan with black hair locks.

Is this a Jew? was my first thought.

They surely didn't look like that in Linz. I observed the man stealthily and cautiously. But the longer I stared at this alien face, examining it feature for feature, the more my first question was transformed into a new conception: Is this a German?")

Seven artists stood in the courtyard with their easels. Two of them were busy painting something for what appeared to be five tourists. Refocusing, Dolphie decided to seize an available spot in the corner of the courtyard before any other artists arrived.

One artist had just completed a watercolor street scene for a tourist and was about to wash off his brushes in a water-filled coffee can when he noticed Dolphie. He was short and wore a beige tweed coat with a white handkerchief to impress the well-dressed visitors at the museum.

"You from around here?" he said as his aluminum-tipped paintbrushes made an annoying clanking sound while he stirred.

"I'm staying across town," said Dolphie. "This is a good spot. Is it always this busy during this time of day?"

"Yes, sometimes even more when the school tours come through. They don't pay as much, but you can always scratch out some postcards for the students for a few coronas."

"I was once on a school tour here. We spent the day at that museum over there," said Dolphie reminiscently, almost as if he were only talking to himself.

"That museum generates a lot of business around here now. Say, there's usually a funny guy who comes around here a few times a week, and he sets up right where you're standing, so be ready to move if you see him coming."

"Move? Why? Aren't these places for whoever comes first? That's the way it is at the other plaza."

"Sure, but you're not going to want to get into any discussions with this guy. Best just let him have his way, and he prefers that spot for some reason."

"He can just as well do his work from any other plaza in the city. This isn't the only artist spot."

"No, no, you've got it wrong. He's not an artist. He's a, a type of magician or something. He sets up a table with pamphlets and talks to the public about mystical things. I'm not sure what he wants, because he doesn't ask for money. All I know is that he's passionate about what he says and likes to invite people to group meetings or something."

It was two o'clock at this time. "Men of Austria, men of Austria, listen to me," a megaphoned voice echoed toward the plaza from down the main street. A small figure, wearing a dingy brown coat like most of the local men, was approaching the plaza. He sauntered behind a huge conical speaker that dipped and swayed with every other step he took.

"What has become of you? And what on earth will become of you? You have assumed the position of a groveling suitor. You search for truth and yet fall victim to following in the ways of the bramble around you. You have descended from your rightful place in the underworld. It was a right place. It was a fitting place. You are Aryans. Aryans from Atlantis, I say. You were meant to rule. You are of a noble race. Purify yourselves and come back to your origins. Come back to your place. Atlantis still reigns. Look around you. You've become a despicable lot; swine that wallows in filth. Come back. Your time is now."

His name was Edgar, and as he approached the artist courtyard people began to make a pathway for him like street pigeons avoiding foot traffic. Dolphie, however, remained at his selected spot, indignant. *What right does this loudmouth have in disturbing us*, he thought.

The man stopped in front of his usual spot now preempted by Dolphie. "Are you from Vienna?" Dolphie asked undauntedly.

"I am from Vienna by birth, but my origins, like yours, come from Atlantis, my brother."

Up close there was nothing extraordinary about the man's appearance. He had a prominent nose, which arced away from his face, and squinted eyes, which gave the impression that he needed to wear bifocals. He was thin and almost gaunt looking, yet when he spoke, his voice commanded your attention and provoked a response.

"Sir, I am an artist, but I've had some schooling. Atlantis is a mythical island, and no one's origins can come from there. Why don't you try to sell souvenirs or something if you want to make a living?"

"You say you've had some schooling, and to this I agree. You've only had some. Have you heard of Plato?"

"The philosopher?"

"Yes, he was a mathematician, too—in addition to being a genius—and wrote about this so-called mythical place."

"Well, and what does that mean?"

"For someone with only a little schooling like yourself, it probably doesn't mean much. If you were to read about other philosophers like Philo and their works, you would know that certain claims about Atlantis have been verified throughout history."

By now a small crowd had gathered around the two men. Though Dolphie dared to challenge this public heralder, who was seen as little more than a public embarrassment, the crowd understood Dolphie's line of questioning and took interest in the conversation.

"Even if this is so," Dolphie continued, "what bearing does it have now? Will this create jobs? Look around you. Even in this mighty city, people struggle."

"Yes, brother, they struggle. They struggle, yet they don't realize what they are struggling against. You are struggling because you lie along the bottom, and you're looking up when you should be reigning from the top looking downward."

Dolphie found himself at odds with himself. He didn't want to agree with the man, yet inside, he found himself taking in every word and concept. He knew that the man was talking about greatness. He understood what he was referring to in this description of someone who was always looking up. Dolphie's chest started to feel heavy, and suddenly, something happened that hadn't happened since the death of his father. He felt a sense of shame, a conviction for disappointing himself and the whole world.

"Here, take this bulletin. You should come to our meetings. We have them once a week, and we educate people in the things that have been held from them," said the man. "We're having one tomorrow night."

"Like Atlantis?"

"Like Atlantis, and quite a few other things, brother. Just come out."

Examining the flyer carefully, Dolphie asked, "Where is this place? Is it your house? My lodgings are very temporary, and I won't be able to."

"I can meet you at the tram station," the fellow interrupted, peering at him intently. "You'll be able to catch the commuter train from there and make it back before nine thirty."

"I have to get back before seven to be able to keep my place at the hotel." Dolphie didn't want to use the word shelter to add more pain to his feelings of shame.

"Don't worry. We'll be able to bring you back."

The artists and onlookers watched with anticipation thinking that Dolphie would finally reject the invitation. However, only a few moments passed before he folded the paper in half, put it in his left trouser pocket (because the right one had a gaping hole in it), and firmly shook the man's hand. They parted.

7

THE OCCULT

It was a weeknight, which meant to Dolphie that the evening commuter trains would not be overburdened with tourists and weekend travelers.

Riding the commuter train during nightfall was a different experience. Streetlights were dim from low levels of electrical power in the area. The effect was eerie all along the boulevards. Ghostly figures flounced up and down the sidewalks in fading shadows. All the while, the tram would click and send sparks as its connecting wires skipped over phase breaks in the drop cables.

Click-clack, click, click-clack-click, click-clack, click, click-clack-click; the cable phase breaks, installed at every street intersection, enabled a passenger to tell how close he was getting to his destination by counting the noisy buzzing and clicking sounds from station to station—many children had memorized the number of rhythmic clicks it took to get to places like their homes, the town center, or school.

The clicking and buzzing was becoming less frequent, and Dolphie knew this meant he was reaching the outer suburbs of the mighty city. Fewer pedestrians were visible outside, and most of the passengers had exited the tram. Only the incessant shudder of the train and the occasional screeching stops kept him from being lulled into sleep.

Coasting now, the tram jerked, shuddered, and came to another stop. It was one of the last stops on the line, and there were no outdoor sounds to be heard. Dolphie peered through the window and recognized Edgar from the plaza. He was still grim-faced, but seemed to be pleased to know that Dolphie had kept his rendezvous. Dolphie stepped off the train.

"I see you've made it," said Edgar. "You look hungry."

"Never mind about that," said Dolphie. "I said I would come, and I have. Is your office far from here?"

"No, it's not far, but let me introduce you to a few people before we talk about that. I'm sorry, what was your name again?"

"Adolf. Adolf Hitler."

"Herr Hitler, I'd like you to meet some other young men who will be attending the meeting along with you," Edgar said, motioning to four others. "This is Gustav. This one is Colbert. Over here we have Faron, and this one is Barend. One other person will be meeting us later, so that will make six of you in total."

All of the young men feigned a warm greeting with a socially acceptable nod. They were all hungry, tired, and generally discontent.

The group walked slowly away from the tram station. Dolphie and the four others walked a pace behind Edgar. None of them was familiar with this side of town, which was hardly impressive. The houses were modest and not very well maintained. The occasional passersby were dressed almost traditionally, very simple. It certainly had a different feel when compared to Vienna.

Then they came upon a huge structure that overlooked a grassy incline. It was a real castle, though now a run-down relic from Austria's medieval past. Stone buttresses adorned the tops of four pillars in the front. The castle was dark gray, almost black, caused by local coal burning.

In times past, the city council maintained the grounds of such places by keeping foliage trimmed back and small leaks in the roofs patched up. However, times were different now. A volunteer group of local neighbors was responsible for upkeep, and anyone who labored as a volunteer knew how to secretly gain access through the main entrance.

The young men were relieved after finally reaching the top of the brick stairway, which led through the garden. Then they all stopped to examine the two figures ahead of them. A well-established looking man, along with another youth, was waiting for them just in front of the perpendicular archway, which supported huge wooden doors. The well-established looking man was blond and formally dressed.

"*Willkommen,*" he said with a genuine smile. I am Julius. It's so good to see fine young men like yourselves come to visit us this evening."

"These are the ones I was talking to you about yesterday," said Edgar. "May I present, Gustav, Colbert, Faron, Barend, and Adolf."

The young men all gave another socially acceptable nod to acknowledge the welcome.

"And this is Rhienhart," continued Julius, referring to the youth next to him. "He's not from Vienna, like all of you. He comes from Salzburg." Julius tenderly placed an arm around Rhienhart's shoulder and continued in a low tone, "It's wonderful to see how we are now spreading out to other big cities. But please, do come in, won't you?"

Julius ambled in front of them through the huge doors, and Dolphie noticed that he was carrying a book in his left hand. The cover had the picture of a stout woman dressed in black, which he found intriguing.

He led them to a small alcove near one of the front rooms. It was filled with books, which were neatly arranged along bookcases and desks.

"We can all sit here for the time being," said Julius. "Edgar, why don't you get our young men a few refreshments?"

"Of course," he replied, and disappeared through the doorway, his fading footsteps echoing down the hallway.

"My uncle has that book," said Gustav, noticing now the hard text in Julius's hand.

Appearing almost startled, "Your uncle? Oh, yes, your uncle has this book? Well, he must be well-read," Julius said.

Julius then seized the moment as an opportunity to segue into a meeting. He turned the cover over so that the book faced the young men, who were all sitting across from him in a semicircle. It was like being in school, and Dolphie thought about the wonderful stories shared by Father Eisenbraun at the abbey.

"Have any of you heard of this woman?" he said, thumping the book with his index finger. "Her name is Helena Blavatsky, and she's an exceptional authoress. She is very well traveled and very intelligent. Now, I know some of you are probably thinking, he's not going to peddle off a bunch of books after we've come all this way to get here. But this book is special, because it speaks about each one of you. It's called 'The Secret Doctrine.' Do any of you know what a doctrine is?"

Dolphie sat up, "A doctrine is a type of teaching or lesson; they teach you that in Sunday school."

"Very good, very good," replied Julius. "Then a secret doctrine would be a type of hidden teaching, would it not?"

The young men simply stared at him, expressionless.

"Let me tell you young men something. I know why you are here. You may not quite know why you are here, but I know you are here to discover more about yourselves, and this secret doctrine is going to help you do just that."

Faron spoke up. "Sir, I study Greek history at university. Edgar talked with me about the lost city of Atlantis and new evidence about its existence. I just wanted to…"

By this time, all of the young men were affirmatively nodding their heads in agreement with Faron, implying that they were not particularly interested in any discussions on doctrines.

"Young man," Julius now intoned gravely, "Atlantis does indeed exist, and it exists through all of you. You see, the secret doctrine is just this: Certain superhuman men survived the destruction of Atlantis. They are called Aryans, and they are your forefathers. But, you all can now tap into this superhuman power if you want to. And isn't this the cause of all your problems—the lack of real power? This is why you cannot get a job. This is why you fail. This is why the less desirable folks in our country are now leading us into an abyss. Each of you can connect with a guiding spirit from Atlantis, and your lives can be changed for greatness."

"Is this some kind of political party?" asked Gustav. "Why are you doing this?"

"We have no party affiliations whatsoever," he said with a forced chuckle. "Politics are the workings of mere men. We're a small club, and we're supported by the Thule society, but let me say, we do consult with local politicians about things like preserving our customs and culture. And we are privileged to be able to meet in this glorious castle. It's symbolic to us. Look around you. Isn't this a beautiful place?"

Slow footsteps, which began as a whisper, were now echoing toward them from down the hall. They were the shuffling sounds of someone who slightly dragged his heel. They all suspected that Edgar was returning with some type of refreshment.

Edgar appeared at the doorway with his arms full. He was carrying what appeared to be refreshments on an unpolished silver tray. There were seven small, partially filled glasses containing absinthe, which were not watered down, and thick onionskin reefers of cannabis.

The young men were delighted to be treated as adults, but worried about where this was headed. They had all seen their parents sip and savor absinthe at social parties, but no one ever smoked cannabis. This was a substance that was always associated with brothels, criminals, and perverts.

"Ah, here we are," said Julius. "Thank you, Edgar. Boys, I mean, young men, feel free to have a glass. You certainly must be a little dry."

Rhienhart, who was slightly aloof from the rest of them, took the initiative to grip a glass. "Thank you," he said. "In Salzburg, our house servant always serves absinthe on Saturday evenings before dinner." He raised the glass to his nose and breathed it in. It smelled slightly stronger than the watered down version he had become accustomed to since he had turned sixteen. He hesitated for a moment and then dared to sip it. The others, watching his every move, felt cowardly when he then turned to them and grinned.

"Come on, boys," said Julius, "don't be shy. Take one."

It was like playing Russian roulette. They were still timid, but the boys each stretched forth their arms to take hold of one of the small, ornate crystal glasses. Then they slowly sipped and savored the alcohol. They felt the cold liquid run smoothly down their throats and warm their stomachs. Gustav hiccupped out of nervousness, but everyone thought it was because he had gulped too quickly.

Julius smacked his lips, "Mmm, *das est gut, ya*! But this is only the first part. Now comes the finishing touch. This will help you relax a little." He picked up a cannabis reefer, lit a match, and brought it to his mouth. He inhaled intensely with his eyes shut, swallowed, and then exhaled. He did it again, and this time, the funny onionskin paper generated a bright orange glow as it burned.

"This is a true art form," Julius said. "Now there's one for each of you, so put down your glasses and try it."

By this time, Gustav noticed something unusual about the thin paper that enveloped the cannabis. There was small writing on it; all of the reefers were wrapped in something that resembled pages out of a book. He picked one up nonchalantly and brought it to his face to read the small inscription.

"Were these pages from a Bible?" he asked in shock. They all took a closer look at the thickly rolled reefers. "Yes, yes they are," said Faron. "Look, in the beginning God created." Faron began to unroll his reefer, reading the unfolding verses before him. He smudged away the residue of the cannabis leaves and read as much as was visible on the remnant piece.

The boys felt embarrassed. Only uncivilized pagan tribes could have thought of using a holy book as common paper. They felt as if they had accidentally caught someone in the act of undressing. But then Colbert said soberly, "Why would you use the Bible for this? My dad kisses our family Bible every night before going to bed. Don't you think there's something wrong about making reefers out of it?"

"Gentlemen, relax a little. All of you are too tense," said Edgar. "We have to use pages from books to make these cigars burn well, and only certain types of paper will work. We have a collection of books that have been in this castle for years. Most of these dusty old books have lost their covers, so we really don't know what they are about, and we don't bother to read them for content. We simply rip out some of their pages to burn."

Rhienhart chimed in, "Nobody ever pays attention to the writing."

"But I don't feel right smoking this when it's been wrapped in pages from the Holy Bible," said Faron.

"Boys, look at me. Look at me now," said Julius, who was visibly shaking. "I've already told you that I know why you're here. You're here for greatness. You're going to have to die to your old values and your old way of thinking if you want to achieve true greatness. Don't you want power in your lives? Don't you want to fulfill your noble destiny of supremacy on this earth? It's possible, my friends, oh, it's possible. But you have to have your own renaissance. You have to be reborn."

There was dead silence among the boys. Every time Julius spoke, he somehow captivatedly stirred them into a false sense of shame for doubting him. He was like the father whom they might have wanted to have: gentle, firm, and self-assured. Dolphie still felt that his father had never thought he could ever achieve anything great. He still felt the cold hand of his father from the grave repressing him, dragging him down into a life of mundane, meaningless drudgery and bureaucratic boredom.

Then, without any provocation, Dolphie's voice cracked through the silence like thunder.

"Do you hear the footsteps? I said, do you hear the footsteps, my brothers? I hear the footsteps, not of men, but of mighty giants."

All eyes were upon Dolphie now, who seemed to be in a trance-like state.

"They're crushing goosesteps, and they will burn an imprint into this continent and abroad, and yes, I do see it now. I do see and accept this renaissance of spirit and soul."

It was then as if they all started moving in slow motion. Dolphie first took a reefer and imitated Julius's every gesture in inhaling and swallowing. Then Rhienhart followed, which prompted the rest of the young men to clamber as they all reached for reefers at once, their hands colliding into one another as Edgar balanced the tray to keep the items from falling to the dusty floor. They began to laugh and pat each other on the back as Julius refilled a glass of absinthe to toast the group.

Before long, their eyes were glossed over, their minds were numb, and their sense of resistance had vanished. They mumbled to each other and laughed. But it was darkness, it was sedative, it was self-liberating from any inhibitions—and it was addictive.

As if on cue, Julius and Edgar led the boys out of the alcove to a large room near the foot of a spiral stairwell. The stairs appeared to ascend into gray nothingness. The second story of the castle was nearly in complete darkness, as only the occasional flickering of homemade candles illuminated the busts of statuettes hung above the doorways.

Most of the floor was made of white tile, but a huge circular mosaic portraying the head of a black timber wolf sprawled from wall to wall. It was sixty feet in diameter and dominated the room.

"Young men, I want to initiate you in your quest for greatness," said Julius. The boys, huddled together near the center of the mosaic, were now ready to accept whatever was to come.

"Come with me, each of you. I want to show you something," said Julius. He walked them to the inner edge of the mosaic outlined in black tile. Six open coffins had been neatly laid along the outside edge of the circle, and they were all pointing toward the image of the wolf.

"In a symbolic gesture of your new birth, I want each of you to lie in your own coffin. Don't worry, it's comfortable in there. You see, in order to have access to the spirit world as mighty Aryans, you have to die to yourselves this way."

"Nobody is going to close it on you, gentlemen," said Edgar "but I want you to repeat this special chant to yourselves as you lie down and as you get up. You only need to be in there sixty seconds or so."

Edgar smiled as he gave each underling a card printed with an ancient Semitic chant. None of them understood the words, but each one began to verbalize the funny poetry and stepped into the black silk-lined coffins without a second thought.

The young men created a collective chorus of mumbled hums as they went over their verses again and again from within their death boxes. When they stepped out after a minute or so, they did indeed feel different. They we alert, they were older, and a dark seed had been planted.

Suddenly, Dolphie stood up quickly again. "Do you hear the footsteps?" he shrieked. "Brothers, they're coming."

Years later, Dietrich Eckhart, an active leader in the Thule Society, would say of Hitler on his deathbed:

> ***Follow Hitler! He will dance, but it is I who have called the tune. I have initiated him into the 'Secret Doctrine', opened his centers in vision, and given him the means to communicate with the Powers. (Rule by Secrecy)***

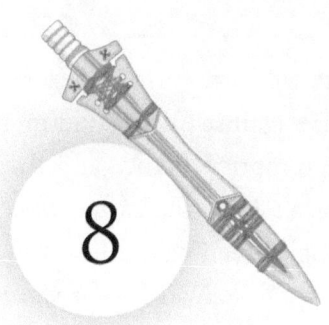

8

WWI & REINCARNATION

....

It was no man's land, but it was anyone's land. Any man who dared to approach this desolate, war-ravaged stretch of abused earth usually felt the numbing dead weight of emptiness in his soul. It was a horrifying contrast to Austria's rolling lush green valleys and crisp, frosty-tipped, picturesque mountain ranges. Austria had continued to increase as an empire in the recent years, occupying the Ottoman provinces of Bosnia and Herzegovina. It was joined with Hungary, and many attributed its growth and power to economic success. Others thought that Austria's strong alliances helped to keep any enemies of the empire at bay—and still there were others, like Dolphie, who knew that it was Austria's possession of the spear that allowed it to have such hegemony. By this time, he had the compulsive habit of visiting the Hofburg museum to simply gaze upon it. An ill-fated public visit to Sarajevo by the Austrian Archduke and his wife changed the world. Some Serbians had demanded to have their own empire, so a Serbian rebel named Princip wielded a semi-automatic pistol, approached their stalled vehicle in a motorcade, and shot Archduke Ferdinand and his wife, the Duchess of Hohenberg, dead—the Archduke's lifeblood poured out of a six-inch gaping wound in his jugular vein, staining his royal apparel.

It spread like wildfire. Austria declared war on Serbia, provoking Russia to mobilize against Austria. Germany responded by mobilizing against Russia, prompting France and Britain to take a stand against Germany. It wasn't long thereafter when the lifeblood of French, German, and Englishmen would begin to stain the battlefields of no man's land during World War I—the war to end all wars.

At the time, George Patton was a second lieutenant in the US Army, with the experience of a veteran soldier and a skilled athlete. He had chased Pancho Villa around Mexico on a "Punitive Expedition" ordered by President Woodrow Wilson, and learned to love action. He had been in gunfights. He had been in newsreels. He had been singularly made an aide-de-camp by Brigadier General of the US Army, John Pershing.

He had been trained to play hard for the US Olympic Pentathlon team in 1916, as the games were expected to take place in Berlin, Germany, but all of these climatic achievements came to an abrupt interruption, and now he was "over there," on the edge of no man's land.

Pap-pap-pap-pap-pap-pap. Under the distant sound of gunfire, Patton shouted to his troops, "Listen, everybody knows that we're here because these d----d French people couldn't even fight their way out of a crowded marketplace if they had to. They're not a fighting people. Somebody else will probably always have to fight their wars for 'em. I think they like the color yellow so much because it matches the color of their own blood."

Several of the men chuckled among themselves.

Patton had been given the privilege of organizing the first tank brigade to see combat (the 304th Tank Brigade). He and his tanks were a part of an offensive involving over 500,000 US soldiers and French troops.

"But listen to me," he continued. "You are the first American tanks to see combat, so you'd better settle it in your minds right now that American tanks do not surrender to the enemy. As long as your tank is able to move, it must go forward. Now, you are the first American tank unit, but we will not be the only Yanks out there. General Pershing has informed me that he has assigned an American colored unit to fight under the French command. Their helmets are French, but they wear US uniforms."

"Sir," a master sergeant interrupted, "I've heard about them, they call them the Hellfighters from Harlem, or something like that. Are we to fight alongside the coloreds if we meet them in the field?"

"They can all go right back to hell," shouted a corporal. "You will all honor any man wearing an American uniform, no matter how competent he may be as a soldier," Patton insisted. "Don't be distracted by their skin tone. And remember, our role is a subordinate role to the foot soldier. The most important rank in the army is the rank of private first class. If any doughboy gets wounded but wants to ride on your back, let 'em jump on. Our tanks will be able to protect our ground troops and outmaneuver the enemy on any terrain. If your gun becomes disabled, use your pistols and squash the enemy with your tracks. If your engine stalls, remain where you are and wait for help. Any questions?"

There were none.

On the other side of no man's land, a light rain started to drizzle. Lice, mud, vomit, and human waste were all mixed together in a brownish goo that remained on the floor of the trenches where Austrian soldiers impatiently waited. The Austrian army had become unnerved at the news of American units joining the war on the side of the French. They therefore hunkered down and waited for favorable intelligence reports before deciding to devise a strategy.

New war technology had made it possible to slaughter large military units in minutes. The mobilization of airplanes, long-range artillery, machine guns, and tanks were a top priority for both sides. However, intelligence-gathering remained in antiquity. Only volunteer runners who dared to cross minefields riddled with potholes and barbed wire enabled high-ranking officers to calculate favorable strategies based upon the latest news of troop mobilization. They were low in rank and had a high mortality rate. But one such seemingly invincible corporal got the attention of higher ranking officers for bravery and evading sniper fire. It was Dolphie.

Dolphie had enlisted in a Bavarian regiment at the age of twenty-five and appeared to have great luck avoiding life-threatening injuries. On more than one occasion, he had slipped away from a particular area where moments later a big shell exploded, killing or wounding everyone there. Thus, he was promoted to corporal and functioned as a dispatch runner. He tirelessly ran the latest messages back and forth from the high command staff in the rear to the fighting units on the frontlines. To the surprise of everyone, he would even take out his hidden watercolors and calmly paint the landscapes of battlefields during a lull in skirmishes.

"Corporal Hitler!"

"Yes, First Sergeant."

"Put away those color things and listen! We need this coded message delivered to Captain Schultz's unit on the other side of that ridge. There has been sniper fire reported in the immediate area, so keep your head down and your helmet strapped tightly. Do you have any questions?"

"No, First Sergeant."

"Get going then."

These were the types of orders that Dolphie had become used to. Fear was never a factor because he believed his time to die had not yet come. Dolphie had continued in his studies of the 'secret doctrine' and called upon guidance from the powers of darkness during wartime. Though by any account he was an incongruous soldier, with sloppy mannerisms and unmilitary bearing, he was nonetheless always eager for action and felt he had assurance of safety from his guided spirits of Atlantis. He was convinced that these guided spirits would enable him to one day possess the Longinus to usher in his destiny. Until that day came, he knew that nothing could kill him. Therefore, he was always one of the first to volunteer for dangerous assignments, even after several narrow escapes from sure death. To his comrades, he became known as a likeable loner, notable for his good luck.

But Dolphie's hands were shaking now because he was holding a crucial message. He knew how important this message would be to every field commander waiting for the right moment to plan an attack. Devising an attack always required foreknowledge of the enemy's resources and capabilities. But this came without expectation. The message read: *Large African troop disembarkation in Brest, France. Units appear to be wearing a blend of American and French combat uniforms.*

Reading this caused confusion. The US did not have any close enough ties with African allies to want to put them in American uniforms. However, the French did, but why would they be wearing a blend of French and American uniforms? Moreover, German occupied territories in Africa regularly reported on the status of international troop mobilizations. No such reports of African troop mobilizations validated the message. Did this deployment of units go unnoticed by German intelligence?

"Your unit commander needs to see that message right away," said the young field commander. "No telling how much time we'll have for any counteroffensives."

"Yes, sir. Right away."

Dolphie responded and headed into the open area. Clumsily, he leapt from hole to hole of no man's land. The coded message in his inner pocket had been folded over five times. The mud was so deep in some spots of this vast field that a soldier could sink up to his waist and remain stuck. Allied long-range artillery had produced hills and holes deep enough to send mobile armored tanks sliding downward in a nosedive for nine or ten feet. Therefore, the only real threat was that of falling into one of these abysses or being shot by long-range sniper fire.

He sprang forward in a low crouch, attempting to land on his side to prevent his head from plunging into mud holes; the grainy soil would painfully impair his vision if it got in his eyes. The buzzing sounds of flies hovered over the ground, and Dolphie knew that massive swarms meant a soldier's decaying body was nearby.

Sometimes, only a pale body part was left with visible shrapnel wounds. At such encounters, he would hold his breath and avoid looking at any remains.

His gas mask dangled alongside of him and was now caked in mud. He had been warned to don it at the slightest suspicion of a German mustard gas attack—one only had a matter of seconds to secure it tightly before acidic chemicals would begin to burn the lungs and esophagus beyond repair. Even though he had cut off the side edges of his mustache to be sure the mask would seal tightly enough against his face, sometimes the cheap material itself would tear if handled too briskly.

Still, he pressed on, chanting dark mystical prayers under his breath, springing, flopping, and landing into the thick earth, one hand holding his gas mask to his side, the other outstretched for balance.

He lay low and attempted to crawl on his belly when he heard the high-pitched sounds of whizzing bullets. They sank into the earth all around him, making a wet, splatting sound.

Dolphie rolled, crawled, assumed a crouching position, and sprang forward again. He persevered under fire for 150 yards before sliding over an embankment, dropping downward, and falling into the middle of a huddled group of Austrian soldiers.

"We had a lookout with binoculars follow your every move," said an impressed captain. "You must be the dispatch the colonel was talking about."

"Sir, I have an urgent message," Dolphie said with bated breath. He then gingerly wiped the mud on his hands against the side of his trousers, unbuttoned the top of his jacket, reached in and produced the folded note. The captain unfolded the message and frowned.

He mumbled to himself as if thinking out loud: "Hmmm, African units mobilizing in France?" When were you given this message, corporal?"

"Sir, about two hours ago."

"Did the field commander mention anything about artillery or tanks?"

"No. sir, not to me, sir. I only know what the message says."

"Captain," a young lieutenant interrupted, "there was an intelligence report about auxiliary enemy troops from the Netherlands, from Haarlem that were joining with the French."

"No, no, no. That must have been an error, lieutenant," said the captain, dismissively waving his hand in the air. "This message says *African* troops. Have you ever known black people to come from Haarlem, Belgium? Besides, the Belgians are neutral in this war."

"Sir," the lieutenant continued, "couldn't there be another Haarlem somewhere?"

9

THE HARLEM HELLFIGHTERS

....

When they marched, it was rhythmic. When they ran, it was a different, springy type of run. They were from Harlem, New York, over 3,600 miles from France.

The only encounter with Europeans that any of them had had was with first-generation Italian immigrants who didn't care to see Negroes on their side of town.

They knew the Bronx, they knew New York City, and they knew Harlem. They knew racial segregation, they knew injustice, and they knew hatred. They were the 369th,, an all-black combat division from the New York Fifteenth National Guard unit, referred to as the Harlem Hellfighters. They were assigned to fight under the French command because US segregation policies forbade them to fight alongside whites in the armed forces. However, they were to leave an indelible impression in Europe all by themselves. At the end of the war, their recorded 191 days in combat would go on record as being the longest period in combat experienced by any US military unit in World War I. Moreover, 171 of the men would be awarded the coveted French *Croix de Guerre* medals for gallantry in action. They were the first to drive the German army all the way to the Rhine River without ever losing conquered ground or releasing a captive soldier. They were true fighters—but most of all, they were good musicians.

About half of the three hundred thousand African American soldiers were sent to France. There was Terry, a young bronze-skinned athlete who worked valet parking in a big garage. He was a quiet adolescent and a deep thinker. Terry felt comfortable behind the wheel of any vehicle because he had experience parking nearly every type of automobile at the garage.

There was also fair-skinned Napoleon, known as Nappy, who was able to work in a meatpacking slaughterhouse. He had roots from Louisiana and spoke French. He was known for having come from a religious family of "holy rollers," and he wrote to his father whenever he could.

There was James Reese Europe, whose father was a former slave. He was originally from Alabama, but moved to New York City to be a nightclub pianist. He produced a blend of ragtime and jazz music that made people want to dance. He received a commission as a lieutenant for the Hellfighters.

And there was Troy. He was an enormous thick-necked man weighing nearly 250 pounds, all of which was muscle. His skin was so dark that, at times, it appeared to reflect a purplish hue. Troy was an angry soldier because he had witnessed a racist mob attempt to lynch a relative while he was visiting the South one summer. The experience had left an emotional scar on his conscience, and Troy was in Europe to fight a personal war.

"Brutha, I ain't fightin' no white man's war," he would say. "I'm here to wup whitey's *you know what* and you don't need to give me no gun to do it. I'll go hand-to-hand with 'em."

Though the Hellfighters had black officers, they also followed the orders of a white captain. Captain Hamilton Fish had gained the respect of all his men because they knew he had their backs. He protected them from racist attacks from within the military and usually encouraged his men to rise above racial prejudices. He was tactful and diplomatic.

After the war, Captain Fish would become one of the longest-serving Congressmen in US history. The troops were all commanded to march at ease as they disembarked from the naval transport in Brest, France. They had hushed conversations as they stepped on foreign soil for the first time.

"Captn?"

"Yes, private."

"I want to ask you something, sir."

"Go ahead."

"Why can't they let us fight with the regular army? Why do they have to do us like this, sir?"

"Now private, you know there are some in the military who are not ready to see whites and Negroes mixed together. Besides, it would cause too much of a distraction from field strategy. There would be no order."

"Captn, can I ask you a personal question?"

"Go ahead."

"Do you think we're fit to fight? There's some a saying we ain't fit for nothin' but running supply lines and cleaning toilets over here."

Captain Fish turned to him and tried to hold back his tears. Rarely had he seen such raw talent to maneuver and fight like these men had displayed during their drills. It caused him pain that they had to bear a stigma that was so removed from reality.

"You listen to me, private," he said matter-of-factly. "You men are going to prove your capabilities, not only to your brothers in arms, but also to all of Europe. I don't intend for any of you to waste your talents on shinning anyone else's boots but your own. You got that?"

"Yes, sir," the private replied grinning. "Besides, I really think they all know what we're capable of—ever since Jack Johnson wupped their Great White Hope before the fifteenth round. That man Jeffries should have stayed in retirement, don't you think so?"

"Okay, okay, private. I see where you're going. But not every Negro can box like Jack Johnson, remember that. And I don't want to hear any more about the 'Fight of the Century'."

"Yes, sir. Thank you, sir."

"And private?"

"Yes, sir."

Turning his head to face his trooper marching now at attention, Captain Fish said, "I won fifty dollars after that fight, and I put my money on Johnson."

The captain gave his private a slight wink and a nod, acknowledging the silent bond that existed between him and all of his men. His commitment to them was undeniable.

The troops continued to march at ease, headed north of Brest. After about 200 yards they met a French group of officers that appeared to be a modest welcoming committee. They were accompanied by seven French infantrymen in battle fatigues. They all were holding rifles with fixed bayonets.

The captain raised his arm signaling the multitude to come to a halt and to form ranks. One could hear their boots shuffling in the dirt from yards away before forming perfectly aligned ranks.

"*Bienvenue, bienvenue, nos frères* Yankees! *Nous sommes tres content de vous voire finalement!*" said a colonel. (*"Welcome, welcome, our Yankee brothers. We are so happy to finally see you!"*)

Standing in closed ranks, someone whispered to Nap, "What's he saying? Is he the company commander?"

"I don't know," Nap said. "These cats are always formal about everything. He's just giving us a welcome, saying he's glad we're finally here."

"*Permettez moi de vous laisser un traducteur expliquer nos plans,*" the colonel continued.

(*"Permit me to allow a translator to explain our plans."*) The colonel stepped to one side and allowed a stiff diminutive looking officer to step in front. He had the appearance of a small wind-up toy soldier, which prompted a few men to chuckle. According to the insignia on his forearm sleeve, he was of a lower rank, and when he spoke, he exaggeratingly raised his pug nose upwards, exposing his nostrils. He began to speak English in an awkward French accent.

"You men of the three hundred and sixty-ninth are very welcome here. We welcome you as equals, and you will be trained with our French infantry. This is a secured area. We will march for ten miles in a southeastern direction to our camp, where you will rest and then undergo brief but intense training. We will all march at ease to the camp so as not to be heard in the villages."

Captain Fish spoke up, "Sir, we understand that the Germans have resorted to using gas attacks in the field. Will we be trained to engage in combat under these conditions?"

"Yes," said the translator, "you will be issued masks, and we all will train in trench warfare."

"Thank you," said Captain Fish. He then turned to the multitude still standing at attention and commanded, "Battalion, at ease. March!" The French officers smiled as the men set out, stern faced and apparently ready to take whatever would come. Thankfully, the men were relieved to march at ease for the ten miles. It allowed them to talk quietly and encourage each other as they passed through small villages in farming communities.

People would come out to greet them spontaneously. Some approached them and kissed their hands. Some gave handpicked roses. Others would kiss the palm of their own hands and wave to the troops.

One middle-aged woman wearing a yellow smock screamed, *"Merci, merci, nos freres, nous n'oublerons pas ce jour!"* ("Thank, you, thank you, our brothers, we will not forget this day.") She then began to sing part of the French national anthem, *"La Marseillaise—attendez vous dans nos companies, mugir ses verocet soldats… ils viennent jus, ce qui dans nos bras… engulfer nos filles no companies, aux armes cityonnes… formez vos battaillons, marchons, marchons…."*

The private first-class walking next to Nap said, "She's kinda cute. You see, why can't we get this type of treatment in our own home? Even the dogs don't bark mean at us here. We gots ta come all the way over here to be appreciated, and a lot of us probably won't be going back."

Nap glanced at him but continued to walk in silence. He didn't want to think about the possibility of being killed because of what it would do to his family. However, the risk of dying induced no personal fear because of his deeply-rooted faith in God and the promise of salvation described in the Book of Romans. He had to memorize it in his father's church as a child and now had the habit of reciting it out loud when he sensed anxiety among his buddies. There was the time while in the large military transport crossing the Atlantic Ocean when everyone knew that a German sub would torpedo them. Unlike the transports for the white troops, they had not been given any gunship escort and were desperately vulnerable. They had all talked about how long they could last in the water before Nap would start, *"If you confess with your mouth the Lord Jesus and believe in your heart that God has raised him from the dead, you will be saved."*

"I don't know how that's gonna save me from sharks, my brutha," they would say, trying not to sound too irreverent. Nap finally came out of his bubble and turned to the private next to him, "Man, you gotta take every day as it comes and enjoy every moment no matter where you are. Some folks are getting lynched back home who should be safe there. It might just be safer here for some, ya know? God is always in control."

The private looked at him, started to say something, and then turned his attention to a small group of boys waving French flags.

Seeing French peasants reminded Nap of kinfolk in Louisiana. The women wore their smocks the same way his Creole Aunt Josie had, folded high on top just over the forehead and tucked neatly behind the ears. Unfortunately, no one in the family had discussed their French heritage with him as he was growing up; there was always a sense of shame about the topic. He was simply a Negro like everyone else. But passing through the small villages, he could smell familiar aromas of homemade bread and garlic, which made him feel different from the rest.

The men were feeling tired when they finally reached the dusty camp—especially those who had lost their lunches due to seasickness on the transport. It was a tent city dotted with a wide scattering of brown camouflaged field tents, a field soup kitchen, five horse watering troughs for washing up, and five campfires that had already been started. One could hear artillery in the distance, which sounded like thunder.

"Men," the captain shouted to his battalion, "you will all be paired up according to squads and assigned a tent with a buddy. You will have forty-five minutes to rest before starting practice for field combat maneuvers and trench warfare. Your squad leaders will break you down into pairs. Company commanders, out!"

The company commanders took over. Captain Fish was exhausted but didn't dare reveal his condition to his men. He had carried the same field pack, worn the same boots, and ate the same bland food rations during the last ten miles. He began to think of how he wanted to write his father about his experiences and sat down to reflect for forty-five minutes before field practice.

When Nap and Troy fell out from ranks, they both knew their squad commander, Lieutenant Europe, would pair them up as tent buddies. He had been keeping an eye on both of them and was always bothered by Troy's temperament. He reasoned that Nap was the type of man who might be able to help him take better control of his anger. He called them over. "I want you two to take the first tent in the second column. Both of you make sure when we drill for trench warfare that your buddy gets a good seal on his mask. Troy, you're much taller, so you're going to have to squat down a little to check your buddy's mask fit."

Both men gave a "yes, sir," saluted, and headed for the tent, kicking up dust in the wind as they went.

"Well, here it is," said Nap. "Just like camping outside. Did ya ever go camping?"

"Camping? Naaa," said Troy, "our people don't camp."

"Why not? It's good getting to feel all close to nature. My dad used to take us with the church group."

"Man, black people don't camp. Besides, we'd be likely to have our tents raided overnight by whites," protested Troy.

"If you just camp on the black side of the grounds, you'd be all right."

"You don't understand, Nap. White folks do all that camping stuff. And if they do it, I don't wanna do it."

"Troy, you're an angry black man."

"Ya bet I am! What about it?"

"Nothing, hey just listen. You can't take that kind of anger to a battlefield. It's not the place to get emotional. You've got to be clearheaded. We're men!"

"Man, those people almost lynched my cousin right in front of my eyes. They nearly strung him up like beef on a hook. Ain't I supposed to be angry?"

"Well, why didn't they lynch him in the end? What stopped them?" Troy stopped to think for a moment. His continence changed, bearing a look of defeat. He would have liked to continue in his heated ranting, but became almost soft-spoken. He looked down at his boots and started to mumble. "Man, this old white man jumped in and started to hug him. I think someone called him a parson, whatever that is. See, my cousin was accused of taking someone's wheelbarrow. It was a new wheelbarrow with a polished frame. When this man came up to the mob, they was already fixing a rope for my cousin. Then this man said that it was his wheelbarrow and that he let my cousin borrow it. I can't tell you if my cousin knew him."

"That white man saved your cousin's life?"

"Uh Huh."

"He's lucky. They could have easily lynched him, too."

"I know."

"Troy, look, everybody is at war with everybody else. Ain't nothing new about that. We're over here fightin' this war where white folks are killing white folks. You've heard all them stories. That's the way the world is! And they would have even put a rope around Jesus' neck if they had one. Instead, they put him up on a pole then speared his body, and he never did anything wrong. All I'm saying is that it isn't right to want to go out there just to kill someone. That makes you just like them.

"Naaah. I hear what you're saying, but it ain't the same thing. I ain't like them."

"Brother, if you keep carrying on like that with all that hatred in you, you'll be worse than they. And evil is evil in God's eyes. It don't matter who started it."

"Man, you keep going on about all that religious guff and don't you know that this world is being torn apart because of peoples' religion. That's what's causin' these wars."

"Oh no, brother, you've got that wrong! But there is a conflict between good and evil though, and evil has a destiny just like righteousness has. But don't you remember what happened on Christmas day a couple of years ago?"

"You talking about the race riot in Detroit?"

"I'm talking about right here. Don't you remember that story the lieutenant told? On Christmas day, the Tommies and the Huns had a ceasefire to exchange gifts."

"Oh yeah, that was crazy."

"They sang Christmas carols, exchanged gifts, and even played soccer for a while."

"So they were homesick. What do that prove?"

"It proves how a common religious faith brought people together rather than tearing them apart, even in a time of battle. Man, they was killing each other but stopped to honor something bigger than themselves, bigger than their countries, and bigger than the war. Religion don't tear people apart. The conflict is always 'bout good and evil."

Troy sat and thought about it. He knew that once Nap started talking from a religious perspective, that it was no use arguing.

"All right, it's almost time for field practice," said Troy, changing the subject. "Let's get to the field before they call everybody else."

The two men rose from their rolled-up wool blankets to get an early look at the training field. It had every essential component necessary to launch a small war: there were deep trenches, suspended silhouette dummies for bayonet practice, whose dangling, swaying movements still reminded Troy of how his cousin was almost lynched, boxes of live grenades, rifles, gas masks, and boxes of food rations.

A bugler sounded a rallying call, and all the men formed ranks. Once all were accounted for, they were paired up as buddies and marched to the field for intensive training. For most of them, this was the fun they had waited for.

They trained several hours in grenade launching, target shooting, hand-to-hand combat, and defensive gas attack maneuvers. They trained with full packs on their backs, and they trained in T-shirts and khakis. They trained in trenches twenty feet deep, and they trained sliding on their bellies at ground level. They were trained how to render the enemy unconscious using their bare hands, and they were trained how to break a human neck using their forearms. The French officers and infantry were very impressed and even envious of their abilities.

By the end of the day, after six hours of training, fatigue set in. Night was beginning to fall, so the company commanders brought them in for a hearty meal.

Though Captain Fish only oversaw the events of the day, he too felt exhausted. But at last he could have sufficient uninterrupted time to write his father. He sat down at the desk in the officers' tent and began:

Dear Father:

I hope you will forgive me for not writing more often, but I am busy every moment getting my company ready for a tour of duty in the trenches. We expect to be ordered up in ten days, and naturally there is a lot of polishing up to be done so that we can give a good account of ourselves on our introduction to the Boche. *After all our wandering and experiences, it is difficult to realize that we will be facing German bullets and, I hope, taking German helmets before you get this letter. I understand helmets are the only things that we are allowed to keep, and also to send home.*

Our regiment is the most envied American regiment in France and has the greatest opportunity to make a wonderful record. We are the only American regiment with the French Army and have the incomparable advantage of the instruction and experience of the French. We are to all intents and purposes a part of the French Army and supplied by them with all of our rifles, bayonets, helmets, gas masks, knapsacks, food, and ammunition. The men look splendidly in the American khaki uniform and French leather equipment and brown helmets. I wonder what the Germans will think when they take one of our boys prisoner and find that he cannot speak French and comes from Harlem. I am a great believer in the fighting quality of the educated American Negro, provided he is well led. If the regiment does not make a splendid record, it will be the fault of the officers. I believe, if the censorship regulations were abolished, the 15th New York (now the 369th US Infantry) would be as well known as the Rough Riders were in the Spanish-American War, before peace is declared…

Please do not worry about my being hit, as it will not do either of us any good. There is no such thing as dodging a shell or a bullet, as the one that hits is never seen. It is a good deal a matter of luck, or as the French say—"bonne chance."

We went through throwing hand grenades without an accident, although one man dropped his and had the pluck to pick it up again and throw it out of the trench. Our boys already excel the French at grenade throwing on account of their baseball training. The hand grenade is one of the most important features of the present war and has taken the place of the rifl e to a large extent in trench warfare. Several of our men can throw dummy grenades seventy-five meters, which is ten meters further that any of the best French grenadiers. Grenade throwing for distance, accuracy, and speed is the war sport of France and has taken the place of football and other games....

We declared war just one year ago, and all reports indicate that the American nation is aroused and enthusiastic for the prosecution of the war to victory.... I am confident that the farmers—the back-home folks, the plain people—whose sons are in khaki, will bend every energy and make every sacrifice to bring this terrible war to a quick and successful conclusion.

With love to all,

Your affectionate son,

HAMILTON
Capt. Hamilton Fish Jr.
369th US Infantry, A.E.F
Postal Secteur No. 54 (1918)

10

CORPORAL HITLER

Corporal Hitler didn't have any answers to put the field commander at rest. Sometimes the messages of a dispatch runner created more confusion because of their terse nature. There were always unanswered questions and unforeseen assumptions. Thus, when the field commander predictably directed Dolphie to return to his last post with detailed questions, he could only respond with "yes, sir."

"Coporal, you're hungry and tired. But I need a few questions answered so we can know how to mobilize. Take a 15 minute ration break. We're going to have you head back in 16 minutes." A 15 minute ration break for a complete meal would have been very rushed for the regular foot soldier. The German rations consisted of: preserved meat, an egg biscuit, cheese and dried vegetables. Sometimes the jerky-like meat alone was so dry and tough that it might take nine to ten minutes to soften using steam over an open fire. However, to the surprise of many, Dolphie had become accustomed to a self-imposed strict vegetarian diet. He therefore grabbed an extra helping of cheese, nine ounces of dried vegetables and two egg biscuits.

"Corporal, won't you need more protein in that diet to sustain yourself?", asked a food supply sergeant in the makeshift kitchen.

"My diet is fine," responded Hitler "I can maintain sustenance from other energy sources."

Men began to crowd around him to watch him eat. It was all done in a methodical, almost mechanical fashion. He took a bite of cheese, masticated six times then swallowed. He bit into half of an egg biscuit, chomped six times then swallowed. He drank six swigs of water, returned to devour the other half of the biscuit and finally had six spoons full of dried vegetables. He was meticulous about his eating habits and conscientious about his eating manners—so as other soldiers watched him he would simply nod at them to avoid talking with food in his mouth.

"Corporal," the field commander said upon his return," we need you to go now. Take this note to that field captain. In case you lose it you should know what it says. It requires the captain to estimate about how many of these auxiliary African troops are to be expected and describe any type of field artillery they may have—oh yes, and clarification of their nationality if possible: are they African troops, French troops or American troops. I see you've finished your rations."

"Yes sir."

"Then get going."

Once again Dolphie strapped his helmet on tightly, checked his gas mask, checked his pistol, folded the note five times before placing it into his inner pocket and set out. He started on a slightly different course than the one he had taken to arrive. Actually, due to the allied bombings, the terrain was constantly changing. There were no fixed visual reference points to indicate that he was headed in the same direction. He could only rely upon his compass, the position of the sun and the sounds of bombs to reassure him of his whereabouts; he had learned how to distinguish between the explosive sounds of German and French artillery and this kept him from entering enemy territory.

Again, he sprang forward keeping his head low to avoid any possible sniper fire. The sporadic sounds of gunfire were less intense this time which could only mean one of two things: the enemy was taking time to reload and check arsenal inventories or, he was approaching an enemy ambush.

Dolphie was continuing cautiously but confidently when he approached the outer edge of an enormous bomb shell crater. He was glad to have noticed it before falling in but then he saw something move. He froze and waited. Though the fields were now full of rats he reasoned that it probably wasn't a rat because they usually came out in the evenings. Then it moved again. It appeared to have the color and shape of a French combat helmet; and the way it was moving clearly indicated that it was resting loosely on top of someone's head which was concealed at a lower level of the crater. He soberly considered the massive size of the crater which could easily have sheltered a half dozen French soldiers who might be either trapped or waiting to lure someone like him into an ambush.

Immediately, he thought about the 'Old Shatterhand" comic series and how the Indians had always used an element of surprise to successfully catch the American cowboys off guard. He was inwardly compelled to try it (*after the war, Hitler would receive a medal for this achievement*).

Rushing to the edge of the crater and then circling around it Dolphie spotted a group of distraught looking French soldiers. He held out his pistol and started to shout in German, "BEWEGT EUCH NICHT SCHWEINE ODER ICH WERDE EUCH ALLE PERSÖNLICH NACHEINANDER HINRICHTEN. AUF DIE KNIE! ICH SAGTE AUF DIE KNIE, SOFORT!" (***Don't move pigs or I will personally execute you all one by one. Drop to your knees. I said drop, now!***

Though their rifles were still slung over their shoulders across their backs, the soldiers were caught by surprise. Each looked to the other to see who would take hold of a rifle first. No one did. They all assumed that there were other German soldiers accompanying Hitler above ground, hidden from plane view, so, their hands went up and they fell to their knees.

"LEGT EURE GEWEHRE IN EINEM STAPEL -EINS NACH DEM ANDEREN. LOS! DU GEHST ZUERST!"

("Lay your rifles down in one pile—one by one. Move! You go first!,") Hitler directed each of them to lay their rifles down, clasp their hands behind their heads and slowly climb out of the crater squatting like ducks. The group of petrified soldiers consisted of inexperienced young men who had been freshly added to the French infantry. They were separated from their unit and desperately lost. Once they were all above ground, Hitler directed them to sit akimbo in one column--except for the oldest looking soldier. He found it rather opportune to have stumbled across them while en route to retrieve timely information about their auxiliary units, so, he began his own interrogation.

"WIE GROSS SIND EURE AFRIKANISHEN EINHEITEN UND WELCHE ART VON ARTELLERIE HABT IHR? EH? ICH WEISS DASS DU DEUTSCH VERSTEHST- DU FRANZÖSICHER SCHWEIN. ANTWORTE MIR!"

"*How large are your African units and what type of artillery have they? Eh? I know you understand German-- you French pig. Answer me!*"

The young man looked blank faced. They all had practiced their facial expressions and rehearsed what they would say in this type of situation. According to the Geneva Convention they were only required to give their name, rank and serial number if captured. The soldier thus began, "Je m'appelle Victor Depardieu. Je suis sergent. Mon numero de serie est: six, neuf, neuf, zero, sept, quatre, deux." (*My name is Victor Depardieu. I am a sergeant. My serial number is: six, nine, nine, zero, seven, four, two.*)

Frustrated, Hitler pointed the pistol at the sergeant's perspiring left temple and repeated the question. He considered all French soldiers to be cowards and thought that aggression would break them. However the sergeant could only dutifully offer the same information.

"Corporal Hitler, Corporal Hitler," a familiar voice sounded and a head appeared from a trench. "Bring them this way," the voice continued. It was a field sergeant who had once helped him prepare one of his earlier dispatch messages and he was shouting from 15 feet away .

"This is wonderful. Bring them over here for questioning," he continued. Two other German soldiers appeared from nowhere with rifles pointing at the French group. They were noticeably impressed.

"This group was cut off from their unit after the gas attack," said a field sergeant, " good job corporal! Perhaps we can get some questions answered now."Motioning to the group he brandished his rifle and yelled, "get moving!" The field sergeant then turned to Hitler and said "only you could have walked through this war zone without tripping any land mines or being blown apart by a British shell. I've heard about you. Where does this kind of power come from?'

Hitler hesitated as his face folded into an awkward grimace. He was becoming used to this type of attention around the trenches and found it both uncomfortable and flattering at the same time. Then, peering at the field sergeant square in the eye he said, "this power doesn't come from me and it has yet to be made complete. You will hear much of me. Just wait until my day comes."

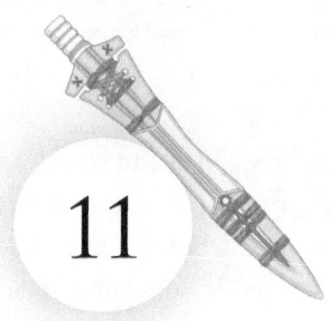

11

VICTORY FOR HELLFIGHTERS

For Patton, if anything had already been made complete in his mind, it was the outcome of the present battle—he could smell victory at hand. He had craftily planned a tank attack against a great German pocket of infantrymen that had begun to overrun Allied lines. Both sides were in the heat of battle not far from no man's land, but the rain-drenched terrain became a hindrance to routing the enemy. After spotting several of his tanks bogged down in muddy shell holes, he decided to personally come to their aid. He put his binoculars away and undauntedly left his commander's observation post to walk toward the tanks that lay mired in mud roughly two miles ahead of him. He didn't bother to take cover or even duck upon hearing the shell bursts around him because he didn't believe in dodging fate. When it was his time to die, he would welcome it bravely, but now was not the time.

While walking, he had a very odd sensation. The flanking movements of the enemy tanks were surreally familiar, like armed chariots in a dreamlike cavalry raid. And though he had practiced combat tank drills on French soil before, he felt that what he was about to do had never been a part of any recent training, yet he had done it before.

For a moment he stopped and stared upon the earth, fixated, until his head felt heavy from an uncanny sensation that he knew not only how the battle would end, but that he had even fought on the very same terrain before. He thought out loud while trudging through the field.

"Yes," he said, "it was here. It had to be here."

If ever Patton had a sense that his belief in the transmigration of souls was valid, it was now.

"It was mine. I took possession of something and hid it, and it was done around here. But what was it?"

Blurred visions and loud noises came to his mind. The noises sounded like garbled mumbled recordings played at a slow speed, and the visions appeared in flashes of yellow hue. Obscured images floated and drifted in quick jerky motions.

There were armies dressed in black, charging with fixed bayonets. There were horses braying and galloping over bodies of fallen men. There was a commander at a lookout post orchestrating attack and false retreat maneuvers. He was wearing a black bicorne hat.

It was then when Patton snapped back to reality as if emerging from an epileptic fit. His eyes focused on the present battle.

When he reached the immobile tanks they were like fallen horses unable to lift themselves back onto all four feet. They needed traction, so he quickly turned around to get the field packs and various gear of fallen soldiers he had recently passed by. He returned to the tanks and tucked the field packs and paraphernalia under the left side of their tracks. Then he ordered the tank drivers to gun their engines in first gear. The field paraphernalia created just enough traction to lift the left side of the steel beasts out of the mire, which caused them to careen to the right, the direction of choice. Patton then hopped on top of one tank, still under sporadic fire, and charged the driver to accelerate at medium speed.

Bullet shells ricocheted off the tank's turret, and artillery shells swooshed over his head without fazing him—and the thunder could be heard all around no man's land.

At the southeast corner of no man's land, the 369th had been waiting for the word to launch its attack at a new hostile sector. Captain Fish admitted that the men had been tried, as through fire, and were ready. But they all knew that most battles are preceded by an exaggerated passage of time during which they could only patiently wait. Captain Fish took the time to write in a personal letter to his father:

Dear Father:

I have just come back from a tour of duty in the first line of trenches and enjoyed the experience immensely. We were withdrawn before our ten days were up, in order to move into another sector, and we are now resting before taking up our new positions. The men lived up to my highest expectations and by their fearless conduct under heavy fire, showed that they had the willingness and ability to fight. My company lines were close to the German lines and in some places not more than fifty yards. The troops under my command were cooperating with an equal number of French troops, and were quartered with them. The condition and morale of my men were excellent and all wanted to remain in the first-line trenches when the time for relief came. The first lines are lightly held and are merely outposts of surveillance. My platoons in the first lines were stationed in combat groups and very strongly protected on all sides by numerous rows of wire entanglements, which completely encircled these small strongholds. It would be costly for the enemy to attempt to capture any of them. Practically all the fighting is done at night or in the early morning. My men are contented, enjoy and show aptitude for night work, especially reconnoitering, and are delighted with the cordial treatment of both the French officers and soldiers.

HAMILTON
Capt. Hamilton Fish Jr.
369th US Infantry, A.E.F
Postal Secteur No. 54 (1918)

It was nightfall, and only the very distant sound of gunfire, often drowned out by the closer, incessant sounds of snoring, could be heard in the dugout. Two privates, named Johnson and Roberts, were on duty with three other infantrymen of the 369th. They were all a part of a patrol group assigned to an advanced listening post in close proximity to the front lines. Their mission was to report on any detectable enemy movements. The muddy incline upon which they were settled, however, made it difficult to detect sound, and this gave the enemy an advantage.

While three of the infantrymen were sleeping, having fulfilled their observation shifts, a twenty-four-man German raiding party furtively crawled through the mud toward the outpost. The slippery earth allowed them to painstakingly push and slide themselves upward without producing an audible sound, though they were equipped with rifles, hand grenades, and wire cutters. Their mission was to launch a barrage grenade attack and capture prisoners for interrogation.

The leader of the group stopped near the top of the incline. He had come upon barbed wire, so he slowly took out a pair of wire cutters and quietly snipped through the twisted strands one by one. Then he slowly pushed and bent the wire entanglements inward to avoid snagging his equipment on them. Once he entered through the barrier, he was close to the outpost. He signaled to his task force by raising his arm. This meant that each man within the immediate squad after him was to unclasp a grenade from his belt. Then, he gave another command by visibly bending his elbow, meaning that they were to remove the grenade pins and wait for him to throw his grenade first. They had only five seconds before the explosives would detonate.

When privates Johnson and Roberts suddenly turned around, they were met by a barrage of exploding grenades: Cablaam! Cablaam-Cablaaam! A grenade exploded yards behind them, rendering their sleeping fellow guardsmen senseless. Another one exploded next to Johnson, sending rocks and fragments in the air and ripping through his lower body. Roberts was shot, at point blank, but purposely rolled three feet to land next to their hidden ammunition stash. And still more grenades exploded.

There were four seconds of silence however when Johnson and Roberts, though seriously wounded, turned the ambush completely around. "Turn out the guard," Johnson yelled and picked up his rifle, shooting blindly in the direction of the approaching enemy, killing several.

A German soldier jumped on him, attempting to subdue him in a chokehold, but Johnson broke the hold and scrambled to pick up his rifle. Unable to outstretch his rifle at such close range, Johnson slammed the rifle butt across the enemy's head and repeatedly pounded with all of his might, bludgeoning the man to death. Roberts, having found the grenade stash, threw the grenades like baseballs into the wave of attackers, prompting several enemy soldiers to leap upon him. They were choking him when Johnson decided to take out his bolo knife. Johnson sprang on them like a wild animal, clefting the skull of one soldier in a single stroke and pressing an attack on the others, fighting against the odds.

By the time the three fellow guardsmen emerged from the shock caused by the grenade detonations, the enemy had retreated, leaving behind dead comrades, rifles, grenades, wire cutters, and automatic weapons. Johnson and Roberts, though seriously injured, remained in good spirits and considered the experience to be one of the greatest adventures in their lives. (Johnson would later be cited by former President Theodore Roosevelt as one of the five bravest Americans during World War I.)

A squad of seven Hellfighters arrived looking confused. Nap spoke first. "What happened? We heard a million grenades go off, and you two are still standing?"

"Look at these soldiers," said Roberts to Johnson, "always showing up late for a fight. (Motioning to one of the fallen German soldiers,) It looks like the Kaiser is gonna have to train his boys in hand-to-hand combat."

"You're hurt," said Nap, "You'd better put some pressure on that," pointing to Robert's leg wounds, "and I'll talk to the lieutenant so you can get to the medical unit."

Nap and several of the others walked over to examine the dead. "Ain't nothing gonna cure that headache," said one, mockingly referring to the soldier with the cleft skull. "Hey look! This one is moving. This one is still alive." One of the German soldiers was emerging from shock. He was barely able to move, but he began to pant loudly.

"Take his ammo belt, and tie his hands together," said a squad member. "We may have got ourselves our first trophy."

The soldier was beginning to moan when a group of four Hellfighters removed his ammunition belts, wrapped them around his wrists, and buckled them together. They gently picked him up—two men holding his arms and two holding his legs—and placed him upon level ground so he could breathe easily and not roll over on his face.

"Hey, Roberts," Nap began, "I'm sorry we couldn't make it to you guys sooner."

"That's okay. Don't worry about it," Roberts said, beginning to wince now because of the pain in his lower body. "I'll be thinking about you mugs while I'm in sickbay surrounded by beautiful nurses."

"I want you to know, Roberts," Nap said, "when we heard all those grenades go off, and we knew the sounds were from around this post, I started praying for you guys. I prayed that God would strengthen you and protect you from all evil."

"It looks like he did just that," said Roberts thoughtfully.

12

WOUNDED IN HOSPITAL

....

Their white, modest, leather shoes squeaked with every footfall against the waxed wooden floors. Sometimes, they slipped on spilled blood, and sometimes they were stepped on by the hobnailed boots of wounded soldiers. But they were always kept immaculately white.

Injured members of the 369th were not allowed to be treated alongside white US soldiers at the field medical unit, so they were taken to a local French hospital to be treated and convalesce. The facility was actually a Catholic monastery whose entire main wing was devoted to tending to injured soldiers. A mother superior helped run the medical wing, which was staffed with nurses, priests, two doctors, and a Red Cross volunteer staff of four local girls, named Giselle, Salome', Annett, and Sophia. Nurses and female volunteers all knew each other very well, and they all had to remain clothed in white from head to toe while on the facility.

Though Sophia was known to have come from a local village, she kept it secret that she had been born in French Morocco and was biracial. She was part French and part Berber, from the indigenous Amazigh tribe, and had come to France to live with an aunt.

Sophia had an olive-brown, smooth complexion, with large gray eyes and thick dark hair, which could naturally curl in ringlets if she let it. Unmistakably, she was the most attractive female on staff by far, and the envy of her colleagues.

When the two French doors at the main wing entrance were opened, two gurneys were slowly wheeled in carrying Johnson and Roberts. They were still sleeping because their squad leader had given them large doses of pain medication that induced drowsiness.

The army medics had tied blue cards to their ankles, describing their injuries in French, as well as Basic English, since no one at the facility spoke English. The note also informed them that a military translator would visit in three days to follow up on their status.

"Are these the ones who fought off that large German group?" whispered Giselle, raising a penciled eyebrow.

"Yes," replied Annett, observing the gurneys. "They're the Yankee Negroes."

"Hmm, they don't look so heroic to me."

"It's always the ones who don't look so heroic that do the greatest damage," said Annett.

"Maybe. Well, why don't we put them in room four, where they'll have a lot of sunlight?"

"Okay, let Salome' know that they'll be in room four so that she can tell Doctor Rousseau. He ought to have a look at their wounds right away."

"Okay."

Salome' was always diligent in preparing the convalescent rooms. Everything had its place. Sterilized bed pans were stacked neatly under the beds five bowls high, towels and soap were set in the corner of the window seal to remain dry and bacteria free from the aid of direct sunlight, a small bouquet of flowers was always meticulously arranged on a small table against the wall facing the beds, and a ceramic water pitcher was always kept half full on corner tables adjacent to the beds.

Giselle walked in quietly. "Guess who's coming this time?" she said childishly.

"Not another wounded German trooper!" she gasped. "No, the Yankee Negros."

"Oh, I heard about them. How many?"

"Two."

"Can they walk?"

"I don't think so—lower body injuries. They're in the foyer on gurneys, asleep."

"Does Doctor Rousseau know?"

"No, that's why I came to you."

"Okay, this room is ready. Have someone bring them in and place them on the beds. I'll get Doctor Rousseau."

Giselle and Annett were summoned to wheel in privates Johnson and Roberts. Though the blue tags dangling from their ankles made them appear as corpses, both men seemed to be regaining consciousness.

"Let's put the skinny one on this bed first," said Annett.

"All right, I've got his ankles," replied Giselle.

Annett delicately slid her hands through Roberts's armpits, bent them upwards at her wrists, and balled her fists.

"All right, we'll lift on three. One, two, three."

They swung Roberts into place, apparently without causing him any pain. "Hey look," said Giselle, pointing at the blue card, "have you read this? It says: 'POINT TO WHERE IT HURTS, OUW ARE YOU FEELEEENG? YOU ARE LOOKEENG BETTER.'"

"They wanted to be sure the doctor could communicate with them, so they wrote those translations," said Annett.

"Not a bad idea," admitted Giselle. "Those Americans think of everything. Too bad we didn't have translation cards for that German trooper. We could have at least insulted him and the Kaiser properly before patching him up," she continued sarcastically.

"Giselle, you know what the Geneva Convention says about tending to the injured, even if they're the enemy, right?"

Salome' and Dr. Rousseau came in just as Annett and Giselle were finishing their discussion while placing Private Johnson on his bed.

Dr. Rousseau was a tall, stout man with a very thin face. His thick black hair was cut short, which gave him the air of a military commander. His large, deep-socketed eyes rested behind wire rimmed bifocals and were able to spot the slightest hint of a wound not properly mended, or an otherwise imperceptible grimace of pain on a patient's face.

"Salut, salut tout le monde," (Hello, hello everyone.) "And I gather that these are the Americans."

"Yes, doctor," said Annett. "We've just placed them on their beds."

Staring and the dangling blue cards, the doctor asked, "And what are these?"

"That's what I was talking about," said Salome'. "The American medics thought it would be helpful to give their diagnoses and help us out with a few expressions."

"You know, those Americans think of everything," marveled the doctor. Giselle looked at Annett and giggled. He then took two minutes to read the diagnoses. "It basically says that they've been treated for shrapnel wounds and trauma. Let's have a look at those wounds."

Lifting the hospital sheet, Dr. Rousseau exposed Private Johnson's right leg, which was dressed in a patchwork of bandages up to his hip. Some wounds were still visible, as not all of the bandages had been well placed. His right trouser leg had been deliberately torn along the side to keep his wounds from snagging on the fabric.

The doctor then focused sharply. "See there?" he said to Salome', pointing at the leg. "That puncture wound there still has shrapnel in it. You can tell by the puffiness and puss. It appears that they probably weren't able to remove it all. We'll have to take him to the operating table."

By this time, Private Johnson was conscious enough to be aware of his surroundings. His eyes quickly darted from the ceiling, to the wall, to the floor, to the bed, and finally to the entourage of medical staff standing before him. He then smiled at the female staff.

"Hiyaa, dolls! Am I in heaven?" he said.

"Owe are you feeleeeng?" shouted Doctor Rousseau. Private Johnson simply stared at him without making a reply.

"*Ca doit etre la phrase correct,*" (That must be the correct phrase) he said to his staff. Doctor Rousseau then took the blue card attached to Johnson's ankle and studied it. *Oui, je le savais.* (Yes, I knew it). He then tried shouting again: "Owe are you feeleeeng?"

"I'm feeling okay, doc, but you don't have to yell," said Johnson. Impressed by the breakthrough, Giselle, Annett, and Salome' all smiled in celebration.

"He said, okay," said Annett. "He said, okay, but what was the other part he said?"

"It doesn't matter," said the doctor, "point to where it hurts," he continued. Still annoyed at the heightened level of the doctor's voice, Johnson frustratingly pointed to both of his ears to indicate the source of his pain.

The staff stared at him. "Maybe his eardrums were injured by the loud explosions during the battle," said Salome'. Johnson's frustration was escalating. But he knew that the doctor would only continue in his loud interrogation if he didn't cooperate. Thus, before the doctor could raise another question, Johnson quickly pointed to the wound in his right leg.

"Yes, you see," said the doctor. "It is as I said. That wound is slowly becoming infected, and it's causing him pain. There is still shrapnel in there."

Doctor Rousseau then examined Johnson more carefully. He touched him tenderly on the chest, arms, and legs, all the while repeating: "Point to where it hurts." Johnson consistently pointed to the same area.

"Salome', please tell the staff in the operating room that this patient will be there in fifteen minutes," he ordered.

"Yes, sir, should I let them know the nature of his injuries?" she asked.

"That would be fine."

Salome' then turned to Private Johnson and gave a reassuring smile. "Don't worry," she said in clear French, "we are here to help you, and we practice the Carrel method, so you are in good hands."

Giselle was beginning to roll her eyes, "I seriously doubt if he even knows what the Carrel method is or understands any French," she said.

"It doesn't matter," said the doctor, "Salome', please, let's not waste time."

"Yes, doctor."

Doctor Rousseau then took hold of Johnson's blue card to peruse it. He turned to the remaining staff. "It says that they are going to send us a military interpreter in a few days, but according to the date marked on the back, he should arrive tomorrow. They must have had a delay in transporting these two soldiers here."

Roberts was beginning to stir by this time. Though he wasn't experiencing any pain, he needed to shift his weight in the bed for better comfort.

"Doctor, I think this one is awake now too," said Annett. Anticipating the doctor's line of questioning, Roberts blurted out: "I'm feeling okay, doctor," which prompted everyone to laugh.

"This is good. This is good," said Doctor Rousseau. "Let's see your blue card." He lifted the card and bent down to read it carefully. "It appears he has the same diagnosis," he said. "Annett, would you come here, please, and lift the sheet?"

Annett dutifully walked over and with two hands, lifted the patient's sheet. She started to feel embarrassed as Roberts was watching her intently. As she and the doctor stood at the foot of the bed, she raised Robert's sheet high enough to block their face from his view.

The doctor studied his wounds, lightly touching them. "These stitches look good," he said, "no sign of infections or internal shrapnel fragments." He then peeked over the raised sheet to look Roberts in the eye when he said, "Point to where it hurts." Roberts remained still. Again, the doctor tenderly touched the areas of his wounds, all the while repeating, "Point to where it hurts." Roberts continued to remain still. Then the doctor decided to apply more pressure to his impressions—and Roberts never flinched.

"This one is fine," said the doctor. "Let him rest, and he'll be ready to get back to the war soon."

13

PATTON AND HITLER GET IT

....

The army field medical units were often more efficient than the local hospitals, especially the units for officers.

The medics at both the Allied and enemy camps were respectively motivated by a continual sense of urgency and an esprit de corps to get their brothers in arms patched up and back on their feet.

At most times, these units were filled with laughter, jesting, and fanciful war-wound storytelling in between surgeries. For Patton however, he had to endure a momentary indignity of having his bare posterior suspended in the air by a makeshift easel, as he lay spread-eagle on an operating table. He was now a casualty.

On foot, Patton had successfully led a tank charge in the battle of *St. Mihiel Salient.*

While others were petrified by the intensity of machine-gun fire, Patton, gazing skyward, had seen visions of his warrior forefathers in the clouds, encouraging him onward. But that is when it happened.

A German round had dug deep into his left thigh. It drilled through flesh and muscle as a hot firebrand and exited, of all places, near his rectum. He then went down.

Ironically perhaps, Hitler endured the very same type of injury during the same time. Near Bapaume, a shell exploded near his foxhole, seriously injuring his left thigh.

He, too, became a casualty, requiring a prolonged period of hospitalization. Both soldiers received historic medals for their bravery and injuries—Hitler received the Military Cross with merit, and Patton received a Distinguished Service Cross and Purple Heart. However, the untimely injuries of both men would regretfully cause them to have to spend considerable time healing as the war drew to a close.

At a base hospital near Dijon, Patton tried to rest but couldn't. Every day, he fought against his own will for continued tactical belligerence on the battlefield. He was still haunted by visions of his forefathers and the déjà vu of battles from a bygone era.

"Chuck!" he said to the medic, who wore the rank of a captain. "When am I going to be able to get back into the fight? It's been nearly a week, and I know that I'm ready."

"George, you're gonna have to let me make that call. The type of wound that you have is going to take a little more time to completely heal, and your insistence on getting up and walking around will only prolong things."

"But I feel fine now. Don't you medics ever listen to your patients? I wouldn't want to go back out there if I thought I couldn't be effective."

"Right now I'm looking at my own effectiveness as a field medic. What kind of medic would I be if I allowed my patients to diagnose themselves and sign their own outpatient plans, eh?

"A pretty smart one if you're following my directions," retorted Patton.

"Sorry, George, it ain't gonna happen. But I will give you my word that I'll try my best to get you back out there before things come to a close."

Patton looked up at the medic from his bed. "All right," he said, "but see to it that I start getting a daily account of what's going on out there. I need to know how things are going with my men." Smiling, the medic replied, "I'll do my best, George." Patton showed a half expression of resignation to the field medic. Even if he had outranked him, deep down he knew he wouldn't be able to force him to sign early discharge papers, but perhaps if he annoyed him enough the doctor would simply relent for peace of mind.

He decided to reveal to the doctor what was weighing heavily on his conscious for his own peace of mind.

"Chuck?"

"Yes, George."

"Listen to this and tell me I'm not crazy. There were visions out there—I saw 'em. Men in my family appeared to me on the battlefield, spurring me on. That's the last thing I saw before I was hit."

"What you saw is not uncommon, George. Many men start to see things when they're in the thick of it—sometimes it's just battle fatigue."

"No, Chuck. Not this. These were the faces that I remembered seeing of my uncles when I was a child. And they appeared in the clouds as clear as day."

(Sighing), "An hallucination, George."

"I'd figured you would say something like that. Well, I know the difference between an hallucination and an apparition. And I'll tell you another thing, there are regions out there where I know I've fought before."

"You couldn't have, George. We've never battled in Europe 'til now."

"There you go again, stating the obvious! I know I haven't physically battled here before. But I tell you, being on that terrain brought back memories—like I've lived another life. And I had been entrusted with something. I was protecting something very valuable and had to hide it, and all this was in the midst of a seventeenth-century battle."

"A seventeenth-century battle?"

"You heard me. But I can't understand what it was that I was concealing. (Talking more to himself) This is all over my head, like an unsolved mystery or something."

"Well, it's completely over my head too. But I think you ought to rest a little more. You'll feel better after more rest. Can I get you anything, George?"

"Yeah," he said with renewed vigor, "you can get me my discharge papers so that I can join my men in driving those Germans to the Rhine River."

The Rhine River promised strategic advantages. It was wide and deep. The transport of ammunition as well as military watercraft could be dispatched to several hostile internal or embankment locations from the Rhine. While controlling this body of water was a chief priority for both the Allies and the Axis, another lesser-known river became the place of contemplation for Hitler; it was in Pasewalk, Germany, near the modest Uecker River.

Hitler pondered and cursed the changing tide of the war while peering into the Uecker. He had been sent to Germany to recover from his wound, and it had been years since he had seen civilians. He now detested the sight of them. They had carried on as if Germany had no interest in Austria's wars. Some even appeared to be profiting financially from it. They apparently were not interested in victory but in buying and selling.

The staff at the hospital had treated him well and allowed him free time to walk outdoors once his leg had healed enough. Nonetheless, Hitler rarely spoke to them. He simply wanted to return to the war front to dispatch secret messages and help win victory for Germany and Austria.

Still dressed in uniform, he stared into the glassy reflection from the Uecker and chanted dark prayers. Passersby thought he was an estranged soldier contemplating suicide, so a local businessman approached him, placing his hand on his shoulder. "Dear fellow, are you all right?" he said. Hitler flinched his shoulder out from underneath his hand and peered at him angrily for interrupting his prayers. He then turned his face back toward the river to continue in his chanting. Finally, he decided to return to the hospital.

The rooms at the local hospital were filled with wounded soldiers. Several had limb amputations. Morale was low because it was generally known that the war was taking a turn in favor of the Allies. The Kaiser appeared to be less confident in newspaper interviews, and there was political talk about Austria becoming a republic.

"Nurse?" inquired Hitler.

"Yes, sir."

"But I want to leave now," he said.

"Sir, according to your orders, you won't be allowed back to your unit for a few months now."

"Yes, yes, I know. I want to leave here. I want to leave this place," he insisted.

"And where would you go, if I might ask?"

"Vienna."

"I'm sure the doctor can release you to Vienna to be closer to family, but you'll have to do follow-up check-ups at the military hospital there," she said.

"Yes, yes, all right."

The loneliness for any person, friend or family member, was the farthest thing from Hitler's heart; he needed to return to the museum. He had to see the spear once again and renew his hopes for the future. He remembered how he had felt when he first saw it, and then the many times he had returned again to see it before the war began. Somehow the spear represented assurance and stability though everything around him appeared to be beginning to crumble. He needed encouragement.

"I'll prepare your discharge papers, and the doctor will sign them in the morning after a brief check-up," said the nurse.

"Thank you," said Hitler.

A good night's sleep and hot coffee in the morning were enough to keep him in relatively good spirits until he reached Vienna by train.

Through his eyes, the city was reminiscent of his years as a struggling artist. Though certain foods were now rationed and the cable car timetable had changed due to the war, most things were unchanged. There were still businesses. There was crowded foot traffic around the town center, there were artists desperately attempting to peddle watercolor postcards—and there were the Jews in black caftan attire—many were becoming more prosperous. He stood at a distance seething with internal rage as he took it in. He would much rather have been at the war front fighting than watching the present scene.

Across the street, a storeowner was putting up a poster. A cartooned image of a proud Austrian citizen was wrestling an enormous black snake that was apparently attempting to devour him. The banner read: *Nieder mit dem Bolschewismus*. (Down with Bolshevism.) Hitler decided to inquire.

The owner was still standing on a stepladder pasting up the large yellow poster board when he heard a sharp voice say, "I can think of better notices to pin up for Austria."

He then looked down at Hitler, who stood staring at him, stone-faced.

"Oh, you can, can you?" he said. "I gather that you've come from the trenches. How long have you been here, young man?"

"Long enough," he replied.

"Then you should understand by now that there are two wars going on. You know about the one in the trenches, but there's a political war brewing."

"The Kaiser will take care of any political wars," asserted Hitler.

"The Kaiser of Germany? He is only a puppet on a string, my friend. I'm afraid his days are numbered."

Hitler couldn't tolerate any more. He felt as though a terrific measure of momentum was gathering that would usher in the end of the present age. He wanted to be able to respond to the storeowner's appalling defeatist attitude, but nothing came out of his mouth. He simply turned and walked away.

He walked past children, he walked against traffic signals, and he darted in front of horse carts to get to the museum. It had a stoic presence in the sea of confusion around him, and opening its huge doors was like entering through a walled city for a haven of rest.

He was still breathing heavily when he stepped inside, but the stillness of the great halls calmed him. The rate of his heartbeat slowed slightly, and he began to breathe in through his nostrils.

Most of the pictures on the wall were the same. A few new modern exhibits were visible, however. And student tours were now taking place, led by younger tour guides.

The student groups were too large for Hitler to pass through, so he decided to follow them all the way to the religious wing.

The young tour guide spoke with authority, describing artwork, artifacts, and archeological findings as they advanced through the great halls. Hitler had visited the museum so often that he remembered just about every word and gesture for this part of the tour. However, approaching the Spear of Destiny, the guide said something a little different this time.

"Good students, gather near," he said. "What I'm about to show you has great significance for our present state of affairs.

I'm going to raise a question, so I want to let the teachers know that it will be permissible for the students to speak at this time." The students gathered near the glowing spear protected in the glass box. Its ageless beauty and majesty were still enthralling to Hitler.

"What is going on in Austria and Germany today? Raise your hand if you can answer." A student raised his hand and was called upon. "Germany and Austria are at war against the French," he said.

"Very good—but not just the French, I might add, but the British and Russians as well. But why would these European neighbors be against Germany and Austria, hmm? Why would the world come against us when it was our Archduke who was first assassinated?"

The guide waited for an answer in silence before he continued in answering his own question.

"It's because they want to keep Germany and Austria separate at all costs. And they want to keep us separated at all costs because they know we are a powerful people with a noble past."

At this time, Hitler was a student again. The words he was hearing confirmed everything in his troubled soul. They were the words he always wanted to say.

"Now, raise your hand if you know the answer to this question," the guide continued. "Who was the last Holy Roman Emperor?" A hand shot up. "It was Francis II of Germany, and he had to dissolve the empire because of that Frenchman, Napoleon."

"Very good, very good indeed. Can you tell us more?" said the guide.

"Well, sir, our history teacher taught us that Austria and Germany were united in a big empire, but that the empire was lost at the battle of, uh, Hausmerliz?"

"That would be the battle of Austerlitz, but you are quite right," the guide continued. "The battle of Austerlitz brought an end to the last of the Holy Roman emperors, and in that battle, Napoleon went searching for this object behind me."

There was silence as they looked upon the golden spear shimmering amid artificial lights.

"This was the spear used to crucify Jesus Christ—it is the Spear of Destiny. Legend has it that whoever possesses it can use it for either great good or evil. When Napoleon defeated the last Holy Roman emperor, he went after this holy spear to use it for great evil, but he never found it in Nuremburg, Germany—that's where it was originally sheltered. Some say he might have conquered the world with it to become a world emperor or dictator. But we know he was later defeated at Waterloo."

"Why not?" Hitler's adult voice bellowed out, causing all heads to turn around.

"Excuse me, sir," responded the guide.

"Why couldn't he find it? The victor always gets the spoils of war," he said.

"That's a good question, sir. I'm sorry I didn't see you there. Napoleon could never find it because one of his admirals, Michel Ney, had turned against him and hid it from him. It was smuggled from Germany through the battlefields of France and eventually brought to Vienna. Ney was a great warrior. Napoleon had called him the bravest of the brave, and Europe owes a debt of gratitude to him."

Hitler's mind was racing fast. It was becoming very clear now. In order to restore Germany and Austria to their rightful place of political hegemony in Europe, one would have to reunify Germany and Austria as one people—and only the Spear of Destiny could afford an opportunity for such an undertaking. The glory, majesty, and crushing power of Rome could be supernaturally restored at the historical location of the last sector of the Roman Empire if the spear were brought back to its original place, Nuremburg, Germany.

"But, sir?" another student's hand went up in the group. "What happened to the original soldier who owned the spear? Why didn't he use it to conquer the world?"

"Another good question. I see this is a sharp group. I'm afraid that you'll have to talk to your parish priest about him. His name was Longinus."

14

THE LONGINUS

....

Nap stood in front of the local monastery, wondering where the hospital was. They had taken him there by an ox-drawn cart over unpaved roads and his back now felt sore.

He also was beginning to feel bothered by the thought that he might not be able to translate in French as well as he had wanted for privates Johnson and Roberts.

He had arrived a few hours late because there were unexpected detours along the way; many bombshells had created huge craters in the area, which made travel nearly impossible. Nonetheless, he was happy to be away from the trenches for a little while on this special duty.

The facility appeared to exist in its own private world. A small green garden was well kept on the side, and the outside walls looked freshly painted.

Nap walked up the stone steps and was met at the door by the mother superior, who had been watching him from a window. She recognized his American uniform and was glad to see him.

"*Soyez le bienvenue! Nous vous attendons depuis longtemps!*" (Welcome, we have been waiting for you a long time.) "*Merci, je suis desolé de mon retard. J'ai dû prendre quelques détours.*" (Thank you. I'm sorry for arriving late. I had to take some detours).

"We understand, my boy. We must take each day at a time.

We all have gotten used to detours around here. But do come in and let me take you to your comrades."

"Thank you," said Nap, now adjusting his walking pace to her leisurely stroll. "How are they doing?"

"Oh quite well, quite well now. There was a little problem with one of the lads. I think he had a few fragments left in his leg, which was beginning to get infected, but the doctor fixed him right up."

"That's good news. (Observing the halls) This is an amazing building. I feel like I'm in an art gallery. I wouldn't have thought that it was a hospital at all."

"Yes, well it's actually a monastery."

"A monastery?"

"Yes, it's a type of indoor community where we come to study and devote our lives to God while we serve each other and people who need us. Since the war, some of our occupants have relocated to make room for a hospital wing. We even have Red Cross volunteers here."

"It feels so peaceful here. And it's so clean! I would never think that a war was going on outside if I stayed here."

"That's God's presence, my son."

"Yes, ma'am. I agree with you."

The mother superior escorted Nat down a long corridor. His hobnailed boots made accentuated squeaks on the freshly waxed floor, but no one seemed to notice.

She walked him past four rooms to the priest's den, which served as both a waiting room for visitors and an instruction room for blind children. It was very well decorated and furnished with three desks, special books on Braille, and two soft comfortable red velvet chairs.

"Sir, I'm going to leave you here for the moment and see whether or not the time is right for you to see your men. If you'll just wait here, please."

"Thank you, Reverend Mother. I'll be fine."

He walked over to examine one of the huge decorative chairs. It almost looked too good to sit upon. However, for the sake of his sore back, Nat sank down in it, releasing an audible sigh of relief. It was an ornate handcrafted piece of furniture fit for royalty, carved from thick cedar wood with a chocolate colored stain.

Directly across from him hung a captivating wall-sized painting of a Catholic saint; an image of a bearded man with a long pointed staff. Though majestic, it made him feel slightly uncomfortable. And as depicted in most Catholic artwork, a golden halo encircled his head as his large expressive eyes gazed heavenward.

"Excuse me, but aren't you the American who came to translate for your men?" a voice from behind him sounded.

Turning from the painting, Nap was now enraptured by the large expressive eyes of the most strikingly beautiful woman he had ever seen. Sophia had a naturally modest beauty—nothing feigned or forward. And she had a way of illuminating a room when she walked in. Perhaps the most attractive thing about her was that she didn't consider herself to be so beautiful; she was too busy thinking about helping others to be preoccupied with herself.

"The mother superior told me that you were waiting here. But I'm sorry, let me introduce myself. My name is Sophia."

"Hello, I'm—my name is Napoleon."

Sophia smiled. "I never thought I'd meet an American with such a French name."

"I'm from the South—Louisiana. My name is common there, I guess, because the French were once there. But where are you from?"

"I'm from Marseille."

"Why do you look different from all the other French women I've seen?"

(Slightly flattered) "I don't know, but I'm sure you haven't seen very many French women in the trenches. You were looking at that picture on the wall when I came in. Do you like it?"

"Yes, there's something interesting about how the artist drew the eyes," he said.

"That painting was done by a local artist. He donated it to our tutoring room for blind children. He's a patron saint for the blind."

"The artist is a patron saint?"

Giggling, she replied, "No, I'm sorry. Are you Catholic?"

"No, I'm not."

"Let me explain then. That is a painting of Saint Longinus. He's a patron saint for the blind."

"What's a patron saint?"

"The patron saints are usually early Christians who had unique trials which, Catholics believe, can help people today with similar trials."

"So he was born blind?"

"No, he had bad eyesight, but then the blood of Jesus cured him. According to Catholic history, he was the soldier who pierced the side of Jesus with a spear. But when he pierced him, Jesus' blood splashed into his eyes and he became healed."

"What happened to him then?"

"He later became a follower of Christ and was killed for that."

"Miss, I've never heard of these things. You Catholics must know a lot about the early church."

"Well, I'm not Catholic. My aunt is, and she's been teaching me these things in hopes to make me one. But you're right. They study these things a lot."

"So you're a Protestant?"

"No, (becoming embarrassed) I really don't know what I am."

"I'm sorry for prying, but you fit in so well here. I assumed that you were like the others."

"Well, I—my past is a little different. Okay, let me simply explain. I wasn't born here. I'm from French Morocco. Have you heard of Morocco?"

"No, I'm sorry. I haven't."

"It's in the north part of Africa."

"Oh, well I do know about Africa!"

"That's good, and you know, you even look Moorish, too. But anyway, my father was Moroccan, but my mother was French. My father was a gardener at a Catholic school where my mother was working as a nurse's assistant."

"So, your father is not Catholic?"

"Oh, no, no. The people there are not Christian. There are some Jews, but most are Moorish and follow a Middle Eastern religion now. And they don't even believe that Jesus was crucified on a cross."

"Why is that a problem for you?"

"Well, in North Africa, if your father follows this religion, you must follow it too. Their religion teaches this. This is why I had to leave. But I still haven't decided what I truly believe."

"Can I tell you something my grandfather once told me?"

"Yes, please."

"My grandfather was once a slave, but later in his life he became a man of real faith in God. And he told me once that God doesn't have any grandchildren—only children."

"What did he mean by this?"

"What he was saying was that everyone must make his own decision about what he believes—and it doesn't matter what your parents believed. Each generation must choose for itself to be children of God—just like that Roman soldier in the picture who speared Jesus."

"Your grandfather seems like a very wise man."

"Thank you. He was. And now I try to write to my father whenever I can. He's an elder in our church."

By this time, the mother superior was standing at the doorway, peeking over Sophia's shoulder. She had been listening to a part of their conversation and found it warmhearted, though she was uncomfortable and adamantly against her female staff socializing in mixed company without a chaperone.

"Sergeant Napoleon?" she said.

"Yes, ma'am."

"Your men are ready to see you now. Will you come this way please? Why don't you come as well, Sophia?"

The mother superior led the way through the corridor to the patients' room with Sophia walking beside her. She had given Salome' enough time to make the quarters presentable so that the Americans could have a brief reunion in a clean environment before leaving. They all cautiously entered the sunlit room occupied by privates Roberts and Johnson.

"Nap?" exclaimed Roberts. "Hey, it's Nap! So you're the translator? No one told us you would be the one."

"Look at you two grunts lying in bed like civilians," he joked. "It already looks like you've got a lot of physical training to catch up on."

"Brother, after eating French cuisine for two days, I can't go back to that rationed sawdust gunk they give us. Naw, sir, I'm staying right here," joked Johnson.

"You'll soon be going home anyway, solider. The war's drawing down. We were the first to chase the Huns all the way to the Rhine—won't be long now," said Nap. "The lieutenant even had time to put together a small jazz squad, and the captain sent them on a local concert tour."

"Are you serious?" marveled Roberts. "How do the local folks like jazz?"

"I don't know; they probably never even heard it before." At this moment, Sophia stepped into view from behind Nap.

The men noticed her immediately and ceased their joking; they began to feel very awkward.

"Hello, ma'am. And how do you do?" said Johnson in a very slow, deliberate tone.

Sophia smiled and silently nodded her head in acknowledgment.

"Nap?" whispered Roberts. "Do you know this woman?" Nap had a sudden sensation that made him feel he should now protect Sophia.

"Uh, this is Sophia. She's another volunteer here with the Red Cross," he said.

In unison, both Roberts and Johnson waved their hands enthusiastically. "Hello, Sophia. It's soooooooo nice to meet you," they said, smiling.

"Miss Sophia?" Johnson dared to ask. "Have you heard of jazz music?"

Sophia nervously looked at Nap for help.

"Il a dit que est-ce que tu connais la musique de jazz?" said Nap. (He said, do you know jazz music?)

"Moi, mais non. Cependent, j'ai les voisines qui m'ont dit qu'ils ont entendu une petite equip de la musique. Ils m'ont dit que cetais une equip des Yankee Negroes," she said. (No. However I have neighbors who have told me that they heard a little music group of Yankee Negroes.)

"She says no, but that her neighbors heard us at a local concert," translated Nap.

"Well, let's give her a little taste right here," he said, turning to Roberts while placing his hands on a serving tray for a percussion sound.

"I don't know if…." Nap began.

'A one, a two, a one, two, three," Johnson interrupted. "da-da da-di-dat, da-da-da-di-dat. Da-dat dadat dat-dat." Johnson and Roberts then began a jazzy rendition of a popular tune. Johnson slapped and slid his hand across a serving tray, creating a smooth tapping sound as Roberts pursed his lips to create the sound of a muffled trumpet. He blew and whistled the lively melody through his teeth as Johnson steadied the rhythm.

"How ya gonna keep em down on the farm, after they've seen Paris," they sang.

Sophia began to tap her foot and smile as all the volunteer staff approached the doorway to attend the concert. Even the mother superior smiled and gingerly clapped her hands with joy.

The melody of their catchy renditions would be hummed and whistled throughout the medical wing for weeks after their departure.

They were the perfect antidote for the gross realities of war and the strain of political strife. As the Harlem Hellfighters were the first musicians to introduce jazz on the continent, they would forever change the musical culture of Europe—though the social culture around the continent would remain politically restless in search of a savior.

Many hearts in Germany became hardened after her unconditional surrender on November 11th. The Kaiser abdicated and fled to Holland. Treaties were reluctantly signed, displaced people sought to reunite with lost loved ones, and poverty surged, but the spear remained safely in Austrian hands.

15

PATTON AND MARSHAL NEY

He had rested well, but was nonetheless restless. Still walking with a slight limp from his thigh wound, Patton felt that he had missed out on the best part of the war and left many things undone. Now, the new transition awaiting him was mocking his ego. From the booming battlefields of glory in Europe, to the present, quiet mundane affairs of his isolated bureau at Fort Meade, Maryland, Patton was determined to take every opportunity to make the war department officials aware of how indispensable his tanks were in field conflict, and how indispensable they would be for the next war.

He was proud of the opportunity to be on the lecture circuit for the military staff colleges. It gave him an opportunity to refine his presentation skills and conduct research on military history and field maneuvers.

Battle strategies in the European theater was his favorite subject, and he spent several days reviewing historical documents as a film critique might review a script and cinematography techniques for a potential award-winning picture.

He sat slumped forward with a document in hand. It was written in a flamboyant, cursive style: "The attack with four regiments being directed against the right wing of the enemy. The general in command shall march his lines by the left, the battalions shall be formed into columns by platoons, the left in front at whole or half distance. The columns thus prepared shall, in marching forward, take a diagonal to the left and, by heads of columns formed by each battalion...."

Patton paused and thought. Then there was a knock at the door.

"Come in," he said.

A very sharply dressed captain casually walked over to his desk.

"Sir, the commander wanted to talk with you about your visit to Washington this afternoon," he said.

"Oh, hello, Bob," said Patton, just looking up. "But I know that already. We have a meeting at fifteen hundred hours."

"I'm sorry, sir," he said.

"That's all right," said Patton, before changing the subject. "Bob," he said, "don't leave just yet. Come over here and take a look at this, will ya?"

The captain dutifully approached him and was handed a well-preserved document.

"This is from the archive department," said the captain after studying it.

"Yes, I know where it's from. I had it sent to me. But do you notice anything unusual about it?"

"It's handwritten, but since it's a primary source, that wouldn't make it unusual. There are loads of primary sources in the archives," he said.

"Bob, what does it say about the general in command?"

"It says that his left flank should be marched to attack the enemy's right wing."

"Wrong. It says that he is to march his lines by the left. He himself," retorted Patton.

"I see," said the captain. "But what is your point, sir?"

"My point is this. Ever since military school, I've always thought that the commanding officers should lead their battalions from the front, but what do you find today? They get hunkered down miles behind enemy lines where they become less effective."

The captain simply listened in silence.

"This age-old document is music to my ears. It's as if I had written this myself. It's too bad they couldn't tell me who wrote it, because I'd like to use it for my presentations."

"Isn't the reference on the ledger, sir?"

"No, the first chapters have been misplaced. They just gave me this in a random set of other documents."

The captain stepped over to look at the document again, taking note of the handwriting style and phraseology. "Sir, Admiral Ney wrote that in the 1800s," he said matter-of-factly.

"Ney?" Now, becoming awestruck, "Of course! Napoleon's Ney!" he exclaimed.

"I could only tell by the cursive style of handwriting, sir," said the captain.

Patton began to have a flashback. He nervously lowered his eyes to the floor. He put his hand on his forehead and saw flashes of subdued yellow lights. He then started to feel cold and began to speak aloud as if to himself. "The dead were in carts," he said. "We carried the dead in carts so that the Russians wouldn't know how many of us they'd killed. It was so cold the blood was brown on the snow."

"Excuse me, sir," said the captain.

Patton continued, "I saw a small man on a horse riding ahead of us, and he didn't care what happened to us. It was Napoleon."

"I see, you've been studying the memoires of Admiral Ney," said the captain, relieved.

"Studied it!" protested Patton "I've lived it. And now I understand what's been happening to me. Listen, Bob, tell the commander that I'll see him at the appointed time, will ya? There's some research that I've got to do."

"Sir?" said the captain. "Are you sure you're feeling all right?"

"I'm fine. Just do what I've asked, huh?"

When the captain left, Patton immediately put on his hat and made his way across the yard to the military archives department, which was actually a converted airplane hangar filled with protected documents and photographs. Young cadets saluted him as he briskly passed by on the sidewalk, but he didn't even take time to return their salutes. He was on his own secret mission and had only one hour before his meeting with the commander.

"Yes, sir, how can I help you, sir?" asked a staff sergeant appearing at the archive window.

"Listen, I'm here to get as much information as I can on Napoleonic War generals, and on one in particular."

"Would that be Marshal Arthur Wellesley? We've just completed a file on him."

"No," said Patton.

"I'm sorry, sir, but the records are sorted by name. Do you have…"

"I want to look at the records on Marshal Michel Ney," interrupted Patton.

"Napoleon's bravest of the brave! I can help you with that." The young sergeant produced a large binder indicating the aisles and shelves within the department. He steadily flipped through the pages, pausing at items described as top secret. Such top secret items were specially coded, and only the base commander or an official from Washington was allowed to see them.

"Here," he said, pointing his finger at a particular spot on his diagram, "here you will find files on Ney. They're on aisle Delta E point seven. It seems that we have some autobiographical material and other random documents on his battle strategies that appear to have been signed out already."

The sergeant then looked up, noticing Patton's nametag on his uniform.

"Oh, I see, sir, that some of Ney's documents were delivered to you already!"

"I got them," said Patton, "but they were unidentified in a mix of other documents."

"I'm sorry about that, sir," replied the captain. "Once we get those documents back, we'll be sure to keep them all together in the right files."

"Good," said Patton, "but right now I have a little less than an hour, so I need to get in there."

"Yes, sir," said the captain. He issued him a written pass and unlocked the side door from the inside.

When Patton stepped inside onto the concrete floor, he unbuttoned his coat. It was stuffy, and as usual, the temperature inside the hanger buildings was up to ten degrees warmer than the temperature outside.

He walked twelve paces to the end of the building where he was met by a military police guard who demanded to see a pass. Patton flashed his pass, and the guard smartly saluted.

"You'll find the Delta aisle this way, sir," he said.

Patton returned the salute and proceeded toward aisle Delta E. The aisles were divided by gray metal racks, which were built five to six shelves high. The army had designed them with specifications for the archive hanger. They were riveted structures with a strong base to support shelves of boxes and even bulky field weapons, if need be.

In the middle section of the Delta aisle stood a shelf labeled foreign officers. On top of the shelf rested a large plain wooden box whose inside consisted of an alphabetized index list of notable foreign officers and statesmen in a large army green accordion file.

Thumbing through the file from the back to the front, Patton noticed immediately that the "W" section was thick with recent documents, and he remembered that the service staff sergeant said they had just completed a file on Admiral Arthur Wellesley. He continued thumbing through the files alphabetically. Once he reached the "N" section he paused and grabbed the documents inside. He pulled them out and read a biography of Marshal Ney:

He was born in Saarlouis, France, on January 10, 1769. He was the son of master barrel cooper Pierre Ney and his wife, Margarethe. He was raised bilingual and was fluent in French and German. He had a ruddy complexion with red hair. He received his education at the *Collège des Augustins*. He was one of the original eighteen Marshals of France created by Napoleon, and he was known to always display great courage in battle.

Reading through Ney's personal background, Patton decided to jump to his military career in anticipation of finding something personally meaningful to him. He flipped through documents. As he read, he was reminded of the many lectures he had to sit through on war history at the Virginia Military Institute and West Point.

It all began to gradually come back to him—the major European campaigns and Napoleonic Wars. Then he noticed something odd in the list of major battles—something was missing: There was the battle of Elchingen, there was the battle of Jena, there was the battle of Eylau, there was the battle of Guttstadt, there was the battle of Bucaco and Smolensk, and even Waterloo—but where was the battle of Austerlitz? Why was there no mention of Ney at Austerlitz, which was an historic and critical battle? He continued to thumb through documents. One document mentioned that he had betrayed Napoleon and plotted against him. Another document suggested that he had escaped a firing squad after the defeat at Waterloo and traveled to South Carolina in the US under an alias name. The more Patton read, however, the more he knew he was connected to him in some mystical way that he couldn't talk too much about. There was something about his absence at the battle of Austerlitz that intrigued him.

A roving officious guard slowly walked down the aisle. It was his duty to assist military personnel and protect all archived documents and paraphernalia.

"Sir, have you found everything yourself, or would you like some help?" he said condescendingly, to which Patton quipped, "No, I haven't found everything myself, but what I have found is myself, so you'd better see if you can help someone else, son."

16

POSTWAR GERMANY

The mighty German army, for all practical military purposes, was no more. After losing thousands of men in battle, it had to then drastically downsize in compliance with the punitive measures spelled out in the treaty of Versailles.

Moreover, the victorious Allies had presented Deutschland a humiliating bill for war damages that equaled 33 billion dollars in reparations. This caused ruinous inflation in Germany, and many citizens slowly, but completely, lost their minds as nearly everyone lost his life savings.

German currency, the Deutschmark, was losing value fast. It started at four marks to the dollar. However, when the war reparations were announced, it dropped to 75 marks to the dollar, and then further sank to 400 marks to the dollar. Eventually, it fell to 18,000 marks to the dollar before finally bottoming out at 4,000,000 marks for the purchase of one US dollar. A wheelbarrow filled with their hard currency could not purchase two ordinary loaves of bread.

Desperate hunger riots broke out in the streets. Heated political extremist groups began to fill public halls, inciting people to violence with talk of revolution. Since the chaos was too much for the police department to control, the Germany army, which had been reduced to a peacetime militia of veterans, was asked to assist.

Hitler had remained a faithful soldier in the army. Despite the shameful loss of the war, he continued to hope in the greatness of Deutschland and the reunification of Austria and Germany. Now he was assigned to an army education department and was given a special duty to spy on radical groups that advocated revolution.

The place was a common beer hall on a war-torn street where locals could drink their problems into oblivion. The city was Munich, in southern Germany, and the time was nightfall.

Boris, the owner of the beer hall, was unnerved. He had lost three brothers in the war and was left alone to manage the family business. Before the war, his brothers had been the ones to run the daily operations. They managed the appearances of local entertainers, they did the bookkeeping, they did the marketing, and they even did light custodial work in the facility. Boris simply made the beer. Now they were gone, and Boris knew he had to do a little more than make beer to keep his business alive.

As local entertainment was hard to come by during this time, Boris simply offered opportunities for groups to visit and hold public meetings. Some visited to recruit volunteers to help find displaced citizens, some church groups visited to preach the gospel of salvation, and others visited with a political agenda in mind.

While the streetlights were dimming outside to conserve energy, three men, dressed in black leather, arrived. Their names were Anton Drexler, Gottfried Feder, and Dietrich Eckart.

"Good evening, Boris," said Gottfried with a smirk, "and how are you tonight?"

"Well, we're getting low on beer. We're down to only two brands until supplies come in. Other than that, I guess I should still be happy to even have this place."

"Yes, I would agree with you on that," replied Gottfried.

"What are you boys talking about tonight, eh? Recruiting for another labor strike?"

"We're here for a very important announcement," interrupted Anton, "I'm sure several of your clients will be interested. You should listen too, because it might help your business."

"I'll listen to just about anything now. Just take the platform when you're ready." The only sound throughout the hall was that of muffled belches from overindulged clients and the thud of beer mugs being slammed on the wooden tables. There was no music, and there were no conversations. Nearly 200 downcast men gathered there that evening and were open for anything to happen. Some didn't have homes to return to. Others avoided returning to their families out of shame for having no means to support them. And most of them didn't even bother to look up as they guzzled their alcohol.

The three men strode, almost in unison, up to the small platform that once served as a mini stage for pianists, magicians, and showgirls. Gottfried Feder began:

"Brothers, brothers, we'd like to have your attention for just a moment. Some of you have seen us here before, but we have come here tonight on a slightly different occasion. We are here because there is a movement starting that we want to you be a part of. You need to be a part of this movement. We are recruiting members for the German Worker's Party to assure that every man can be restored to his dignity here."

By this time, a few heads were lifted in the crowd to glance at the speaker. "Brothers, there are red flags of communism being raised in our land, and make no mistake, the German Worker's Party stands for work, but not Bolshevism. We need to run them out of our land before it's too late." A few men grunted in agreement and leaned back in their chairs, now paying undivided attention. "We are composing our own manifesto, our own creed for every German citizen now. These are among the principles by which we stand: We think that the government's first job is to make sure that every citizen has a job and enough to eat. If the government cannot do this, people who are not citizens should be made to leave the country. No one who is not of a German race should be allowed to move into Germany. And we want anyone who is not of a German race who started living here after 1914 to leave, even if they have to swim for it. We want all Germans to live in a greater Germany."

During a smattering of applause, Hitler arrived and quietly took a seat near the back. He had only heard the last few statements but was relieved to know that they were not communists, though he wondered to himself how anyone could produce a 'greater Germany' without combining both Austria and Germany as one superpower.

He visually scanned the room, taking mental notes of the faces he saw. There were no women. Most of the men were between the ages of thirty and sixty and were malnourished, scruffy, and unkempt, but then he thought he saw a familiar face. The eyes were still the same, though the man now wore glasses. The face had aged since he last saw it, but it was nonetheless recognizable. He might have seen him in the officers' quarters during the war, or it might have even been from the *Realschule* in Linz years ago.

In any case, it was now one of the faces of the men standing on the platform. "Now," the speaker continued, "we want all citizens to have equal rights and duties, but as we said, we need to reevaluate what constitutes a citizen, because non-Germans are not to own any newspaper companies, and there are many of them in our land."

"And if there are no newspapers, our race will become an ignorant people," Hitler protested loudly.

"Excuse me, sir," said the speaker, "I couldn't hear you. Do you have a question?"

"No," said Hitler, "I don't. I actually agree with your platform. This plan seems good for Germany. But you should not force our people to be ill informed by taking the newspapers away. Why don't you create a German national press and be sure that all editors are members of the Aryan race?"

"Dolphie?" said Dietrich Eckart, adjusting his glasses. "Dolphie, yes, it is you!" Eckart removed his glasses and stepped down from the platform. The hall was silenced and all eyes diverted to him as he gleefully paced his way through the middle aisle to embrace Hitler, still seated at the back.

Eckart was beaming with joy. All of the visitors began to applaud as they assumed that this was a miraculous reunion of family members who must have been separated during the war.

"Yes, yes, it is me," said Hitler accepting the embrace. "I was in the trenches, and the powers were good to me. Now I am here."

Eckart then was reminded of the days when he actively recruited for the Thule society. He had met many young men, but Hitler had always stood out in his mind as someone special.

"Have you kept in touch with Edgar and that little group you were involved with?"

"No, I haven't seen them for years. I've been in the trenches. But I want to say that the work you're doing is good. I agree with this. It is time for a new political party, and I think I'm meant to help you in this."

"Dolphie, Dolphie, listen, come up to the platform for a minute."

The two walked up to the platform together as the crowd started to applaud again. Eckart whispered something to Drexter and Feder, which made them both back away from the microphone to allow Hitler to speak.

Hitler began: "What you are seeing here now is a kind of miracle. I am sure now that there is divine favor for our country. I came here tonight as a spy from the army to report on this meeting, but I must say that it has awakened my spirit. Deutschland has been weak because of her political structure. There has been a privileged class of wealthy folk who have left the rest of us fatherless, uncared for. While we soldiers were at the front, we were stabbed in the back by traitors at home. That's why we lost the war. Who were these traitors? Who reaped the profit? Around us we see a whole nation suffering, but among us some are thriving and prosperous. Who are these people who are getting fat while we starve? Comrades, we all know who they are! I'm here to say tonight that what these men are proposing will help usher in a new Germany for all Aryan people. We were a democracy, but that didn't work. It's time to fix this problem. The time is now!"

The audience rose to their feet in applause. Though it was one of Hitler's first public speeches, he appeared to be well experienced. He had a passion and a flare that seemed to grow with greater intensity as he spoke. And if you sat in the audience, you had the impression that he was speaking solely to you.

"You see, I told you," said Eckart to the others on the platform, who were still applauding, "we've found our spokesman tonight."

Five petitions were distributed throughout the hall as Hitler, Eckart, Drexler, and Feder walked down the center aisle making light conversation with the crowd. They shook hands with the men and encouraged them to sign the register as a member of the GWP.

"Sir, I've got a cousin whose business partner is a Jew from Rumania," said one crowd member. "What would happen if this man had to leave Germany? What would happen to the business?"

"Don't worry, comrade," said Drexter. "Before this man leaves, full ownership of the business should be signed over to your cousin."

"Thank you," he replied.

Drexter and Hitler walked over to a corner of the hall to talk privately while Eckart and Feder continued in greeting newly signed members of the GWP. Drexter further explained the origin of the party and its political agenda. Hitler however was already thinking of grander ideas.

"A workers' party is good, but it sounds too small," said Hitler.

"We don't want to intimidate anyone with a large political machine," said Drexter. "These are very simple people who simply want their country back. We wanted to start from small beginnings and steadily grow."

"Small beginnings work well if you're farming crops," replied Hitler, "but to change the political structure, you must start by making a big impression for people. They need to be overwhelmed to gain confidence. This party needs to emphasize that it is for all Germans, not just for those who are interested in work, but mothers and children, nephews and nieces. It needs to be bigger in name and in function."

"The manifesto explains who we are well enough, don't you think?"

"People won't take time to read a manifesto," said Hitler. "This party should be a national movement. It should be a national socialist party."

"Do you think people would respond to a National Socialist German Workers' Party?"

Hitler didn't say a word; his eyes confirmed all his thoughts. And Drexter knew from that moment that the future of the party would be in Hitler's hands.

Months later, Hitler and top leaders in the GWP penned a new manifesto for the National Socialist Workers Party and aggressively recruited for membership. They highlighted twenty-five points in their new manifesto:

1. We demand the union of all Germans in a Great Germany on the basis of the principle of self-determination of all peoples.
2. We demand that the German people have rights equal to those of other nations, and that the Peace Treaties of Versailles and St. German shall be abrogated.
3. We demand land and territory (colonies) for the maintenance of our people and the settlement of our surplus population.
4. Only those who are our fellow countrymen can become citizens. Only those who have German blood, regardless of creed, can be our countrymen. Hence no Jew can be a countryman.
5. Those who are not citizens must live in Germany as foreigners and must be subject to the law of aliens.
6. The right to choose the government and determine the laws of the state shall belong only to citizens. We therefore demand that no public office, of whatever nature, whether in the central

government, the province, or the municipality, shall be held by anyone who is not a citizen. We wage war against the corrupt parliamentary administration whereby men are appointed to posts by favor of the party without regard to character and fitness.

7. We demand that the state shall above all undertake to ensure that every citizen shall have the possibility of living decently and earning a livelihood. If it should not be possible to feed the whole population, then aliens (non-citizens) must be expelled from the Reich.
8. Any further immigration of non-Germans must be prevented. We demand that all non-Germans who have entered Germany since August 2, 1914, shall be compelled to leave the Reich immediately.
9. All citizens must possess equal rights and duties.
10. The first duty of every citizen must be to work mentally or physically. No individual shall do any work that offends against the interest of the community to the benefit of all.

Therefore, we demand:

11. That all unearned income, and all income that does not arise from work, be abolished.
12. Since every war imposes on the people fearful sacrifices in blood and treasure, all personal profit arising from the war must be regarded as treason to the people. We therefore demand the total confiscation of all war profits.
13. We demand the nationalization of all trusts.
14. We demand profit sharing in large industries.
15. We demand a generous increase in old-age pensions.
16. We demand the creation and maintenance of a sound middle-class, the immediate communalization of large stores, which will be rented cheaply to small trades people, and the strongest

consideration must be given to ensure that small traders shall deliver the supplies needed by the state, the provinces, and municipalities.
17. We demand an agrarian reform in accordance with our national requirements, and the enactment of a law to expropriate the owners without compensation of any land needed for the common purpose. The abolition of ground rents, and the prohibition of all speculation in land.
18. We demand that ruthless war be waged against those who work to the injury of the common welfare. Traitors, usurers, profiteers, etc., are to be punished with death, regardless of creed or race.
19. We demand that Roman law, which serves a materialist ordering of the world, be replaced by German common law.
20. In order to make it possible for every capable and industrious German to obtain higher education, and thus the opportunity to reach into positions of leadership, the state must assume the responsibility of organizing thoroughly the entire cultural system of the people. The conception of the state idea (science of citizenship) must be taught in the schools from the very beginning. We demand that specially talented children of poor parents, whatever their station or occupation, be educated at the expense of the state.
21. The state has the duty to help raise the standard of national health by providing maternity welfare centers, by prohibiting juvenile labor, by increasing physical fitness through the introduction of compulsory games and gymnastics.
22. We demand the abolition of the regular army and the creation of a national (folk) army.
23. We demand that there be a legal campaign against those who propagate deliberate political lies and disseminate them through the press. In order to make possible the creation of a German press, we demand:

(a) All editors and their assistants on newspapers published in the German language shall be German citizens.

(b) Non-German newspapers shall only be published with the express permission of the state. They must not be published in the German language.

(c) All financial interests in or in any way affecting German newspapers shall be forbidden to non-Germans by law, and we demand that the punishment for transgressing this law be the immediate suppression of the newspaper and the expulsion of the non-Germans from the Reich.

Newspapers transgressing against the common welfare shall be suppressed. We demand legal action against those tendencies in art and literature that have a disruptive influence upon the life of our folk, and that any organizations that offend against the foregoing demands shall be dissolved.

24. We demand freedom for all religious faiths in the state, insofar as they do not endanger its existence or offend the moral and ethical sense of the Germanic race.

25. In order to carry out this program, we demand: the creation of a strong central authority in the state, the unconditional authority by the political central parliament of the whole state and all its organizations.

The leaders of the party undertake to promote the execution of the foregoing points at all costs, if necessary at the sacrifice of their own lives.

17

PEARL HARBOR, HAWAII

It was three o'clock, and Patton was standing at attention before the base commander, anticipating a pre-briefing on the do's and don'ts about his visit to Washington. As his heels were perfectly aligned and his body was standing erect, he nonetheless had already mentally checked out. After reviewing the personal history of Marshal Ney, Patton's strategic mind was busy devising his next plan to travel to South Carolina to further investigate his life. He believed the controversial theory that Ney had cleverly escaped his execution in France and established himself only a few hundred miles away from where he was now standing, at Fort Meade, Maryland.

Because Patton had earned a reputation for being brash and whimsical, despite being a brilliant strategist, his commanding officers always felt that they were jeopardizing their own promotions by having him appear in official meetings.

"George," said the commander, "you're finally getting what you've been asking for. The war department wants to hear your personal accounts on the efficacy of tank warfare. Congratulations!"

"Thank you."

"But listen, go ahead and stand at ease, George. I don't want you to think that you can just roll in there and talk to the brass hats like they're a bunch of idiots. This whole thing about tank warfare is still new. You'll basically be talking to a bunch of old US cavalry troopers who won't be too ready to trade their horses in for tanks."

"There will always be a place for mounted horsemen," said Patton.

"You just make sure that you convey that sentiment to them, all right?"

"Of course."

"Now, there's another thing about orders that have come up for you."

"I've never requested any orders," said Patton.

"Soldier, you're in the US Army. Since when has the army sought anyone's request for orders? Now then, they're sending you to Pearl."

Patton was dumbfounded. His personal plans to stay on the East Coast were dissolving before his eyes. He was now going to Pearl Harbor, Hawaii. Yet he knew that the needs of the army always came first, so he bore the shock of disappointment.

"Is there something wrong, soldier?" asked the commander. "No, sir," he said with resignation. "When are they expecting me?"

"You'll have a week to pack. And I wouldn't bother taking any winter gear. A lot of men have put in for this assignment, George. Your wife will have the time of her life. But I'm going to warn you, like I do all of my married men, stay away from Chinatown. The army wants to get you ready for that Assistant Chief of Staff position for intelligence, so stay out of trouble."

"They didn't review my records to put me in European intelligence?"

"There are more things brewing in Japan, George. And the Chinese are getting nervous about the Japanese being in their Shandong province. We have enough European intelligence units, but there are quite a few Japanese Americans in Hawaii that we don't know too much about, so I put your name in the ring to be considered for the job to help keep an eye on things. Out of one hundred and fifty thousand Japanese Americans, fifty thousand were born and raised in Japan. They call them *isse*, and these folks are not citizens, even though they make up one-third of the population on our island."

"It still seems to me that they'd better worry more about the Chinese. They've got warlords, and some of them are talking about communism."

"The Chinese are a very complex mixed group," said the commander, "and their only interest is getting their own house in order. But the Japanese, they're looking to expand territory over there with their samurai culture, and if you look at it, they've got to expand. All they've got are six little islands with dwindling resources."

"I see."

"But at the same time, reports are coming in about the Germans again. They've got some kind of radical party talking about revolution."

"It might be the only solution they have for their economy right now."

"No. It's more than that. They've got this "super race" mentality that's getting people stirred up, and they see themselves as victims of the Versailles treaty."

"We should have done more to put a new government in place after their surrender."

"Perhaps, but what can you really do?" he said to himself exasperatingly. "It wouldn't take too much for a powder keg to form over there. Just the wrong person, at the wrong time, could do a lot of damage. All it would take is someone like, like…"

"Like a Napoleon?"

"Napoleon?" he looked at Patton queerly. "I was thinking more about someone this century, George."

"Of course, sir, but Napoleon came to power nearly out of the same circumstances. And he probably would have become the emperor of all Europe, but he lacked one thing."

The commander sat and glared at Patton. He didn't expect any subordinate to ever attempt to teach him about war history in his own office, but he let Patton continue in his tangent.

"And what would that have been, George?" he asked with feigned interest. "What was the one thing that Napoleon lacked?"

"A talisman of power."

"A what?"

"It was some mystical thing of supernatural power that he was after. But one of his own marshals hid it from him to save Europe."

"George, when we allow you to conduct research and lecture about military strategies, keep your focus on this century, got it? And since I don't think any super bombs had been developed when Napoleon was around, please don't share any of your grand theories about what Napoleon lacked with our friends in Washington."

"Well, of course, sir. Who would expect them to know anything about that?"

18

THE LIST

The local people, short and bronze colored, moved casually to a swaying island rhythm as they went about their day, while the fragrance of a million flowers suffused the warm air. Honolulu, Hawaii, was a brisk island paradise that had become a major international city. It was the "pearl" of the Pacific. A million tons of sweet sugarcane were produced annually. Multiple tons of pineapple were also exported across the Pacific, and the University of Hawaii was growing in its reputation of producing notable graduates in the fields of business and politics.

The fishing industry had also boomed, requiring a need for hundreds of contracted laborers, and there were none as skilled in the fishing industry as the Japanese. Many immigrated to settle there as contracted employees with American businesses around Waikiki, an international port. They were quiet, diligent, and usually appeared to be very cheerful.

They had also left a mark on society as skilled gardeners, tailors, restaurant owners, and educators. One hundred and seventy Japanese language schools had been established to cater to the thousands of Japanese children, born on US territory, whose parents insisted that they keep their Japanese heritage and citizenship. They were a society within a society.

Tamiki Hirata was unusually tall for a native Japanese.

He had been on the island for ten years and had a lovely wife and three intelligent children who attended a predominantly Japanese elementary school and a language school. He was a skilled fisherman who owned the latest model of a fifty-four-foot steel commercial vessel, and most of the fishing companies around the port of Waikiki knew him as very easy-going.

Hirata now was rushed however. He had decided to pick up his daughter, Noriko, immediately after school, while his other children were attending the language school. It was the time of Setsubun, a Japanese holiday celebrating the beginning of spring, and he promised he would take her to the local temple to see her friends. So, he pulled up to the school in his blue 1925 Chevrolet Tourer and beeped the horn.

"Noriko, Noriko, come now," he said, spotting her amidst smaller children.

Noriko obediently came running, her right hand holding her hat on top of her head of jet-black hair.

Noriko was a modest girl who was very well liked among the teachers. She was very eager to please, as many Japanese girls were. However, she had an appearance and sociable demeanor that attracted even the non-Japanese. Her eyes were not as slanted as the other girls' eyes were, and that made her appear partially Hawaiian. Her skin was not as pale and didn't turn red in the sun. It kept a healthy glow. Her Hawaiian friends, though there were only a few, felt open to talk with her about their own families and traditions. There was Adamina, a girl two houses down, who loved to go with her grandfather to the sugarcane fields. She made stick dolls out of sugarcane pieces and had a collection of them hidden under her bed, despite the fact that her mother insisted that she not bring them into the house because of the ants. And there was Abira, a neighbor from the opposite side of the street who frequented the big Hawaiian church of Protestants downtown. She always invited Norkio to accompany her there. Her father was an usher at the church and had studied Japanese culture as a student in Kyoto.

"Climb in," Hirata instructed, "or we'll be late like last year." Noriko delicately climbed in and plopped herself next to her father. They drove off.

"How are you, father?" she asked. "I'm fine. And how was school today?"

"It was fun. The teacher told us a story about Setsubun in Nagasaki, where she was born."

"This must be that new teacher."

"That's the one. She told us a lot of things about the emperor that I had never heard."

"Oh? Like what?"

"Oh, like things about him and the temple, and god." Hirata started to become slightly nervous. He and his wife had decided to raise their children in a nominal Japanese tradition without explaining the religious implications of Shintoism; which was growing more controversial among non-Japanese on the island.

"Go on, Noriko, what did she say."

"Well, she said that the emperor represented god on Earth and that every Japanese has a duty to honor him as god."

"Did anyone ask her any questions?"

"No, I don't think so. But is this true, father?"

Hirata said nothing. They had just pulled up to park in front of the temple where a crowd was gathering near the courtyard. Many school children had arrived early to be able to sit close to the platform because the closer one was, the easier it was to catch the soybeans during the theatrical bean-throwing part of the event.

Noriko and her father walked hand-in-hand and pushed forward to get as close as possible to the temple platform. By this time there was only standing room left. On her tiptoes, however, Noriko could see some of her friends on the opposite side of the courtyard.

A melodious high-pitched shrill in Japanese riff came from a bamboo flute within the temple. Then there were the dull percussion sounds of someone beating a goat-skin drum. The ceremony had begun. The temple priest slowly led a procession of five men around the platform, chanting ritualistically in a baritone voice. He was robed in layers of a white garment with a black box-like cap on his head. It was so small that it had to be strapped by a string under his chin to be kept in place. Over his shoulder, he and the other processors carried twigs from a cherry blossom tree as they steadily walked in rhythm set by the thud of the drum. They encircled the courtyard and chanted prayers designed to drive away evil spirits. Then someone wearing a demonic paper mask appeared on stage. He growled as he approached the processors, which prompted the priest to direct the audience to shout in unison:

"Demons out, good luck in, demons out, good luck in," as they drove the masked demon from the platform. Finally, the processors threw soybeans at him, which were supposed to keep him away. The audience of giggling children and smiling parents jostled under a rainfall of white soybeans that were meant to be taken home to purify their dwellings from evil.

Amid the festive crowd, Noriko was surprised to see Abira standing toward the back with her father, Kale. Though she knew that her father had studied Japanese culture, she had never seen them at any previous ceremony.

Kale was known to be a part of a large custodial cleaning business called 'Island Hoppers,' which the US military had contracted to work at the Hickam army base. No one would ever have suspected however that the FBI was commissioning him to spy on Japanese nationals in the community, and no one would ever imagine in their wildest dreams that this pleasant Hawaiian-born socialite was there that day to spy on Hirata and his daughter.

Abira had caught a handful of soybeans and was showing them to her father. "Look father," Noriko said happily, "that's Abira."

"Oh? Does she go to school with you?" he asked.

"No, she's the Hawaiian girl who lives on our street. Can I go and say hi?"

"Yes, but let's go quickly now, because traffic will start to build up soon."

Noriko and her father waded through the crowd as the stage performers slowly returned to the temple accompanied by the ceremonial music. Many children were still looking for scattered soy beans in the grassy area of the courtyard, so Hirata carefully walked around the youngsters without acknowledgment. He was not used to talking to or socializing with either the Japanese or the Hawaiians, as neither group was part of his daily routine at the workplace.

His workday began, during most days, at five o'clock in the morning at the American-owned fishery near the port. He had become used to working for them. On board his ship he kept a shortwave radio to be able to speak with them, from their office on shore, and with his wife, who kept a radio at home aided by a tall antenna atop their house. This constituted the extent of his daily social interactions.

"Hi Abira!" said Noriko enthusiastically, "I didn't think you would really come."

"Yes," said Mr. Hirata to her father, "it's unusual that we might find you here at the temple."

"I've always loved Japanese culture," said her father, Kale, "ever since I studied in Kyoto years ago. But I've always been too busy to attend public ceremonies here."

"I see your daughter got a few soybeans," he said, looking at Abira, who was still examining them suspiciously. "You know, you're supposed to use them to drive evil from your home," he said to her.

"Yes, I know. But we were thinking more about planting them in the garden," said Kale jokingly.

"Mr. Himala?" asked Noriko sincerely, "aren't you afraid of the evil spirits?"

"Well, I suppose I might be if my church hadn't assured me that we have the protection of angels and the Holy Spirit. I don't think they are going to bother us," he said dismissively. Kale then looked up directly at Mr. Hirata. "Do you practice Shintoism, Mr. Hirata?"

Mr. Hirata was becoming uncomfortable now. "We have our own family traditions, Mr. Kale, and some of them go back for centuries. You must have learned about these things when you were in Kyoto."

"Yes, yes, I remember many ceremonies like this one we saw today. And I remember that even the emperor would attend some."

"The emperor is god on Earth," said Noriko with a smile, "that's what our teacher was talking about today. And every Japanese must accept being Shinto."

Hirata let out a forced laugh, "These children take things so literally!"

"Oh, but I've always been intrigued by the religious part of the culture," said Kale. "And I do remember having many discussions in Kyoto about it. It seemed that everyone took it literally, and that the emperor was esteemed to be a type of son of god, on Earth, and no one ever questioned anything he did."

"I think you'll find that the Japanese community here in Hawaii is a little different," said Hirata conclusively. "But I'm afraid we are going to have to leave you now as I have to pick up my other children. It was nice seeing you!"

"Likewise, Mr. Hiratata."

Noriko and Abira grinned at each other and waved goodbye while Hirata led Noriko away into a swirling crowd of giddy children. Abira didn't exactly understand why her father had acted strangely toward Mr. Hirata. He was usually very reserved in discussions with the Japanese. Listening to their discussion had left a funny taste in her mouth, and she hoped that the exchange would not come between her and Noriko. She was almost sorry she told her father that Noriko and Mr. Hirata had planned to attend the ceremony.

On Monday morning, Kale Himala was standing in a cold, private room at Hickam army headquarters before three men who wore gray coats and fedora hats. They were accompanied by Major George Patton.

And Kale was responding to several questions pertaining to Mr. Hirata's religious background.

"So why was he there if he's not a Shinto?" asked one agent. "This seasonal bean festival can be done at parks and schools, too, why did he choose to go to the temple?"

"That, I cannot answer, sir," said Kale. "Perhaps they were meeting friends there. I saw his daughter talking with a few girls who appeared to be classmates. But I'm personally still not clear as to why Shintoism creates a national threat."

"It's about loyalty, Mr. Himala," said one agent. "A true Shinto is loyal to the emperor at all costs. He'll be loyal to the emperor before showing loyalty to his own government. Now Mr. Hirata is a very private man," he continued, "I don't think that he was meeting anyone at the temple. But he goes out to sea every day as a contracted fisherman and keeps a short-wave radio on his boat. It is quite possible that he can be communicating with other sea vessels."

"I don't know who he would be communicating with, sir," said Kale.

"Gentlemen," said Patton, "this man knows his way around the harbor and rubs shoulders with American businessmen on the island. There's no telling how much scuttlebutt he knows about US interests here and naval maneuvers. Mr. Kale, you just keep watching this monkey. He's not the only one on the list that we need to continually watch. I'm drawing up plans to conduct war maneuvers here for the army, and we're going to simulate an attack by Japanese imperial forces, which should shake a few commanders out of their slumber."

Comfortably nestled at the foot of the Waianae Mountains, the Schofield barracks at Fort Shafter were to be barren for three days. They were constructed in 1908 for the army to be able to have a mobile defense for Pearl Harbor, and now, Major Patton endeavored to use all 17,000 acres for war games to simulate such a defense. The army, the national guard, and reserve units were mandated to take part in an enormous chess match of military hardware.

It was dawn. Patton and his personally selected team chose to assume the role of the enemy. Patton played the part of the emperor and his Japanese army was called the "blacks." His team was composed of seven hundred men equipped with tanks, jeeps, rifles, and most importantly, aircraft. Their mission was to capture an area of land representing an island near the Pearl Harbor capture zone.

As the enemy, they were given the advantage of initiating a first strike. The games would not begin until they launched an attack. They had from dawn to dusk to decide when and where to commence.

"Now a surprise air attack would be the most probable course of action that the Japanese would ever take," he said to team officials standing three miles away from the capture zone. "You pilots need to remember that if they can keep you in their sights for seven seconds within a range of 400 yards, you're dead, so keep maneuvering. Once you see an official red flag waved, you're out of the games. We'll launch an air attack from their left flank when the sun is directly in their eyes, and that'll give us an advantage. For each flyby at treetop level, you will eliminate twenty of their infantrymen, but you'll need to barrel roll out of there after you strafe, so they don't shoot your backside. Give the officials time to get 'em out of the way when you pass. When we've eliminated enough ground forces by air, the infantry units will take land. I'll signal the field for an all-out ground attack when we're ready."

"Sir, how will we recognize the officials at ground level?" asked a platoon captain who had missed a previous briefing.

"The ground officials will be carrying red flags, and they'll be wearing yellow stripped helmets. Now, remember, the emperor expects the most dauntless courage for all of his officers. When our ground forces outnumber theirs, we've won."

The early morning mist hovered over the ground for hours, at which time Patton's team was expected to launch a ground attack. Every man remained hair-trigger ready as early morning passed into early afternoon. Then, against a cloudless mid-afternoon sky, the lookout squad detected the humming sounds of fighter planes.

"Captain, enemy aircraft detected at Oh, ten hundred hours—approximately four thousand yards away," reported a young ground defense lookout.

"That's outside our effective shooting range. Wait 'til they're at least at six hundred yards to start lining them up, and radio Captain Bolger in the field," replied the captain.

"Sir, they're arcing right against the sun now. We have no visual capability—too much glare."

The captain then turned to the official next to him, who was trying to suppress a grin. "Is that in the rule book?" he said helplessly. "Can they get strafing points when we can't even see them? They'll wipe out ground troops in five minutes!"

The humming of aircraft grew louder, sounding as an approaching swarm of violent insects.

"Captain," said the game official, grim faced, "any side may use topography, weather conditions, or any natural elements to his advantage in a state of war."

As the humming grew louder, the captain shouted to his ground-defense squad leaders, manning twenty-millimeter cannons, and to his radio operator. "Okay, listen! We're probably going to lose quite a few ground troops in their flybys over the next few minutes, but be sure to get them when they pass. We'll knock them out of the games in the flybys. Turn your guns around now."

The sound of plane engines revving in high gear from the skies signified to everyone that they were beginning to dive. The men scrambled and fumbled as they started to muscle the heavy guns 360 degrees to be able to line up the planes in their sights as they passed. Some of the gunners lingered however, and attempted to line up the partially visible aircraft against the sun.

The first enemy aircraft successfully swooped down at treetop level like a bird of prey and did a wild barrel roll, thus eliminating twenty ground troopers. Official scorekeepers were perched behind the twenty-millimeter ground gunners as eager baseball umpires ready to call a hit, but ground defense participants failed to keep the aircraft steady in their sites before they exceeded 400 yards, which put them in a safety zone. Then, four more enemy planes came screaming down at them.

"Aim at the nose when they start to pull up," a gunner yelled. "You'll be able to keep the body of the craft in your sights if you aim high first before they roll."

Patton stood on a hillside watching the maneuvers through binoculars. All was going according to plan. Only six aircraft had been eliminated, but twelve had successfully strafed enemy ground troops resulting in their loss of 240 infantrymen. His infantry could now outnumber theirs in a ground assault. By chance perhaps, all of the heavy guns were still turned around targeting aircraft. This clearly provided an advantage for a frontal attack led by tanks. He thus signaled the tanks for a lightning speed ground attack toward the capture zone from three miles away.

"Captain, he's released his tanks!" shouted the lookout, "and they're moving at top speed."

"How far away are they?"

"Approximately two and a half miles."

"Our effective range is one point two miles. Still too far. Radio Captain Bolger to send in the tank units."

"Yes, sir."

Ground defense tanks appeared from bushes and camouflaged regions on the terrain, but they started out too slow. By the time they were within effective shooting range, Patton's tank divisions had progressed just outside of enemy territory with cannons blazing.

Enemy tanks were hit and eliminated at a ratio of four to one. Then, finally, he released his eager infantry units in an all-out attack. They came running as they hooted and hollered at the obvious victory they had accomplished in record time. They poured onto the capture zone area like a spilling flood, and the war game officials scrambled to toss red flags into the air signifying hits, eliminations, and disqualifications. The mock Japanese army had effectively invaded.

A siren sounded, indicating that the games were over. Patton's army of "blacks" happily broke out in songs of victory. Senior officers and enlistees were impressed with their strategy. Opposing sides turned toward each other to shake hands when, from a distance, Patton appeared. He was walking through the combat zone onto the capture zone area to take center stage, as a playwright might address an audience at the close of a theatrical production. His men erupted in cheers and a great round of applause. Then a senior officer handed him a megaphone.

"Men, what you have just seen is the future of war maneuvers. The next war will begin in the air, and it will end in the mud. And I think we've all seen that there's work to be done in ground defense tactics. But we didn't come here today to play sport. In the coming years, you will be a part of a new army—and you'd better be ready. Before the US Army is dragged into another war, be it from Europe or even Asia, the US Army had better be ready."

In the following years between 1935 and 1937, Patton continued to handle questions of national security with a sense of urgency. As Assistant Chief of Staff in Hawaii, he composed a list of 128 Japanese and two Caucasian individuals on the island who he believed posed an imminent threat to the US. This was around the time when Japan had entered a treaty with Germany against communist expansion. He advised authorities to arrest his identified suspects, but they never did. His list was later deemed obsolete and discarded before 1940.

19

THE OTHER LIST

They were the names of other condemned men. A different list of suspects now was tightly clutched in the hand of Hitler, and the names written thereon were not Japanese, but German, Dutch, and Bulgarian. The brown sheet of paper had been dampened in the wet palms of its bearer, but the names remained nonetheless legible—and many would be surprised. Some claimed that they were only scapegoats used as pawns, but others believed that these were the communist perpetrators who set fire to the Reichstag parliamentary building in protest of the ever-increasing Nazi party.

Four weeks prior, Hitler had become a German citizen and was sworn in as the newly appointed chancellor. Their National Socialist Worker's Party manifesto had captured the minds of many, creating the groundwork for the new Nazi party. Hitler had met statesmen, community workers, and dignitaries. He restlessly pushed his philosophy of Aryan superiority while blaming Jews, communists, and gypsies for economic troubles, and his speeches were becoming more supernaturally charged with dynamism. Fear, pride, hatred, and discipline were common themes diabolically interwoven into the fabric of his political platform. He had even gone so far as to stage a mock revolution in one of the beer halls where he often orated, but this incident only resulted in his brief imprisonment, allowing him to write a book about his personal struggles. The book earned him over a million dollars. He was unstoppable. And that's when it all started to crescendo into a fiery storm.

As chancellor, he had asked the president, Paul Von Hindenburg, to call for a new parliamentary election. A new election would have helped him win a majority in the government, and a majority of Nazis could then allow him to legally drive out the communist party and abolish democracy. The crafty details to this tentative plan were still being discussed on that winter night in the apartment of his friend, Dr. Joseph Goebbels.

"Why then couldn't some form of socialism be retained," asked Goebbels, in a politically charged discussion. "The German people know what communism looks like, and they don't really want it, but there are precepts in socialism which could suit us." Goebbels was a scrawny, club-footed man with high political ideals. Despite his frail demeanor, he was known for his political astuteness and journalistic writing talents.

"The mere association that socialism creates is poisonous," argued Hitler. "The Nazi party must stay away from it for that reason alone. We must purge every branch…"

Before Hitler could finish his response, the telephone rang, and Goebbels rushed to answer it. The heated discussion came to a standstill in response to the sense of shock in Goebbels voice.

"Hello? Yes. Who? How do you know? Completely? How many names? We're leaving now!" he said.

"What's happened?" asked Hitler.

"They've actually done it, those communist pigs! They just burned down the Reichstag."

Hitler lowered his head and turned to face the opposite wall where no one was standing. He was pensive for a few short seconds before turning around. Then there was an air of contentment about him.

"This is a sign to us, so we are not to worry," he said reassuringly. "Their party won't have a chance of survival now. Let's go there."

The main streets near the town center were blocked, which required them to walk two miles to get to the Reichstag building. When they arrived, the flames were beginning to dwindle. The main legislative chambers had been gutted and charred, and the stench of sulfur lingered in the air.

Local police officials who were friendly with Nazi party members were gathered near the structure, keeping onlookers from coming too close. Then one young officer approached Hitler.

"You will want to see this, sir," he said, handing him a brown sheet of paper bearing several names.

"Who wrote these?" asked Hitler.

"We knew who they were before this thing happened," he said, "and we know about others, too."

Their names were scribbled in black running ink. They were: Blagoi Popov, and Georgi Dimitrov, two Bulgarian communists, as well as Vassili Tanev, Ernst Torgler, and Marinus Van der Lubbe. All had been a part of an international communist movement, and Van der Lubbe was known to be a kingpin.

Van der Lubbe was an unusually strong man from Holland who was understood to have a mental illness. He had worked as a bricklayer and was nicknamed "Jack Dempsey" after the American prizefighter.

"Where are they now?" asked Hitler.

"They're being held in protective custody. I don't know where they are now, but they'll be tried in court. But there's not a lot of evidence against some of them."

"Someone needs to see to it that at least one of them hangs."

"Yes, we've been talking about this already," said the police officer.

Though the flames of the Reichstag had been extinguished, flames of fear and anxiety were being fanned from week to week. There was a sense of anticipation about what turn the government would now take. Street demonstrations grew.

As chancellor, Hitler asked for a special emergency decree from President Hindenburg, and he received it. The Reichstag Fire Decree gave him special powers, allowing him to suspend many civil liberties in Germany, and the Nazis also used it to ban publications that were not considered "friendly" to their cause.

Street demonstrations thus ceased.

Despite the fact that Marinus van der Lubbe claimed to have acted alone in starting the fire, Hitler now announced that the event marked the beginning of a subversive communist plot to take over all Germany. Nazi newspapers heralded these suspicions, resulting in societal panic and the social isolation of communist party members. Thousands of them were imprisoned.

With communist electoral participation now suppressed, the Nazis were able to increase their share of the vote in an emergency election, giving them and their allies a majority in the Reichstag. Hitler would now be voted dictator. The government now would be changed forever.

At the trial, each judge on the panel glared at Van der Lubbe. They had used the word scoundrel against him several times, but it didn't seem to bother him anymore. Van der Lubbe knew that some kind of execution awaited him, and he was ready to die.

"How could you even dare to think that the German people would respond positively to such a criminal act?" questioned a panel judge.

"German people, like my own people in Holland, are a disciplined people, but they are a vulnerable people. They're hoping for a savior to come now and solve all of their problems, but these Nazi devils from hell won't solve anything. They don't want to help Germany, they just want power."

"So who sent you to do these things?"

"No one sent me. I acted alone. I saw what was going on myself, and sometimes I think I'm the only one willing to face the truth."

"Well, now you're going to have to face judgment," retorted another panel judge. "You should have moved to the Soviet Union to live out your sick communist fantasies," he said. "Boy, you're a fool, and you'll die a fool's death."

An official guard was called upon to take Van der Lubbe back to his cell. He grabbed the young man by the right arm and dragged him across the courtroom like a rag doll. Van der Lubbe then ceased resisting and began to walk in pace with the guard. With head inclined, he was looking at the passing tiles on the floor with each step until he saw the iron bars of his cell at his feet. The guard opened the cell, pushed him to the cement floor inside, and locked it.

The panel of judges had previously decided that a public execution would not be in the best interest of the Nazi party at this time; it would appear to be too vindictive. Thus, the following morning, Van der Lubbe was awakened at dawn by a guard who was standing over him. The guard nudged him with a nightstick, smirked, and then yelled, "*roust, roust*," to alarm him. Van der Lubbe was slowly waking up when another guard quickly slipped a cloth sack down over his head and pulled a slipknot tightly around his neck.

He could barely breathe. The two men then each took an arm and dragged him into the courtyard. The air was brisk, and the ground was still covered with settled ashes from the Reichstag fire, which had happened a half a mile away. Van der Lubbe was forced to kneel and rest his head against a wooden stump. He could feel deep jagged crevices in the stump against his face, but he remained motionless, fixing his eyes on the inside of the cloth sack, which was bleach white. Then everything went black. An axe fell, and Van der Lubbe's head rolled to the ground, kicking up a puff of grayish ash from the Reichstag fire.

Without any opponents to hinder him, Hitler's eyes were now focused on Austria as his mind tenaciously held on to the possibility of a restored Roman Empire in all of its glory.

All it would require is the friendly annexation between the two nations and the possession of the spear. He waited.

20

THE HAKOAH CLUB

The anticipated handball match at the Hakoah Sports Club was the talk of the town in the Jewish community. It was the only sports club in Austria where Jewish men were allowed to join as members, and several boys had already excelled to international stardom. The club had been founded by a Jewish Viennese Zionist and was already the home to many Olympic medal holders of their faith. In addition to famous medalists, local names such as Alexander Fabian, Max Wortmann, and Joseph Stross were the pride of the community.

For Baruch Finklestine it was a safe haven away from the bullies of racial prejudice and religious intolerance—an island of acceptance where everyone understood each other. He enjoyed playing team handball and had become one of the top five athletes at the club. He could jump higher than anyone, and he could whip the ball at fifty-seven miles per hour.

His teammates were looking forward to having him lead them to victory in an international competition, which was to be held in London. The competition was one month away.

Though the complex was the pride of Jewish culture and athletic achievement, a few non-Jewish young men also frequented the club. There was Franz, who was third place on the swimming team, and Eric, who was fifth place on the fencing team. Victor was also a new member and had just recently moved into town. Though he was unfamiliar with team handball, his large shape and broad shoulders made him an ideal goalie, so he was considered to be another team asset.

Since his father had worked in the civil service as a diplomatic aid, Victor's family was often exposed to various ethnic groups from Eastern Europe. He thus learned to fit in with whomever he could, and he couldn't understand racial prejudice or religious hatred.

His family recently moved into a villa near the great Heldenplatz Imperial court, and his father was now a new local member of the Austrian Nazi party.

"Victor, listen. When you see the ball holder run over to your left, you know he's going to try to throw a tight shot into your right corner. That's his best option. But you're going to have to anticipate whether he'll throw it high or low," explained Baruch in a practice game huddle.

"I know, I know. But how can I tell? That's the problem.

Sometimes our own men block my vision," replied Victor.

"Listen, if he takes a jump, and he's in the inner circle, he's more than likely going to throw it in your lower right corner. It's not easy to throw it high and be accurate after you've jumped. So be ready to kick your foot out 'cause he's probably going to try to shoot a tight ground shot."

"I got it."

Baruch turned to another player. "Samuel," he said, "you're playing left back, so try to look for me when you can. I can whip it in from the outer circle, but I need you to block when you can. If you don't see me, pass it to Ezra. He's usually open."

The boys spent the whole afternoon that Thursday drilling offensive and defensive plays. They practiced dribbling, passing, and using their bodies to block attempted shots. Victor was becoming used to the technique of shifting his weight to lean sideways to absorb attempted goals. He learned to stay light on his feet, and he learned to read the body motion of the players.

By evening time, the boys had had enough. They were able to put in double hours of practice as they knew that the sports club was open extended hours on Thursday nights to make up for shorter business hours on Fridays, the days of the weekly Jewish Sabbath feasts. They thus dragged themselves into the shower room. They showered off, packed up, and bade each other goodbye until Sunday.

Victor shouldered his tote bag containing his team uniform as he stepped off the tram. He always enjoyed crossing through the famous Heldenplatz plaza on the way home because it made him feel as if he were in a grand stadium. The Imperial Palace and stately historic buildings surrounding the great plaza put him at the center of all Austria, if only for a few moments. Since his family had moved into the area, it was his idiosyncratic custom to stop for a second or two to appreciate the scenery. But it was now cold, and his aching muscles begged him to sit down, so he hurried home.

"Victor, Victor, is that you?" his mother's voice sounded from the kitchen.

"It's me, Mom."

"Why are you so late, huh? Your supper is cold."

"I'm sorry. I thought I told you that I would be practicing late tonight after school."

Victor's father was reclining in his den. The door was left ajar, and he was reading the local newspaper. He had only arrived ten minutes before Victor, as it had become his habit to return home late in the evening. He was now waiting for his wife to warm up his dinner.

"Victor, Victor come here, son," said the father from his den.

Victor entered, apparently tired. "Hi Poppie," he said.

"Sit down, son. You look tired. I've been meaning to ask you how you are doing at the new school, but I've been very, very busy these days."

"School is fine. It's not that different from the last school, except they don't have any organized sports."

"But your grades, how are they doing?"

"My grades are fine, Poppie."

"Well, I hope you'll be able to continue in good spirits, despite not being able to play any sports."

"But I am playing sports, remember? I told you that I was going to join that sports club and play team handball after school. That's why I'm late."

"What kind of team requires boys to practice until late in the evening on school nights?"

"We have to practice late on Thursdays because it closes early on Fridays for festivals."

"Festivals?"

"Not real festivals. I mean, the people take Fridays off for family traditional things."

"What's the name of this sports club?"

"It's called Hakoah."

"What did you say?"

At this moment, Victor's mother gingerly entered the den to summon them both for dinner. However, she stood motionless for a moment as she caught a familiar expression of distress on her husband's face. Victor's father was well educated and knew immediately that Hakoah was a Hebrew word. But he was hoping that his son had not joined the notorious Jewish sports club.

"Victor, did you join that Jewish club?"

"I really don't know if it's Jewish. No one told me I had to be a Jew to go in. But it's a great sports club. I get along all right with everyone."

"Who's the captain of this team?"

"The unofficial team leader's name is Baruch."

Victor's father glanced at his wife in disappointment. He felt as if they had betrayed him during his long hours of being away from home every night.

"Honey, why didn't anyone tell me about this?" he said. "I didn't know it was Jewish, dear."

He turned his face once again toward Victor. "You are not going to be a member of that club, do you hear me?"

"But, Poppie, I'm the team goalie. We're practicing for a big game, and I don't care if they're Jewish. What's that got to do with anything?"

"Son, they are Jews. They are different from you and me, and I don't want to talk about that right now. You'll have to find some other club."

"But, Poppie, there is no other club around here, and so what if they're Jews. Why does everybody keep talking about Jews all of a sudden, just because that chancellor in Germany sees them as a problem? This is Austria, and I don't have any problem with them. I just want to play sports."

"That chancellor in Germany will one day be a chancellor of Austria, son. He was born here. And the party has already agreed to..."

Victor's father stopped himself because he saw that his wife was slowly slipping into shock. Her lurking fears were apparently true. The two of them had discussions about the local Austrian Nazi party and its political agenda. Now it was all beginning to make sense: her husband's late-night meetings, the local editorials in the newspaper extolling Hitler and his triumphs, the growing animosity over Jewish Austrians. Germany and Austria were going to become one.

"The party has agreed to what, darling?" she asked.

He was caught. Victor's father had wanted to be able to break the news to his family in a more gradual, softhearted way, but it was too late. The best he could do now was explain himself and the intentions of the Nazi party in the most benevolent way possible. He asked his wife to sit down.

"Listen, you may not have heard the news, but Chancellor Hitler is now a dictator in Germany, and the Nazis are doing good things for Germany. Since Hitler has taken office, the economy has improved. And he's restoring dignity to the people. You remember how it was not too long ago?"

"Okay, Poppie, but what are you saying? We can't move to Germany now, we just got here."

"No one is moving anywhere, son. But what I'm saying is that Germany and Austria are going to be united again. It's already been planned. He's going to do for his homeland, Austria, what he's been doing for Germany, and it's about time for it! But that Jewish sports club as well as the Jewish community centers will be closed up."

"But why, Poppie, why? What have they done? Aren't they Austrian too? The guys at the sports club…"

"Never mind about the guys at the sports club. There's not going to be any guys at the sports club soon. It's going to get dangerous around there. But they'll be given an opportunity to leave the country."

Victor and his mother were feeling mixed emotions. Was this something to celebrate? It was true that Germany had experienced a noticeable turnaround economically, but there was something shamefully dark about the Nazis and their ways. Their rallies had become more commonplace in Vienna, and their swastika posters had become more noticeable at the tram stations, but they still appeared to be an efficient secret society with hidden agendas. Victor grew worried about his teammates at the club.

There was very little talk at the dinner table that night. Victor, though he was instructed not to reveal this information to anyone, felt compelled to warn his friends. He thought of what he might say. Victor's mother worried about the future of her child as well as the future for her nephews and nieces.

By Sunday afternoon, the initial shock had subsided, and Victor was dressing for church service. His parents had always hypocritically insisted that he attend while they stayed home on the premise of catching up with affairs. Victor's personal plans however were designed to miss the service and meet with his teammates to talk.

Though his father forbade him from ever returning to the sports club, he couldn't let the team think he had simply given up on them.

Tightening his necktie, Victor walked into the kitchen to cut a slice of apple strudel and wash it down with a glass of milk. Both his father and mother were in the den, as he could hear their muffled voices.

"I won't be gone too long," he said opening the door. "Okay, son, say hello to the priest for me," yelled his father. The crowded city tram was not as alluring as the open sidewalks that day. Victor needed to walk. It helped him relieve stress. How could he tell his friends on the team that they might be in danger soon—for playing sports at a Jewish club? He thought deeply. He walked through the great *Heldenplatz* plaza without even looking up. A church bell tolled in the distance, prompting him to imagine what the priest in his own parish might have talked about that day at the service. When he arrived at the sports club, there was a long line of mostly young men in front of the main doors. It hadn't opened yet, but his teammate Ezra, nicknamed Ezzy, was waiting at the end of it. He waved as he approached him.

"Ezzy, it's good to see you. Where are the others?" he asked, shaking his hand.

"They're not here yet. You look like you've just come from a church. Aren't you a little overdressed for practice?"

"Yeah, well I can't go to practice today, and I have to talk with Baruch."

"He'll be here, but why can't you come? You know we got a big match next week, and that's the last match we'll have before finalists go to London."

"I know, I know. Listen, can you come with me for a moment—please come."

Ezra was reluctant to lose his place in line but knew that there was something seriously bothering Victor. He decided to walk with him, away from the crowded entrance doors.

"What's the problem Victor? Are you trying to drop the team?"

"No, I'm not trying to drop the team. I have to drop it, but there's something even more important than that. I think everybody here will be in danger soon. You should tell your families to start making plans to leave Austria."

Instinctively, Ezra understood what Victor was talking about, though he didn't want to accept it. The Jewish community had become so accustomed to ignoring insults and discrete methods of persecution that they no longer could respond to threats with a sense of urgency.

"Victor, we are aware of what's going on in Germany, and we know that there are people like that here, too. But things will settle down, so don't be worried. You can still play here."

"No, you don't understand. I'm telling you that even this club is in danger. It won't be long before this whole country will be changed." Baruch had just arrived from the tram and, from a distance, saw his two teammates talking. Noticing Victor's formal attire, he suspected that he wouldn't be able to practice on account of a family wedding or funeral. He was already planning in his mind whom he could ask to stand in to be the goalie when an unrecognizable figure appeared from within the sports club. He was frowning and didn't even care to make eye contact with anyone standing in line before him. He spoke in a monotone voice.

"Today, this club will be closed," he said frankly. "It is under inspection, but will be opened tomorrow on normal schedule."

One of the members standing in line spoke up. "Is there anything wrong, sir?" The man simply rolled his eyes and repeated, "Today, this club will be closed. It is under inspection, but will be opened tomorrow on normal schedule. That is all."

Members of the crowd looked at each other, mumbled, and returned frowns to the stranger still blocking the doorway. Someone suggested that the city fire marshal was probably inspecting the structure for code compliance. Another man said that city officials never work on Sundays. Someone else said that he had seen the same man before, talking to his rabbi at the synagogue.

While the crowd was beginning to disperse, Victor sought the opportunity to talk with Baruch.

"Baruch, I'm so glad to be able to talk with you," he said. "It looks like all we'll be able to do today is talk. They've never closed this place on Sundays before. Did you know this would happen?"

"Me, how should I have known?"

"It's just that you didn't suit up for practice."

"Oh, well, my father told me that I needed to attend church this afternoon. But listen, I came here to warn you, something bad is going to happen in Austria, and I think you should tell your father that it might be best to get away for a while."

"What are you saying?"

"My father works closely with local politicians, and, uh, they're trying to change laws that might affect the sports club and even the Jewish community."

"Do you know how long people have been talking like that?" he said. "My family goes back two hundred years in Austria, and people have always wanted us out."

"Okay, maybe that's true, but things are changing quickly, Baruch. And the things going on in Germany today will start to affect us here. That's all I can really say."

Baruch stared at Victor. He had never seen this side of him and wondered if he really knew him. For Baruch, however, nothing was as urgent as preparing for the upcoming match, which would determine who would make the playoffs in London. That, to him, came before any political controversy occurring in Vienna or Germany.

"Victor, are you dropping the team?"

"I don't want to, but I have to. I'm sorry."

"It'll be hard to replace you, you know. You're the right size for a goalie," he said jokingly.

"Thank you. But I think I need to give my father a little time. I'm going to try to come back, but you shouldn't count on me for the big match next week. I'm sorry. And please believe me about getting away for a while."

The conversation was naturally drawing to a close when the two men began thinking simultaneously whether or not they would see each other again. They hugged and they shook hands. Baruch simulated attempting to make a goal with an imaginary ball in his hand, and Victor responded by leaning sideways and kicking out his foot. They smiled. Then Ezra approached him and gave him a pat on the back, and they all started to go their separate ways.

It felt too early to return home, despite the fact that if he had attended the church service, he probably would have been returning home about this time. Victor decided to walk past his church to see if any of his friends might still be lingering there. If he could talk with them about the afternoon service, at least he would be able to impress his father that he had been there.

Ironically, his parish was just four blocks away from the sports club in a southwestern direction. Though he had never walked through that area of town before, most of the dispersing crowd was headed that way, so he decided to go along. No one noticed him tagging along several paces behind. However, Victor began to notice a stark change of scenery as he walked. The tall, perpendicular stone architectural shapes were slowly disappearing and were replaced by small bread shops, shoemaker shops, and kosher butcher shops. The pace of life changed, and the people changed. It didn't feel like a Sunday anymore, but he felt like a foreigner as people began to steadily walk past him.

Victor could see the tall spires of his church half a block away on the left side of the street, so he decided to pick up his pace to get to familiar ground. There were familiar cars still parked not far from the church and groups of families walking around; but something gave him the impression that the church service had been unexpectedly cancelled. A steady stream of disappointed looking people began to pass him. They appeared to be headed in the direction of the local tram stop. One young man around his age stopped him.

"You're going the wrong way. No service today," he said.

"No service? Why?"

"No bishop."

"Is Bishop Schmidt ill?"

"I don't know—I don't think so. My brother said that he wasn't here anymore."

"Well, did anyone ask any of the priests inside?"

"There were no priests inside—just a sign on the doors. It looks like some other bishop will be here next week. Someone said that he's coming from Germany."

Victor's thoughts began to reaffirm his increasing anxiety. The sports club was closed, and his own church was closed. There was a silent invasion-taking place, and he was certain of it, but the enemy was still invisible at this point.

"Thanks for the scoop," he said. "I guess I'll be able to catch up on a few things at home today."

Victor raced home on foot. He didn't want to return by the tram this time because it was too difficult for him to remain still. His conscience bothered him to the point that he couldn't look anyone in the eye, now realizing that he had been privy to highly sensitive information that would change people's lives forever. The end of Austria, as he knew it, was beginning to unfold right before his eyes.

"Poppie, Poppie," he yelled upon entering their villa.

"What's the matter?" said his father.

"It's happening. It's happening now," he said with bated breath. "They closed the church up, and they're replacing the bishop with someone from Germany."

"Bishop Schmidt wasn't there this afternoon?" asked his mother.

"No," he said, "and the whole church was closed."

Victor's father looked at both of them. "There really is no cause for alarm. I expected that this might happen."

"What, darling, what is happening?" responded his mother. Victor's father sighed and inclined his head. "The Nazification of the church," he said. "Bishop Schmidt has probably been reassigned because he refused to accept new policy changes in the church."

"Policy changes? Honey, you never mentioned anything like that. What type of political policies would involve the church?"

"Poppie, are we going to be able to live the way we've always lived?" asked Victor.

"Stop being alarmists! Any time you have a new government, you will have new public policies."

"But the church, darling, the church! The church should stand above politics, unless you're talking about those hideous state-run churches like before the Reformation."

"Well, the church, the people, and everybody else is going to have to get used to pledging allegiance to Nazi policies and Hitler as the head of the Reich's church. I'm sorry, but I can't change that!"

21

THE ANCHLUSS

The silent pre-revolution continued furtively without causing any noticeable disruption in daily affairs.

The sports club reopened, and new, Nazi-approved bishops were being installed in the local churches. The men's handball team lost the playoff match, which was a significant disappointment for many, but eight days later no one would even remember it because the new political changes came like a thief in the night—the *Anchluss*, or annexation of Austria and Germany was here. It was the day that many had secretly longed for. For Hitler, it marked the long-awaited beginning of prophetic megalomania.

It was a display of self-determination like the world had never seen. International news agencies reported it as an invasion. Austrian citizens however received it as a parade. Breaking all prior international treaties, the two nations set forth a new vision for a new empire. Thousands began to fill the streets in anticipation of seeing German troops. Vendors gave away small swastika flags. People danced. Squadrons of German military cargo planes began to fly overhead, dropping paper swastikas and leaflets. Every radio program was interrupted to validate the recently rumored annexation. They encouraged citizens to gather at the Austria/German border for ceremonies to welcome German troops.

At the borders, hundreds of smiling Austrian guards lifted barrier gates to allow the expected German convoys to enter. Then they came: big trucks carrying troops, the latest Panzer tank units, convertible automobiles carrying statesmen and high ranking officers. There were miles and miles of vehicles that rushed in like a rising tide.

Then, Hitler arrived. As the passenger in a black 1936 convertible Mercedes-Benz 500K, he stretched out his arm in salute to cheering crowds as he crossed the border near his birthplace. It was mass ecstasy; the crowds seemed drugged in jubilation. Hitler's time had finally come, the day he had dreamed about. He was headed to the Imperial Palace near the *Heldenplatz* to deliver a speech while young people ran alongside his motorcade.

"I can't find my tie. Victor, have you seen it?" Victor's father and mother were expected to attend Hitler's public address at the *Heldenplatz*.

"It's in the basket in the laundry room," replied Victor. "We'd better get moving now. There'll be no place to stand near the plaza if we wait here another ten minutes," continued his father.

"Poppie?" asked Victor, "do I have to go? I really don't feel very well."

"He doesn't feel very well," he said with disgust to his mother. "This is only the greatest event to take place in Austria over the last 200 years, and he doesn't feel very well. It doesn't matter that you're not feeling very well. This is history in the making. A new Reich will be established for a thousand years, and you'll be able to tell my grandsons about it. Let's go before it gets too late."

A military band was playing Austrian anthems in the great plaza. Thousands upon thousands attended. As far as the eye could see stood men, women, and children of all ages, and all eyes were fixed upon the balcony at the Imperial Palace. Hitler's motorcade had recently arrived, and he was expected to be in the palace now preparing to speak. Then, in a deafening burst of applause, he appeared on the balcony in his official mustard-brown uniform. He approached the microphone with tears welling up in his eyes. He spoke:

"This land and this people do not come to the Reich with hat in hand. I, myself bring you home. Hence, in this hour, I can report to the German folk, that the greatest orders of my life have been carried out. And as Fuhrer and Chancellor of the German nation and the Reich, I now report to history that my homeland has joined the German Reich. Of all the tasks that we have to face, the noblest and most sacred for mankind is that each racial species must preserve the purity of the blood which God has given it. It is not for men to discuss the question of why Providence created different races, but rather to recognize the fact that it punishes those who disregard its work of creation. And I can prophesy here that, just as the knowledge that the Earth moves around the sun led to a revolutionary alternation in the general world-picture, so the blood-and-race doctrine of the National Socialist Movement will bring about a revolutionary change in our knowledge and therewith a radical reconstruction of the picture which human history gives us of the past and will also change the course of that history in the future." Hitler continued in his fiery speech throughout the day, and his radical reconstruction plan was implemented that evening. Teams of brown shirted young men became visible everywhere, wearing swastika arm bands. Some carried clubs as they went from town to town, heralding Hitler's arrival and intimidating anyone who didn't return the Nazi salute. When they encountered open defiance, they brutally socked and kicked people into submission.

One of the first establishments they visited was the Hokoah club. They entered by force, claiming that the club had been nationalized and that all Jewish members had to leave immediately. There was resistance, Hence some club members were shot. Then, in accordance with the reconstruction plan, they visited the neighboring Jewish community centers and insisted that they be closed. They were given one hour to close them down. Most of the centers complied. However, it was the third visitation that Hitler had longed for and had arranged for with only an inner circle of confidants. The Hofburg museum had been notified days prior to the annexation and was now prepared for the arrival of two Nazi officials.

Though the museum director did not want to relinquish any of his invaluable treasures, he knew he had no choice and counted the loss of the Longinus as a sacrifice for a higher nationalistic cause.

The two Nazi guards were dressed in civilian clothes when they knocked on the doors of the great museum.

"Heil Hitler," said one official as the door was opened.

The museum director fumbled a return salute, "Heil Hitler."

"We are here to collect the spear. Surely you have it ready by now."

"Yes, of course I do. Come in, it's just next to my office." The three men walked ten feet and turned toward the director's office, which was just in front of the first exhibit. "Tell me, sir," said one official as he observed the shimmering spear in its glass case. "The Fuhrer has expressed interest in collecting several pieces of artwork to launch a new renaissance. But why would he be so eager to go after this relic first?"

"Gentlemen," interrupted the director, "the value of the Longinus can't be measured by its material makeup. The history behind this spear marks the beginning of humanity in Western civilization. I can only say that whoever seizes it for its powers must be sure never to lose possession of it. Death and destruction will be certain to come if this happens."

"If this relic is over a thousand years old, it's the perfect relic to bless a thousand year Reich," said the official. "We'll take it from here."

Both men took hold of the case, pushed against the great museum doors with their shoulders and stepped out.

"Heil Hitler," said the director with tears streaming down his face. The Longinus was gone.

22

THE INVASION

"I tell you they can never be trusted!" yelled Patton, slamming his fist down. He was now in a heated discussion at the Fort Myer officer's club, having been recently reassigned to the army base adjacent to Arlington National Cemetery. Since it had no strategic training fields for combat practice, Patton often vented his aggression in social discussions about Germany and Japan. "They've already broken treaty mandates. What more do ya need to see?" he continued, "They're gonna goosestep right into France!"

"George," said an older colonel holding a beer mug, "those Austrian folks see him as their economic savior. They're not complaining about the annexation, so don't get your Irish side in an uproar."

"No, sir. You couldn't be more wrong on that. He may have you fooled, and he may have the British fooled, but I ain't fooled," he said wide-eyed. "I know now that this monster Hitler has got his claws on something powerful, and he's gonna use it.

"The Huns ain't got nothin' but hardware. Oh, they've got good stuff, but I wouldn't worry about any super bombs."

"I'm not talking about bombs," said Patton. "Don't' you remember what I was telling you about Napoleon?"

"Let me think. Oh, yes!" he said sarcastically. "He was looking for some kind of artifact with supernatural power that would have helped him conquer the world, right?"

"Well, I see that you've finally started to listen to me," said Patton. "But I wouldn't call it simply an artifact, old boy. That man must have his hands on it by now, because I recently learned that the Austrians were keeping it in a museum," said Patton heatedly.

"And what was this thing again?" asked the colonel rolling his eyes. "Wasn't it the cup of Christ they used during the Crusades or something?"

"It's the spear used to crucify Christ on the cross. Stop being ignorant."

"Well, I think that spear, being over one thousand years old, ain't gonna be sharp enough today to pose any threats to nobody."

"You're still being ignorant. What about Attila the Hun? He had it and used it. What about Charlemagne? He used it to fight off invaders. What about…."

"That ain't history; that's oral tradition. You can't know if these things are true."

"I do know it, and I know it because I've been there. I know how Napoleon wanted to use it, and I tell you that Hitler will simply try to do the same thing. Even you should know that all history just repeats itself."

"George?" said the colonel, "no more drinks for you." He then turned to the civilian personnel serving near the bar. "Did you hear that, buddy? My friend George has had enough this evening." Patton left the club in silence.

The post chapel on base created the perfect environment for prayer, worship, and meditation. Beautifully done in a red brick colonial style, it had four grand pillars in front, representing the four biblical writers of the gospels, and a high tower, which made it visible from miles around. Patton himself had initiated its design as a personal project. As a commanding officer, he oversaw its completion and took pride in it. Now he needed it for enlightenment.

He was anxious. As long as Hitler had the Longinus, he knew that terrible destruction awaited Europe. If the US were at war with Germany, perhaps he could preemptively curtail mass destruction by seizing the spear. During this time, however, no American wanted to get involved again with Europe's problems. He thus kneeled and meditated alone in the chapel. He concluded, after deep reflection, that the spear not only had to be taken from Hitler, but it needed to remain in US possession, but this would take time.

The bond between Germany and Austria was cemented almost overnight. Residents from the two former countries began to integrate, intermarry, and interbreed while people from German backgrounds in the eastern part of Europe became envious and wanted to somehow take part in the burgeoning renaissance. The citizens of Danzig were such a people.

The small region of Danzig had been created after World War I by the League of Nations. It had formerly belonged to Germany, but was assigned to Poland as part of war reparations. It was a semi-independent country now with a binding relationship with Poland and no relationship with Germany. Though geographically nestled between both Germany and Poland, its population was nonetheless ninety percent German and ten percent Polish.

Many Poles were resentful about this, however, and continued to harass German residents, to the acquiescence of Poland itself. Since citizenship was granted only to the Poles, the Germans became very disheartened, and tensions often flared, producing seasons of violent backlashes. Then, like the spreading of cancer, a Nazi party slowly developed among the majority and the new Third Reich, comprised of Germany and Austria, sought to aid them, creating a pretext for violent aggression in their own best interest.

If the Nazi's claimed that their campaign in Austria was one of annexation, the campaign in Danzig would be one of liberation. The people of Poland, as well as all of Europe, became suddenly terrified at the launching of a new battle strategy. It was called the lightening war, or blitzkrieg.

They invaded with a supernatural, indomitable force. Poland was a helpless, limping, wounded beast surrounded by a pack of ravenous wolves that would maul her to death. They sped into Poland in waves of tanks, machine-gun mounted jeeps, and hundreds of infantry units. They showered buildings with gasoline and set them aflame. They blew up whole villages. Their tanks forded shallow waters where bridges had been destroyed by the fleeing Polish army. They advanced thirty miles a day in accordance with a prearranged schedule, and the most resistance they encountered was from the Polish cavalry attempting to engage them with swords while on horseback.

The German army had mastered every technique necessary for conquest. Every Polish defense unit was completely destroyed either through bombardment or incineration. Now, the world could no longer passively sit and watch.

Patton slammed the front page of *The New York Times* down on the desk of his older colonel friend.

"Look at this! Didn't I tell you? I knew I was right! I knew I was right! Are you now gonna sit on your fat carcass and wait for them to invade the rest of Europe? We've got to get in there. Look at these pictures," he said, pointing to the graphic illustrations.

The older colonel hung his head in apparent shame. "Yep," he said, "it's true, and I don't think we'll be able to avoid this one."

"Avoid it? We're the United States of America! Our allies need our leadership."

"Okay, but it's still not our war, and don't think that Roosevelt isn't looking for a way in that would be acceptable to the American public."

"Listen," interrupted Patton, "the British and French are now bound by treaty to declare war on Germany. I've fought in France. I've even trained their tank divisions. I should be able to go as an advisor, shouldn't I?"

"The war department isn't going to go for that, George, and I think you know it. We still need to wait, and I'm sure that's what they're saying in Washington. Too much American blood has been shed over there in the last twenty years, and Americans don't want to lose any more sons."

"You know what I'm gonna tell those bureaucrats who run the war department?"

"What?"

"Either lead, follow, or get the h----l out of my way!"

"George, you're going to Europe at this time would be a political mistake."

"Political?"

"Yes, political. We're still a nation run by politics, but the time will come. Our getting into this war is gonna have to be caused by something that directly affects American lives, something that would be seen as an intolerable offense. I just hope that it doesn't cost too much or take too long."

It had only taken a couple of weeks before all Polish resistance was crushed. Many simply fled the country. Then, the Nazi war machine continued to kill, steal, and destroy with remarkable speed. Within a year and a half, they launched so many successful invasions that the rest of the world had difficulty keeping up with them. In record-breaking time they invaded Czechoslovakia, they invaded Denmark, they invaded Norway, they invaded Luxembourg, they invaded Greece, they invaded the Channel Islands and Yugoslavia, they invaded Belgium, they invaded parts of Egypt, and they invaded France. All were brought under the submission of the Third Reich while the Longinus was secretly hidden in a church at Nuremburg, secured under Hitler's control.

23

HIRATA

Only the steady sounds of waves slapping the side of his wallowing commercial vessel could be heard as Hirata quietly drifted off the coast of Waikiki. He had turned off his engine because he knew that most schools of skipjack tuna were frightened by the sounds of motors and could detect their vibration from miles away.

Skipjack tuna was his primary catch, and the American fisheries on shore paid him well for them. Sometimes he brought to shore catches weighing almost 1000 pounds. Hirata didn't even like communicating by radio in these waters for fear that the tuna could hear his voice. However, during the last two weeks, a Japanese vessel had been contacting him every other day or so to inquire about fishing laws and international waters. It felt good for him to communicate with fishermen from his native country because they allowed him to reminisce about the times he went fishing with his father as a boy. He felt unfortunate however that he was never able to see this anonymous vessel or meet its owner. Whenever they communicated, there was no vessel in sight.

The sounds of a familiar voice came through the static of his short-wave radio.

"Captain Hirata, Captain Hirata, are you there? Over."

"Yes, this is Hirata, you must be Trap Net."

"Yes, this is Trap Net. How are you, my friend?"

"Still waiting for the big catch. Good thing the storm passed over last night. I'd like to get at least 500 pounds today."

"Good, luck! Tell me, were you able to find out the answer to my question the day before last?"

"Yes, if you want to fish within five miles off Hawaiian shores, you need to register your boat in Waikiki. Then, if you want to use any trap nets, you'll have to be at least within one-quarter mile from the shore or any reefs, and of course, stay away from Pearl Harbor if you don't want to be shot at by the US Navy."

"Thank you, but I was talking about the type of nets I could buy."

"Oh, yes, yes, I remember your question now. There are different types of nets available here. Most of us use the rope and twine, but there are more expensive types available. Rope and twine are the strongest though."

"Our dragnet got tangled this morning with some kind of underwater net about seven miles from the harbor. Do you know what that was?"

"Yes, be careful! I'm surprised the Navy didn't stop you. That's the underwater barrier for submarines. It's a protective net to keep any foreign submarines from getting into the harbor."

"Hmm, this seems like the kind of net we're looking for. Do you know anything about how much pressure it can take?"

"I can't tell you anything about this type of net. I'm sure the US government controls that."

"I see. Well, we'll probably have to get the ones on the market sometime. We can probably get the ones we need in Tokyo. How long will you be out today?"

"Oh, until the usual time, I don't mind waiting around for the night feeders, but I'll probably head back around seven. I've got some books to read. How about you?"

"We're going to cruise around for a while—probably won't start working until next week anyway."

"Just don't go after any skipjack tuna—those are my babies!"

"Ha ha. Okay, maybe we'll try the black marlins. They're very popular now in Tokyo."

"Listen Trap Net, I'm going to sign off now. Time to lower the nets. Let's see if we can talk the day after tomorrow, all right?"

"Okay, Captain. Good luck hunting."

Though Hirata was an experienced commercial fisherman by trade, he didn't realize that he himself had been bated, hooked, and trapped as an informant for the Japanese Imperial Navy. During this time, secret task forces within their navy were dispatched to study the US Pacific Fleet at Pearl Harbor, and Hirata had been in communication for two weeks with a Japanese mother submarine, disguised as a commercial fishing vessel. Their main focus was battleship row where dozens of US destroyers and battleships were docked. Their objective was to ascertain how close a midget submarine could come to the harbor without being detected. Hirata, unwittingly, provided them with vital information.

The Japanese Navy had completed its designs for an underwater barrier net cutter. It was a sharp-edged figure-eight slicing apparatus they attached to the front of their midget submarines to break through Pearl Harbor's net barriers.

Periodically, Hirata raised his nets but found very few skipjack tuna—not enough to be worth the labor of hauling them ashore. He thus lowered his nets again and waited. He heard squadrons of American fighter planes in the distance on practice runs near Pearl Harbor and began to think about the future of his children growing up in US territory.

There was such a military presence there that he began to wonder whether or not it would be better for them to be raised back in Japan. Yet, he knew Japan was becoming more aggressive in Asia. His sons would most definitely have to serve in the Japanese Army when they came of age, and this could even mean that they might be called upon to offer their lives in suicide missions. He returned to reading his book.

"Honey, honey, it's me," the soft voice of his wife came through the shortwave. "Captain Hirata," she continued playfully, "do you read me? Over. I repeat, do you read me?"

"Okay, sweetheart, what would you like me to buy before coming home?" he said.

"I wasn't calling for that, but since you've asked, we could use more leeks."

"Okay, but why are you calling?"

"Another storm is supposed to come through tonight. I just wanted to let you know in case you wanted to start coming back."

"The wind has been picking up," he thought out loud. "It might be a good time to head back."

"Have you caught anything?"

"No, I've just been reading a little. Oh, that Japanese fisherman contacted me again."

"The one who wants to know about fishing laws around here?"

"Yes, that's him. But I'm beginning to feel a little funny about him."

"Why? He's probably just trying to be sure how to stay out of trouble with American companies."

"Maybe, but every time we talk I can never spot his ship, and his frequency is strong. It seems that he should be close enough to be able to spot."

"Maybe next time, you can ask him his location on the compass and try to meet."

"That's a thought. Anyway, I'll be coming in soon. I'll pick up more leeks at the market, but can you have a drink ready for me when I get home?"

"I most certainly will," she said dutifully. "See you soon! Over and out."

Mrs. Hirata prepared a half glass of Japanese port wine for her husband. She knew that he would be in a reflective mood when he returned, and port wine was his drink of choice during times of reflection. It had a fruit base, rather than being distilled from rice or grain, and Hirata appreciated that because he didn't believe that a daily food staple should be used to produce alcoholic drinks. To Hirata, rice and grain were for eating only.

She put his wine glass atop a wooden serving table, which also functioned as a food tray, and placed them in his favorite sitting room, the wine casting a purple shadow against the wall as the sun hit it. Though the house had been built in a western, single-story ranch style, the Hiratas dedicated one room to remain purely Japanese, completely fashioned in traditional Japanese décor. On a plane wooden floor it had two sitting mats, soft-lit paper-shaded lamps, which hung from the ceiling, and large sliding doors. Inside, they kept a small Bonsai tree in a corner and a Shoji screen for dressing into robes. It was a room reserved for prayer, meditation, and drinking. Hence, the children rarely set foot there.

With a brown paper sack filled with freshly cut leeks in hand, Hirata opened his front door. Mrs. Hirata met him there but said nothing. She simply smiled, placed her hand gently upon his shoulder, and dipped her head in a bow. She then took the leeks and stepped toward the kitchen. Even when the children were present, there was a code of behavior in the Hirata household, which demanded silence and peace, especially when he came home. Hirata took off his jacket, removed his shoes, and washed his hands in the bathroom before walking into the Japanese room. He smiled when he saw the glass of wine waiting for him and took a sip. He could now relax. It became his custom to both relax on Saturday evenings and sleep in late Sunday mornings. But he sipped again and wondered: *"Why would Japanese fishermen have such difficulty in finding the right nets?"* He remembered as a boy buying nets with his father at the local town market. There were all kinds of nets and bamboo poles for fishing. Every fisherman knew where to get a net. As he remained in thought about the anonymous fisherman, he heard a slight tapping at the door, which sounded like his daughter's knock, so he tightened his robe and went to the sliding doors. When he opened them, he was overwhelmed with the aroma of Miso soup.

"Sorry to bother you, father, but mother wanted to know if you'd prefer to have your soup in here or with us."

"You know, I think we should all have our soup in here tonight," he said.

"Here, in the Japanese room?"

"Yes, here. Let's make it a special night. Tell your mother to bring the pot in and let your brothers know they need to help arrange the mats. You can bring in five bowls."

"Okay, father."

Hirata returned to his tray, finished his glass of wine, and put the glass away. The family had never before sat in the Japanese room to eat together. It had always been for his private silent meditations, but Hirata sensed that the family, on this night, should be together. His two sons entered, still holding school notebooks, as they had been busy with homework from the language school.

"Father?" asked his older son Hiroshi, "Noriko said you wanted us all to eat in here."

"Yes, I do. You and your brother get the extra mats and arrange them around the table. Your mother is bringing in the soup."

"But I don't understand. We're not supposed to come in here."

"Son, I've decided that you can, tonight. Now you two need to start getting things in order."

The two boys looked at each other as if something were wrong. Then, Mrs. Hirata appeared from behind, followed by Noriko holding a stack of five bowls. They squeezed between the two boys.

"I know you two heard your father," she said, "Oh, I forget the table, Hiroshi, go get the low table quickly and place it next to your father."

Hiroshi went quickly to fetch the serving table while his brother Jiro placed five mats in a circle on the floor next to Hirata. When Hiroshi returned, he quickly placed the low serving table next to his father. Mrs. Hirata and Noriko then placed the bowls and adjusted the mats.

"Father," asked Jiro, "why is it a special night tonight? Are you sick?"

"There's nothing really special, son. I simply wanted us all to be here. Now, everyone please sit on a mat," said Hirata in a gentle smile. "Let's bless the food before it gets cold."

He then proceeded in reciting the Shinto prayer *"Itadakimasu."* It was a prayer respecting the divine nature of eating for the sustenance of life. All the family was quiet until the closure of the prayer. When he finished, he sat down among them.

The Hirata family was changed that night. Eating together in the dimly lit Japanese room induced a type of sacred bond between them. Somehow Hirata understood that times were changing, and he felt inspired to appreciate his family more.

However, it would be the first and last time for years to come that they would be able to peacefully sit and eat together in the Japanese room.

24

PEARL HARBOR

Sunday mornings were times for the Hirata brothers to explore. There were no school classes to attend, and they usually tried to complete their homework on Saturday nights to have free time in the mornings. Mrs. Hirata usually accommodated early morning explorations by preparing a late brunch before noon. This usually gave them three hours or so to walk to the beach or jump through a waterfall without missing a morning meal when they returned. On this day the boys decided to visit a pineapple field because one of their friends at the language school helped his uncle on there on Sunday mornings. By seven o'clock, they were on their feet and out of the house.

"Why don't we go to the North Shore?" asked Jiro, "It's too hot to stay around sticky pineapples in this heat."

"We told him we would be there. Besides, he said his uncle would give us a couple of pineapples if we got there before twelve o'clock."

"We've had pineapple before. That's not so unusual."

"I know, but I wanted to bring some home to surprise mom, then she could make us pineapple dessert."

Hiroshi decided to appease his younger brother and took him through a long route to the pineapple field. They played by shuffling their feet and kicking up the red powdered earth all the way to the shoreline where a few morning surfers were preparing their boards. The water was postcard blue and the ocean was calm. But then they heard a faint humming sound that sounded like bumble bees. It grew louder and louder and began to echo off the mountain range.

"Look at all those planes!" exclaimed Jiro, looking skyward.

"Looks like another naval war maneuver," said Hiroshi. The sky was dotted with small planes. They looked like a

huge swarm of fruit flies buzzing around a fruit bowl, and they began to stretch out as far as the eye could see. The treachery of an empire was on the wing.

"But they usually don't practice until noon," said Jiro. There was an explosion near the naval harbor. Then another, and then another. People near the beach thought it was a war maneuver employing live ammunition, but a Japanese air squadron was bombing Pearl Harbor in a ruthless surprise attack. The planes came screaming down, one after another, strafing every US vessel in the harbor.

Seamen were dumbfounded. A siren was sounded and a speaker shouted over a public amplifier: "Man your battle stations. Man your battle stations. This is not a drill. I repeat, this is not a drill."

Some stood there in shock, motionless, but many others desperately scrambled to get to their stations for defensive tactics. They tripped over each other. They jumped from exploding ships into an oil-filled harbor where the water was now on fire. They tried to drag buddies out of the line of fire, but the Japanese warplanes were everywhere at once. There were 181 torpedo bombers and fighters crisscrossing the skies, black with the thick smoke of burning oil, arcing and careening up and down in a frenzied free-for-all. Though they fired random, opportunistic shots to kill any seaman or destroy whatever vessel they could, eight battleships were their primary targets. The USS West Virginia was torpedoed and sank quickly. The USS Oklahoma turned over like a turtle and sank. The USS Arizona was mortally wounded in her ammunition compartment, creating an explosion killing over one thousand crewmen at once—the greatest loss of life on any ship that day. There were screams of pain and there were screams of rage as the men frantically fought for their lives and the lives of their buddies.

"Oh my God!" yelled Hiroshi. "That's real. Look at those flames!"

Just then, a misguided artillery shell came screaming at them as they stood watching at the water's edge. It hit near the shoreline, sending two bodies of civilians flying into the air.

"Let's go. We've got to get home. A war is coming," Hiroshi said.

Women screamed and men scrambled to their cars as Hiroshi and Jiro ran as fast as they could, retracing their steps.

They clamored through brush and fields on the way home. It wasn't long before Jiro looked up and noticed a large squadron of low-flying aircraft approaching. A second wave of about 170 warplanes was headed toward the harbor, apparently to finish the job that the first wave had begun. One aircraft flew so low that Jiro could see the pilot waving at him. Then, to his shock, he spotted the Japanese symbol of the rising sun on the fuselage; he was horrified to know that the attackers were Japanese, like him.

"Does this mean that Japan will own the island now?" asked Jiro, looking at his brother.

"I don't know. I don't' think so. But this definitely means there will be a war."

"What about us? What will happen to us?"

"I don't know. C'mon, let's hurry home."

The boys continued in their scramble to get home. They could distantly hear more cannon fire and explosions starting up again near the harbor. By the time they reached their neighborhood, people were standing on their front lawns looking toward the skies. Still under the impression that highly elaborate war maneuvers were taking place, Japanese and Hawaiian residents alike were not alarmed, but found the proceedings entertaining.

The entertainment came to an abrupt end when an army vehicle sped around the corner with two officers inside. It was an open-top government sedan, which was commonplace near the military bases. The soldier on the passenger seat fired his M-16 rifle into the air.

"Get in your homes! Get in your homes, now!" he said, as he continued firing warning shots. Their auto sped up and down the neighborhood streets.

Mr. and Mrs. Hirata heard the warning shots but did not hear the warning to stay inside.

They were still outside looking for their two boys when they appeared from across the street. They immediately knew something was wrong by their expressions.

"A war is starting, father, and it's starting at the harbor," said Hiroshi.

"What do you mean, a war is starting? They have these exercises at least twice a month around here. You know that!"

"No, this isn't a practice. There was fire and explosions, and I saw a Japanese pilot flying overhead," said Jiro. "That's why they're telling everyone to stay indoors."

Mr. and Mrs. Hirata looked at each other with alarm. If this were true, they knew that the life they once had in Hawaii would now be over. They all hurried inside, and Hirata locked the door behind them.

At Pearl Harbor, when the attack ended and the smoke cleared, twenty-one US Pacific Fleet ships were either sunk or damaged, the local hospitals were filled beyond capacity, and two thousand four hundred and three Americans were dead—this toll included sixty-eight civilians.

By late afternoon the island was shut down. There was dead silence everywhere. Teams of active duty servicemen toiled around the clock to rescue dying seamen still trapped in submerged vessels, and army units patrolled neighborhoods ready to shoot any Japanese citizen who appeared to be suspicious of subversive activities.

Before late evening, Hawaii was declared a war zone. The governor signed an order of martial law. Roving military trucks used megaphones to announce that all of Hawaii was under martial law, and that strict curfew hours were being imposed.

All of the members of the Hirata family were gathered around the short-wave radio to hear what was being announced in Japan. The Japanese news stations were discussing an end to diplomatic relations with the US when there was a banging on the front door.

Hirata cautiously cracked the door open and asked who it was, but then the door was violently kicked in by two angry US army officers, and Hirata was pushed back two feet.

"Are you Tamiki Hirata?" one asked

"Yes, I am," said Hirata, in a startled, but calm voice. "You are placed under arrest."

"An arrest? I'm sorry, you must be mistaken. What would be the charge?"

"Come with us, Mr. Hirata. You'll have all of that explained to you."

"No, officer, I can demand to know what charges have been...."

"Mr. Hirata, we are under martial law now. We don't have to explain anything to you, so you'd better get moving."

The second officer had drawn his pistol, and Hirata sensed that he would have no misgivings about using it. But then he noticed a familiar person waiting behind the officers near their parked vehicle in the street. It was his neighbor, Kale, who was watching intently from a distance. Hirata was relieved after seeing his neighbor and thus complied with the military officers. He walked with them to the automobile.

"Is this the man?" one officer asked Kale.

"Yes, it is," said Kale, very grim faced.

Stunned, Hirata was confused. He felt that there was some type of trial taking place and still had no idea as to why he was implicated.

"Please, please, would someone explain to me what is happening?" he begged.

Kale stared at him for a few moments and said, "They found the transcripts. How could you have done this? What pains me most is what I'm going to have to tell my daughter about Noriko's father."

"What are you talking about? What transcripts? You're making a mistake."

"There's no use denying it, Mr. Hirata," said one agent. "The short-wave codes on the transcript identify your fishing vessel. We've got the sub, and we've got Sakamaki in custody now."

Hirata's mind raced back to his last fishing trip the day before the attack. Immediately he knew that they must have been talking about his communication with the Japanese fishing vessel.

"Wait a minute. If you're talking about my communication with that Japanese fisherman...."

"There was no Japanese fisherman, Mr. Hirata. We have a record of you communicating directly with a Japanese mother submarine, which transported mini subs throughout the harbor. And Sakamaki is being interrogated now."

"Okay, okay, now I understand, but let me explain. I didn't know that I was talking with a Japanese sub, and I've never heard of Mr. Sakamaki. Someone was asking me about fishing laws near the harbor, that's all."

"We have it recorded that you discussed underwater nets, Mr. Hirata. The Japanese were able to cut through territorial nets around the harbor and use subs in their attack based upon your information. Now I'm going to ask you directly: Are you a spy for the Japanese Imperial Navy?"

He began to have tunnel vision. Everything around him appeared to shrink, and he felt very far away. How could all of this be true? He looked at Kale, still incredulous to what was taking place.

"It's true," said Kale. "One of those subs washed ashore, and they captured the operator along with information about your conversations in his coded messages."

Hirata thus became linked to the first captured prisoner of war, Kazuo Sakamaki. He was a naval officer who had volunteered to attack Pearl Harbor in a midget submarine. His mini sub was believed to have sunk the USS West Virginia. His mini sub later became disabled and was trapped on a beach in Oahu. He was found by a Hawaiian soldier and taken into military custody.

"Of course, I'm not a spy. Mr. Himala, you know I've lived here for years as a contracted fisherman! I'm innocent, and you have no grounds to...."

Kale approached the two army officers and spoke in a low tone.

"Listen, let me have a word with him for a minute, all right?" Though one officer kept his sidearm drawn with the safety latch unlocked, they both nodded, granting permission for them to speak confidentially. Kale walked with Mr. Hirata a few feet. "Okay, Mr. Hirata, listen to me. It's very important that you cooperate now, because things can take a very serious turn for you and your family. I have been working with the FBI for the last couple of years, and you were put on watch for some time, but they threw out your file because they didn't have anything on you. Now, I believe you. I believe your story, but army intelligence may not be convinced."

"So what am I supposed to do now? Are they going to execute me without a trial?"

"No, Mr. Hirata, they won't execute you, but if we're not careful, they will confiscate all of your property and send you and your family to a detention center in northern California. That's probably the worst that can happen right now."

"Take all our property? What would happen to our children?"

"I couldn't answer that right now, but I'm going to try to avoid that happening. No Japanese family on these islands will be treated like that, if I can help it."

"So, what am I supposed to do?"

"Just cooperate, Mr. Hirata. The Americans are enraged now. They've lost brothers and sons, and the hospitals will probably be filled with dying men for weeks. Already a couple of Japanese Americans were caught helping a Japanese pilot who crash-landed after the attack. He was finally killed by some Hawaiians, but rumors about the local Japanese are beginning to spread. The Yanks may start to take their anger out on you people if we're not careful."

"Okay, I'll cooperate. I tell them everything I know, everything I did, and answer any questions they want."

"Fine. That might save you, Hirata. Now, we're going to get in the car and drive to the army base where they'll be questioning, but don't worry, I'm staying with you. With luck, they'll be finished with you in a few hours, and you can come home."

Kale put his arm around Hirata and gently walked him to the car. He waved and smiled at his family, who were all watching with tears in their eyes from the front door. Kale's smile offered some reassurance that things would be all right. The four men entered the vehicle and sped away.

At the time of the attack, there were 157,000 Japanese citizens and residents in Hawaii, who represented a majority of the island's labor force. On the West Coast of the US, 110,000 would be rounded up and sent to relocation camps in northern California, but fewer than 2,000 of these would be shipped in from Hawaii. Those dwelling on the island became an asset to helping the US prepare for threats of an invasion, and there would be no plans to establish any such camps there.

The following day the Hirata family gathered together again around the radio. The children were worried about their father, who hadn't returned home yet, so they listened intently to the American broadcasts. Within minutes, there was a sudden interruption in the local news as the network announced a presidential address. The president began:

"YESTERDAY, DECEMBER SEVENTH, NINETEEN-FORTY-ONE, A DATE WHICH WILL LIVE IN INFAMY– THE UNITED STATES OF AMERICA WAS SUDDENLY AND DELIBERATELY ATTACKED BY NAVAL AND AIR FORCES OF THE EMPIRE OF JAPAN…"

Hiroshi and Jiro looked at each other and felt awkward. Oddly, though they were still horrified by what they had witnessed, they now felt a slight sense of privilege to have been at the scene of a historic event that even the president was taking time to address. They continued to listen.

"...THE ATTACK YESTERDAY ON THE HAWAIIAN ISLANDS HAS CAUSED SEVERE DAMAGE TO AMERICAN NAVAL AND MILITARY FORCES. VERY MANY AMERICAN LIVES HAVE BEEN LOST. IN ADDITION, AMERICAN SHIPS HAVE BEEN REPORTED TORPEDOED ON THE HIGH SEAS BETWEEN SAN FRANCISCO AND HONOLULU..."

At this moment of the broadcast, the front door slowly opened and Mr. Hirata stepped inside. He was exhausted, having been interrogated under intense pressure for several hours non-stop. He quietly sat behind his family and listened to the broadcast.

"...NO MATTER HOW LONG IT MAY TAKE US TO OVERCOME THIS PREMEDITATED INVASION, THE AMERICAN PEOPLE IN THEIR RIGHTEOUS MIGHT WILL WIN THROUGH TO ABSOLUTE VICTORY. HOSTILITIES EXIST. THERE IS NO BLINKING AT THE FACT THAT OUR PEOPLE, OUR TERRITORY, AND OUR INTERESTS ARE IN GRAVE DANGER. WITH CONFIDENCE IN OUR ARMED FORCES—WITH THE UNBOUNDING DETERMINATION OF OUR PEOPLE—WE WILL GAIN THE INEVITABLE TRIUMPH—SO HELP US GOD...."

"Father!" shouted Noriko, noticing Hirata on the other side of the room. She and her brothers ran to hug him tightly as Mrs. Hirata began to cry. "We thought you would have come back yesterday?"

Though fatigued, a reassuring smile of hope formed on Hirata's face. "Things are going to be a little different here for us, but at least I'm sure that we'll be able to stay here together," he said.

"What happened?" asked Mrs. Hirata. "Were they going to take you away?"

"Never mind," he continued. "No one will be taken away now. Why don't we all go to the Japanese room? Sweetheart, would you and Noriko prepare some tea?"

Then he and Mrs. Hirata entered arm in arm, with the children following behind.

25

PLANS OF ACTION

The war department in Washington, DC was known to have round tables in the conference rooms to make every seated official feel as an equal during corporate meetings; no one could ever sit at the head of any table. However, despite this prearrangement, every officer knew who was in charge at this particular meeting.

Twelve men, smartly adorned in official uniforms, encircled the outer edge of that table, appearing as a multi-colored brick wall of white, green, and gray as they sat nearly shoulder to shoulder. Their eyes would remain fixed on one man, Dwight Eisenhower. He had been appointed the new Assistant Chief of Staff in the operations division for war plans. His eyes were as piercing as an eagle's, and when he spoke, he drilled his very mind into the minds of his listeners. Always measuring his words, when he spoke his hands often reinforced his passion by balling into fists or openly pointing at his listener. Now he was introducing an overview for the first amphibious assault to destroy the Nazi war machine—the place would be North Africa.

"Gentlemen," he said, standing behind a huge map of the western hemisphere, "I know I don't have to describe to you the rate at which the Nazi army has advanced from Europe into North Africa. Intelligence has told us that Hitler knows he's running short on natural resources, so he's looking at Russia and North Africa for oil and phosphates."

"Isn't he seeking world domination?" asked one general. "Yes he is. This character's a megalomaniac who's out to dominate anything and everything he can, but he's also a pragmatist and knows what it's going to take to reach his objectives."

"I don't think he's gonna get too far in Russia, but North Africa could be a different story," said a naval commander.

"You're reading my mind, admiral. Gentlemen, take a look at this map. Morocco is the western-most country in North Africa. In fact, it may surprise you to know that Morocco was the first country to recognize the United States during Washington's administration."

There was grumbling among the officers before Patton spoke up. "They had to recognize us before protecting our ships from pirates at that time."

"Very good, George," said Eisenhower. "Now, the best front to meet our enemy, gentlemen, is right here," he said, pointing to Casablanca, Morocco. "When we get a beachhead here, we'll be able to eventually confront Rommel's desert army in Tunisia, drive them out, and hopscotch from North Africa, up the boot of Italy and into France. The Nazis have already infiltrated Egypt, and we believe Marshal Rommel is building up multiple Panzer divisions in Tunisia right now."

"What about the Vichy French?" asked another officer. "How much of Morocco do they control at the moment?"

"Excellent question. The Vichy French at the moment are concentrated in the western part of the country. We can only assume they have complete control there. And, of course, they've allied themselves with the Nazis to the point of being able to rely on the Luftwaffe for air support all along the coast."

"But will they attack us after what we did for them in the last war? And what about the local people? Do they have their support?"

"That depends on whether you're talking about the French or the Moroccans. Remember, Morocco may be under the French, but the local people have little loyalty to them. And they're quite a mixed group—you have the Arabs, the Jews, and the Berber people among a few others—and there's a great deal of backbiting among all of them. I believe that the Berbers are the originals there. Referring to your first question, we don't know whether or not the French will attack us. We'll simply have to prepare for the worst-case scenario."

"Could there possibly be a way of allying with the Moroccan people for covert operations against the French?" asked an army captain.

"We've looked into that, but it's almost impossible to find someone who clearly speaks their language. The Arabic they use is not the original Arabic, and the Berber people speak an unwritten language all their own. But intelligence task forces are working on that. Needless to say, I can't stress enough how critical it is for us to be able to take Casablanca. This is the only place where we'll be able to build momentum and drive Rommel out of Africa before jumping over into Italy. This plan will light a pathway from Africa, into Europe, and ultimately into Berlin. We've called it 'Operation Torch' for those reasons, and we're assigning General Patton the task of orchestrating command."

Patton nodded and offered a faint smile in acknowledgement. Based upon his recent private discussions with Eisenhower, the assignment truly came as no surprise. He suppressed all feelings of wanting to complain over why it took so long to enter the war and made direct eye contact with the Atlantic naval fleet commander seated across from him. For Operation Torch to be a success, he knew the navy would be indispensable to get his troops to land.

Parachuting into Morocco would be too hazardous.

"Gentlemen," Eisenhower continued, "over the next two days, we will need to draft a preliminary strategic master plan for war in the Pacific, Europe, and North Africa. Both your insight and cooperation will be expected. We've ordered a catered lunch this afternoon, so make yourselves comfortable, because no one will leave the compound until we have finished today's phase of planning."

Roast beef, mashed potatoes, and peas were served—a privileged meal during wartime rationing—but no one ate. For hours, the leading officers of each military branch toiled as a team to hammer out an initial phase of war plans covering every aspect from the types of water crafts necessary for amphibious assaults to the types of food necessary for sustenance on different terrains. There were minor conflicts of ego and some grumbling, but after two days, the entire war, for every theater, had been masterfully organized.

Patton was satisfied with his orders and the plan before him. It would allow him an opportunity to distinguish himself among his peers and allies. This, in his mind, was the ultimate goal, secondary only to winning the war and taking possession of the spear in Germany. He would need 34,000 troops to embark on the shores of Morocco at three locations: Safi, 140 miles south of Casablanca; Fedala, six miles north of Casablanca; and Port Lyautey, 60 miles north of Casablanca. Once landed, all of the ground troops were to converge on Casablanca in a unified assault after fighting off French ground forces.

26

OPERATION TORCH

Infantrymen climbed down wavering cargo nets into landing crafts off the coast of Fedala. The sea was purple, and it was a full moon—time to invade. They were ordered not to fire first in hopes that the Vichy French would welcome them.

Patton firmly ordered a small group of soldiers to enter their Higgins gunboats and motor toward the shoreline first. Each soldier was equipped with an automatic submachine gun, grenades, and ammunition belts that crisscrossed from their shoulders to their waistlines; this way they could keep their ammo dry if they had to wade to shore in waist-deep water.

Patton remained on the cruiser USS Augusta, carrying his trademarked ivory plated 45 magnum pistols and binoculars.

Hundreds of yards ahead, rapid popping sounds were heard and fire-like sparks flew toward the landing crafts. They were tracer rounds. The French were considering the Americans an enemy and had initiated an attack. Then from a port in Casablanca, six miles south, shells from a French battleship begin to fly overhead in a remote attack. The ground forces in Fedala were caught in a storm of incoming projectiles, so the American battleship USS Massachusetts returned fire against the French vessels. They exchanged fire for fifteen minutes before the

French warship was completely destroyed while still in the harbor. US battleships eliminated pesky French enemy aircraft with anti-aircraft cannons. Enemy fire thereby subsided. A Fedala beachhead was secured, though it had cost the lives of dozens of infantrymen.

The Miramar hotel, located a mile in from the shoreline, had always been an exotic resort for French and German tourists. It was noted for its live entertainment of belly dancers, huge trays of traditional couscous dinners, and spicy roasted lamb dishes. There were ten occupants present that evening. However, at the first sound of discernible gunfire, they immediately fled in their vehicles toward Casablanca for shelter. The only person left was the French concierge and his family, who all hid in the wine cellar.

Near the hotel, the darkness was pitch black, but a US army flashlight signaled a squad of seven infantrymen to surround it, with machine guns pointed at the doors and windows. A French-speaking officer took a megaphone and, in a southern American accent, began addressing any possible occupants inside.

"Attention, attention, nous sommes des soldats Americains. Nous avons encerclé cet hotel et maintenant il faut sortir avec vos mains sur vos têtes. Si vous ne sortez pas, nous allons faire. irruption avec nos armes."

"Attention, attention, we are American soldiers. We have surrounded this hotel, and now you must come out with your hands on your head. If you don't come out, we are going to break in with our weapons."

They waited. There was no response, so the squad leader took aim and fired five rounds of his machine gun at the front door, sending orange sparks flying and destroying the lock.

He then kicked the door in while crouching low. Three more soldiers immediately followed him, all pointing their machine guns in opposite directions. There was not a sound. A fourth and fifth soldier entered and found the light switch. They turned it on and found the lobby empty. The prior occupants had apparently left in a rush, spilling their dinner, leaving burning cigarettes, and stealing from the cash register as they fled.

The final two soldiers entered with Patton just behind them.

They all froze to detect any sounds of people in hiding.

"You two, start checking the rooms upstairs," Patton said to the soldiers in front of him. "You, sergeant, go see if that wall phone is still working."

The wooden floor creaked as the sergeant stepped toward the bar to examine the wall phone. A functional landline telephone would come in handy once the three beachheads were established. He began to lift the receiver, but then they all heard a sound. A bottle had fallen and bounced. It was now rolling on a cement floor just beneath them. Then, the rolling abruptly stopped.

"Someone's in the cellar!" the French-speaking officer said.

He began addressing them:

"Nous savons que vous etes au sou sol. Si vous ne sortez pas, nous allons tirez par cette planche."

"We know you're in the cellar. If you don't come out, we are going to start shooting through the floor!"

"Ne tirez pas, ne tirez pas,"

"Don't shoot, don't shoot," a muffled meek voice sounded through the floor. Then soldiers could hear footsteps headed toward the main wall. A trap door in the wooden floor began to slowly pop up, and a young boy gingerly ascended with his hands in the air.

"Are you the Americans?" the boy asked.

"Do you speak English?" answered the officer, pointing his machine gun at the boy.

"Yes, I can speak English, but we thought you were Germans."

"Why are you afraid of the Germans when you are fighting on their side now?" the sergeant asked.

"Not everyone is on their side. Some of us are resisting and…."

"Is there anyone else with you in that cellar, boy?" interrupted Patton.

"Yes, my mother and father are with me. We all work in the hotel."

"Tell them all to come out with their hands up. And sergeant," he said to the translator, "don't lower your gun yet, this still could be a trap."

The boy disappeared through the trap door for a moment. There were muffled adult voices, and then he reappeared. He stepped out, still raising his hands, and held the trap door open for his father and mother to climb out. They all appeared to be rather embarrassed when the father spoke.

"Thank God you have finally come to Morocco. We were hoping that you or the British would come before it was too late."

"Why are you still here?" said Patton. "This is now a war zone. You should have left with everyone else."

"Yes, but this is our home. I'm the concierge, and we feel safer here than in Casa. We heard the ships firing from the port."

"Tomorrow we'll have to arrange for your evacuation. It's going to get dangerous around here, and frankly, I still might add that I don't trust you."

"Yes, I understand, but I think my son was trying to explain to you that not all French people here support the Vichy government. We don't want the Nazis here."

"That may be so, but at the moment, while the French army is still in battle with my men all around this coastal area, you are still an enemy." Patton turned to the American translator and grumbled, "It's a pity, too, because we need to have a local translator with us to work with you."

"Oh, but sir, I could work with you and your translation team," said the father.

"I want a native Moroccan translator who could speak Arabic and French," replied Patton.

"Oh, sir, take my advice. Don't look for a Moroccan translator. You can't trust them. They are pickpockets. They cannot be trusted."

"Well, I have never known the Moroccans to turn against their own people and collaborate with the Nazis, like the French have!"

There was silence. The rebuke brought shame on the family, and they all hung their heads low. The mother then humbly spoke up.

"Sir, it might be difficult to find a local Moroccan who'd be willing to cooperate with you. But the problem is not that they're untrustworthy. It's just that many don't trust foreigners after what we French have done by taking over their country. But I know a woman in Casablanca. She is a French Moroccan and speaks both languages well. She spent some time in France not long ago, but now she's working with children in a small school. I think she would be able to help you as a translator. She once worked with American soldiers in France during the last war."

"All right, tomorrow when you all leave, you can do a service to the US Army by contacting her and telling her to report to me. My staff will give you details on how she can get in touch with me."

The beach at Safi was different from Fedala; the water was deeper near the shoreline. The mission of this landing was to deliver light tanks and armored vehicles.

Once the tanks were placed on shore they would be ordered to dash quickly to Fedala so that Patton could use them in an attack on Casablanca.

At the third point of embarkation, Port Lyautey, landings continued relatively undisturbed until US tanks became engaged by light French tanks. Though Patton had instructed his field commanders to always remain the aggressors in combat, they were now at risk of being outnumbered. Their M5 Stuart light tanks volleyed with the French tanks in a stalemate until a roving US naval reconnaissance aircraft miraculously spotted the battle. The pilot radioed warships off the cost to calculate their cannons and deliver shells against the French tanks. This drove them off and secured the port for multiple US landings. The battle for control of the port however wasn't over. Two hundred and fifty French soldiers remained hunkered down in the nearby Kasbah, an ancient Portuguese fortress with thick cement walls overlooking a hill. Cannon and machine gun fire streamed continuously from the Kasbah for a full day. A special US unit dug in and waited in foxholes near the fortress, reenergizing themselves by eating K rations. They talked about scaling the walls of the fort, but had no scaling equipment, so they decided to rush the fortress in an all-out frontal attack. Two men ran swiftly to place detonation devices against the huge doors, but were cut down by machine guns. The commanding officer then radioed the port to have a howitzer 105-millimeter artillery vehicle driven to their location. The howitzer arrived and fired point-blank at the gate, but the projectile simply bounced off the structure. The ancient fortress was as strong as any modern barrier. Finally, the commander radioed in dive-bombers off a nearby battleship, and the pilots bombed the French stronghold into submission. The survivors came out, amid the dust and smoke, with their hands in the air. They surrendered, but the fortress was severely damaged. The three beachheads would now be secured to unite in a reinforced attack against Casablanca. Operation Torch was an unquenchable flame.

As Patton's Operation Torch was burning brightly in North Africa, Hitler's Operation Barbarossa in Russia was beginning to show signs of fizzling. The Nazi war machine had advanced east, leaving a trail of blood and plunder all the way to the Russian border. Hitler thus masterminded a plan for the largest invasion in the history of warfare, dedicated to conquering the Soviets.

In addition to foot soldiers, the operation required six hundred thousand motor vehicles and up to seven hundred and fifty thousand horses. Surprisingly, though they had made inroads into Russia, they failed to learn from the lessons of Napoleon, who had attempted to invade using the same route. There is no army so great as to be able to fight against a Russian winter. The formidable Nazi war machine got stalled in the snow, and many men began to die of exposure. Hitler was able to advance as far as the city of Smolensk, where he established a headquarters outpost on the Eastern Front.

Once the outpost was established, however, he returned to Berlin, leaving high-ranking officers the responsibility of maintaining his office, where they faced harsh wintry temperatures daily. They felt abandoned as frostbite and trench foot became rampant. With the passage of time, and a daily increase in the death toll, victory began to seem unattainable. Disillusioned and disgruntled officers of the SS formed a plot to assassinate Hitler.

Hitler's field marshal at Smolensk requested that he visit the outpost on a pretext to trap and kill him.

"It's the only solution," said Field Marshal Guenther von Kluge. "It's the fastest, surest way to finish him off. You two officers can meet his plane at the airfield and assume the role of his armed guards to escort him back here. Once his car starts, fire at point-blank range. They'll be caught off guard and won't have a chance."

"But what if it fails?" asked Captain von Boeslager. "Do we have a backup plan if it fails? We've all heard about his mystical powers of escaping death. You remember those stories about the last war?"

"Rumors of rubbish. I don't listen to those fabricated stories. Our plan can't fail; it's too simple to fail," responded von Kluge. "But, in the unlikely event that it should, we'd better be ready to think fast on our feet for a backup plan or face execution with dignity."

"Well, when does he get here? We've been talking about this for two weeks now. Is he going to just show up unannounced?"

"He's coming in two days. He was delayed because the British are beginning to bomb at night. That's all I've been told.

Just be ready when he gets here."

Field Marshal Guenther von Kluge, Colonel Henning von Tresckow, Lieutenant Fabian von Schlabrendroff, Colonel Rudolf von Gersdorff, and Captain George von Boeslager all committed themselves to maintaining this secret pact to assassinate Hitler, even if it meant their own deaths. If they could accomplished their objective, they would then be able to retreat back to Germany and call for all Nazi troops to withdraw from occupied territories. They were in agreement to pursue this as a plan of reconciliation with invaded countries before suffering their own annihilation from Allied forces, but it was not to be.

Hitler's plane was approaching the airfield on schedule. It was an unusually large aircraft, escorted by two fighter planes and another troop transport plane, and this immediately caught the attention of Captain von Boeslager. A troop carrier plane was only used to transport guards and infantrymen. It was unusual to see one as an escort. As the two large carriers landed while the fighter planes continued circling overhead, Captain von Boelsager and Colonel von Tresckow stood at attention near the edge of the airfield, periodically glancing at each other to confirm that all was going well.

The planes then came to a sputtering stop, but then came the unexpected. The side door of the troop transport plane lowered, and fifty SS guards began to descend the mobile ladder.

Everything appeared to have been well rehearsed as they all bounced out, forming two protective rows on the field through which Hitler would walk—these were his armed personal escorts. There would be no opportunity to assassinate him in a motorcade with such guards nearby. Their plans were foiled before their eyes, and Captain Boeslager bit his lip as Hitler approached him.

"Heil Hitler," said Boeslager, extending an outstretched arm in salute.

Hitler returned the salute but was silent.

"Sir, please allow us to accommodate you with a warm meal before going over our strategic drafts," said Boeslager.

Hitler turned to his armed guard next to him and nodded.

The guard then spoke up.

"That would be fine, captain. Please, lead the way to your dinning quarters."

The captain turned to his right to take a quick look at Colonel Tresckow. This was a signal for him to think on his feet. Tresckow had explained how he could be alerted for a backup plan with a simple glance—he would then know what to do.

Assuming that Hitler's fifty guards would not presume to be able to lunch with him, since it was a violation of protocol, Captain Boeslager led him and two of his accompanying officers into a field mess hall tent where they were to dine. Once seated, Tresckow would rise from the table with a pistol and shoot Hitler while he was eating.

Once assassinated, he and Boeslager could then shoot his accompanying guards. It was a simple plan that only the two of them had discussed. But it never took place.

One of Hitler's higher-ranking officers insisted that a meal be prepared for ten SS guards to dine among them. He gave no reason for this gesture, and the sight of so many SS guards in the tent aroused a fear of failure. Tresckow thus aborted the plan, and they all ate a hearty meal with Hitler seated at the head table.

"Our compliments to your field cook," said one of Hitler's guards from across the table. "We can't eat this well at camps back in Berlin."

"Thank you, sir, we try to do the best with what we have here," said Captain Boeslager.

"Well, it's very good. Now remind me," he said, changing the subject, "you need to go over new strategy plans for the Eastern Front, is that right?"

"Yes, after the Fuhrer has finished his meal, we can meet in the next tent where we have prepared maps to show the latest troop movements in Russia."

"Fine," responded the head guard, still sipping his tea. Hitler took a usual extended amount of time to finish the meal. As he was known to be a vegetarian, they expected that it would take him longer to become full, consuming the light side dishes. They waited patiently. When he finally brought his napkin to him mouth, dabbing at the patch of whiskers under his nose, they all knew they would be leaving soon.

The guards were called to stand at attention, and Captain Boeslager led Hitler and his entourage to the next field tent. It was a charade presentation of possible field maneuvers that could be undertaken in the spring, all conjured up as part of a backup plan in case the assassination attempts on the Fuhrer had failed. The presentation was designed to buy time, allowing them to put together another attempt on his life, which Colonel Tresckow had worked out with Lieutenant Fabian. It was meant to be the final attempt.

As the presenters of the spurious plan pretended to stress the importance of their long-winded strategy, Hitler pretended to listen with patience. He had very little interest in their ideas and had no intention of allowing them to initiate any strategies he had not previously authorized.

"This plan can only work if the weather is right, but spring is too far away to wait for an attack, yet I will consider this," he said. "Wait for my orders from Berlin, but take no further actions until told to do so."

"Yes, my Fuhrer. Thank you, my Fuhrer," said the colonel with feigned appreciation.

"Colonel," said Hitler's high-ranking guard, "I think this will conclude our brief visit. The Fuhrer has other engagements in Berlin now, so we should be leaving."

"Of course. Let us walk you to the airfield," offered the colonel as he noticed the sounds of plane engines reviving.

As they walked briskly, Lieutenant Fabian came running after them carrying a box. It was wrapped as a package. He finally caught up with them.

"Sir, please don't leave without allowing us to give you this gift. It is for Colonel Koch in Berlin—our compliments."

The box contained a trick bottle of Russian alcohol with a highly explosive bomb hidden inside. It would automatically detonate with a timed fuse, which was already beginning to burn slowly through an odorless acidic chemical process. The explosion was estimated to take place in fifteen minutes while Hitler would be in flight.

"I'll be sure that he gets it," said the colonel, taking the box. "Goodbye."

Hitler's entourage of officers and guards loaded up, strapped in, and took off. Captain Boeslager waved goodbye to the departing aircraft, still remaining straight-faced.

"Could this actually work?" he asked himself, *"What if the detonation fails? What if they accidentally drop it and everything becomes exposed?"* As such thoughts raced through his mind, they actually became prophetic. The timed fuse was unable to detonate the bomb because the high altitude at which the plane flew made it too cold for it to continue burning—the fuse stopped thirty seconds short of detonation. Upon Hitler's confirmed landing in Berlin, Captain Boeslager and Colonel Tresckow had to make a rushed effort to retrieve the gift before its delivery.

27

CAPTAIN HORN

It was the calm after the storm. There were no sounds of ship cannons or crashing waves from the Atlantic. There was not even a seagull in sight. Some bloated bodies of US soldiers were being prepared for ceremonial burials. Troops that survived were inspecting their machine guns to asses any damages from salt water, but only the distant sounds of US diesel engines could be heard coming from the beaches. The landing craft were now being inspected. Morning had broken.

Though General Patton had ordered his troops to awaken him after seven hours of sleep, he was able to rouse himself out of bed ahead of schedule. It felt surreal to wake up in a luxurious king size bed at the Miramar hotel only hours after shelling the Fedala shoreline into a field of craters. He counted this however as yet another example of adaptation in war that every army soldier had to expect. He put on his steel field helmet.

After deciding to personally assess the damage on the beaches, he walked outside and became amazed at how much the outskirts of Casablanca reminded him of California, particularly the palm trees, which were aligned in neat rows. Then he noticed the damage caused by shells. Local buildings had been bulldozed by projectiles. Even the roof of the Miramar hotel had been visibly damaged. But he suddenly became particularly annoyed when he saw the damage to the palm trees, whose bark had been riddled and ripped through.

"Lieutenant, come here for a minute," he said, beckoning a young officer over.

"Yes, sir?" he responded.

"Take a look at this? Do you see these?"

"They're young palms, sir."

"I know they're young palms, but look at this damage. I want you to organize a task force to cut off the tops. Chop them off just below the shrapnel damage. They'll have a chance to regrow and live if they're pruned right."

"Begging the general's pardon, sir, may I make a suggestion?"

"What's the suggestion?"

"They might be better off if we patched the cavities up with cement."

"How do you know that, lieutenant?"

"I was a medievalist scholar at a university in California, and I studied woodworking, sir. These palms would have a better chance of survival with cement because, over time, new bark will grow over the cement—we could make cement from the sand on the beaches, sir."

Though Patton was impressed with the young officer, he began to notice a foreign accent. He looked again at his nametag.

"Lieutenant Horn, where are you from?" he asked.

"I joined the army in California, but I'm originally from Germany, sir."

"I thought so. You still have family over there?"

"Yes, sir."

"So how are you gonna feel when we start engaging in hand-to-hand combat over there? You're gonna see your own people face to face and may have to use a bayonet on a few yourself?"

"Sir, my squad leader told me he'd keep me out of the combat zone for this very reason. I joined the army as an interpreter, so they want to use me as an interrogator and for special assignments. But I chose to leave Germany when I saw what the Nazis were doing, and I don't consider them my people. I left before the invasion of Poland, but I knew Hitler had plans to conquer all of Europe."

"And how did you know these things?"

"Well, sir, it's like I said. My studies helped me understand what he was doing. I was studying medieval church architecture and woodworking at a university in Heidelberg. One of my uncle's friends was a Nazi, and he told us about how Hitler was going around plundering medieval relics from the Roman Empire, though he didn't use the word plunder. I think he said that the Fuhrer was establishing an historic art collection or something."

"So what, lieutenant? Every conquering army seeks spoils from war?"

"Yes, sir, I agree. But these were different spoils, sir. When the Nazis came to Austria, and he took the holy lance, I knew that...."

"What did you say, lieutenant?"

"They came to Austria and took a holy lance sir. They call it the Longinus. It's a special spear that was used in history for world conquests."

"Lieutenant Horn, I'm very aware of this object, but do you know where he has it now?"

"Probably Nuremberg, sir. That's where the Nazi headquarters are, and that's where they had the spear during the Roman Empire. Hitler is a madman, sir. He's trying to bring back the Roman Empire. Anyone who understands history will see this."

"Lieutenant Horn, when we get to Germany, I'm going to put you on a special assignment. You're going to help me get that spear."

"Yes, sir, but...."

"But what, lieutenant?"

"The spear was known to have a type of mystical power. Anyone who deals with it must be very careful."

"Don't worry. You will be careful, won't you?"

"Yes, sir."

As Patton was finishing his orders to the young lieutenant, a US army jeep was noisily making its way to the hotel. The local town buildings had been constructed so closely together that they created an echo for any vehicles driving on the cobbled streets between them. Therefore, everyone turned to take a look at the loud army jeep, but they were caught off guard at the sight of one of the passengers. She was a very noticeable middle-aged woman dressed in moderate French fashion. Was she a prisoner? Though she had grayish streaks in her hair, she was apparently very youthful and elegant. Onlooking troops were struck by her modest beauty.

The jeep came to a stop, and the two escorting officers stepped down to open her door. One held her gently by her bent elbow and walked her to General Patton.

"Sir," he said, "I think we found the interpreter you were talking about."

"Oh?" he responded, impressed that they would meet her so soon. "What's your name, madam?" he said, not caring to be gentlemanly.

"You may call me Sophia."

"Sophia, I don't know what my officers told you, but the US Army is in need of a local interpreter that could possibly help us with the Moroccan people. You were recommended to me, and I'm assuming that you're going to be willing to serve your people by helping us."

"I am willing, sir."

"Good. Now tell me, are you Moroccan or French? What's your background?

"My father was Moroccan, and my mother was French, so I'm able to understand and speak the local dialect and French. I used to live in France. In fact, I came into contact with an American outfit there during the last war."

"What outfit was that?"

"I don't know the name of their company, but we called them the Yankee Negroes."

"You're talking about that colored unit from New York. How did you come into contact with them?"

"I was working as a nurse at a hospital at the time, and they were sent to us. My aunt in France says they still talk about them."

"I see. Tell me, what were you doing in Casablanca?"

"I was a tutor for an English family there. I was teaching French to three children living near an Anglican church, but the family moved to the northern part of the country when they heard that you Americans were coming in ships."

"Well, I'm going to be frank with you, Sophia. Your country is in great danger of annihilation, and we want to take every possible measure to avoid that."

"What do you mean, General?"

"I mean this; there are fifty thousand combat-ready Vichy French troops in Casablanca. I'm sure you've noticed this."

"Oh, yes, they are everywhere."

"I have about thirty-four thousand combat-ready troops along these beaches, so you can see that we would be outnumbered until further ships arrive, but I'm willing to bet that there may be quite a few local Moroccans who may be recruitable for special assignments, assignments which could ultimately lead to their liberation from the French, of course."

"You want to recruit Moroccan people to help you invade Casablanca?" she asked in disbelief.

"No one is talking about an invasion just yet, madam. But I'd like to explore what types of services we could realistically expect from them."

"Well, many Moroccans might help you if you can convince them that your plans could help their independence. But there are many who are loyal to France. There is a tribal leader in the south named El Galoui, and he's very much in support of the French, and he has many Moroccan followers."

"How loyal are the people to this man?"

"It's hard to say. But everyone respects him, even the royal family. They say that the words of El Galoui break through stones."

"Aren't many Moroccans headed up north now like the British family you mentioned? They realize too that we're coming, don't they?"

"Some are. But it's mostly the Europeans here who are trying to get to Portugal where it's safer. They're the ones crowding the highways and sleeping at the ports near the borders. But I also remember hearing the British family talking about crowds of people trying to get into Morocco from the port near the Spanish border."

"Were they German or Italian troops?"

"They were Jewish families. Yes, I remember now. They were talking about large groups of Jewish families that escaped from Europe who were refugees. You see, last year, some German commandants came here and asked the sultan if he would let them round up the Moroccan Jews, but the sultan said that there weren't any Jews here, only Moroccans. I think many European Jews learned about this and decided to come here."

"Do you know if they've formed an organized resistance?"

"I couldn't tell you anything like that. I think they've only come to survive. My aunt in France wrote me last year about what has happened to the Jews since the invasion. They're being put into large prison camps and treated like animals. She said she didn't know how anyone could be expected to survive like that. It's terrible."

"Well, madam, if the United States Third Army has to invade Casablanca, you're going to have to live with the terrible atrocities of war right here, and many won't survive. Whole cities will be destroyed," he said in a cocky tone.

"Sir, please, I'd like to sit down for a few minutes. May I sit somewhere to gather my thoughts?"

"Captain McRay," yelled Patton, "escort Madam Sophia to the hotel dining area where she can rest and get fresh water. There's still salvageable food in the kitchen, so if she's hungry, ask the cook in company C to fix her something."

"Yes, sir, right away, sir."

The Miramar Hotel was still well stocked with fine wine, fresh vegetables, and cuts of lamb. Captain McRay escorted Sophia up the steps and spoke in a low tone. "I'm sorry if ol' 'Blood and Guts' was a bit gruff with you ma'am. He really does mean well. Are you hungry? There's plenty of food here."

"No thank you. Please, I'd just like to sit down for a moment. May I sit here?"

"Sure, ma'am, but if you want, I could escort you to one of the bedrooms where you can lie down a little."

"No thank you, captain. I'll be fine right here near the lobby."

She sank into the green satin chair, crossed her legs, and tried to rest, but couldn't. The lobby was abuzz with army personnel stomping up and down. Someone was using the telephone to make contact with another army unit. In the opposite far corner, another part of the lobby was being used as an ambulatory station for the walking wounded. It was reminiscent of her experience in the Catholic convent during the last war. These people, she thought, were gearing up for war in everything they were doing, but she could not be a part of it. Her conscience would not allow it.

"Captain," she said to her escort still standing nearby, "I'm afraid I can't be of any real use to your general. I'm sorry."

"How's that, ma'am?"

"I can't help him recruit Moroccan people for war activities. I know what he wants. He wants to form groups of assassins to kill French officers when they fight, and I cannot be a part of that."

"You realize what will probably happen in Casablanca, don't you? They'll have to go from house to house dragging out occupying French troops. It would be easier to have Moroccans working with us on the inside."

"I know, but I'm a Christian. I cannot do this type of work."

"Ma'am, I'm a Christian, too."

"This is your duty, captain," she said, interrupting him. "You have to submit to your orders with a clean conscience, but I have no such orders, except to love my enemies and pray for them. I'm sorry."

"Madam Sophia, our general has decided to launch an all-out invasion of Casablanca on his birthday, November 11th. That gives you two days to think of how you can help us. If you don't want to interpret for trained assassins that's all right, but think of how you might help."

"Sir, I can only think of prayer, which is far more powerful than your Third Army."

Suddenly a strong voice bellowed through the room, "Lobby, teeench-hutt."

The room came to attention as Patton walked toward Captain McRay and Sophia. "At ease," he responded, permitting all staff to continue their busy work.

"Madam Sophia, have you been able to rest a little?"

"Yes, sir, but I'm still a little light-headed. I was wondering if I could simply lie down awhile in one of the bedrooms."

Captain McRay looked surprised.

"Captain, show her one of the suites on the first floor," said Patton.

"Yes, sir."

"And be sure to assign someone to stand guard in the hallway."

"Yes, sir."

The captain waited for Sophia to stand up before walking just ahead of her to a guest suite. Though the hotel lobby had been converted into an army field communications and logistics center, the highly decorated bedroom on the first floor made her feel miles away. It had a large red Arabic tapestry rug in the center of the polished wooden floor. The canopy bed was adorned in pink lace and the chest-of-drawers were a dark chocolate-colored set of fine craftsmanship. Despite the dreamy surroundings, her attention was drawn to the padded footstool opposite the bed.

"Thank you, captain," she said, "I believe I need to rest here a while before I can think clearly about a way to help you."

"Yes, ma'am. We'll have a guard posted in the hallway. Make yourself comfortable."

Sophia locked the door, headed for the footstool, and knelt down. It reminded her of the last time she visited the Anglican church, St John's, in Casablanca, when she had prayed with the British family before their urgent departure. Now she needed to urgently pray for the safety of both her city and the whole country. She started.

"Father in heaven. Father of Abraham, Isaac, and Jacob. Father of my Lord Jesus Christ, I pray that you intercede in this situation. I know that you are a God of love and mercy and that you love all people. You can stop any army. Your word says blessed are the peacemakers. And so I pray for peace for Casablanca. Father, let not destruction come to this city. But I pray that many, both Jew and Muslim, would come to salvation in Christ. Thank you for how you've worked in my life. Thank you that I can have confidence in prayer, knowing that Christ intercedes for his people. I ask these things in the name of Jesus. Amen."

Two hours passed while Sophia remained in the room offering prayers. She paced herself by taking moments to rest on the bed before returning to the footstool to kneel and pray again. Captain McRay passed through the hallway to check up on her and spoke with the private standing guard.

"Has that woman left her room in the past two hours?"

"No, sir."

"She hasn't even come out to ask you anything?"

"No, sir, we haven't spoken at all. She's probably been too busy on the phone."

"What do you mean, private?"

"I mean, I've heard her having a conversation with someone in there. Since she's alone, I figured that she would have to be using a landline."

"Private, that room doesn't have a phone. Are you sure she's alone in there?"

"Positive, sir."

"Then who could she have been speaking to?"

"I don't know, sir. Maybe she was talking in her sleep. I was ordered not to disturb her, so I didn't think about asking."

"Thank you, private. Carry on."

Captain McRay decided not to disturb Sophia because the fate of Casablanca was now planned out. At this point, she could only offer very little assistance as an interpreter as Patton had already decided not to use her. They allowed her to stay in the hotel the following day, explaining to her that once the invasion took place, she could remain there until it was safe in Casablanca. In the meantime, the Third Army was revving up to invade. Armored tanks were filled with petrol. Machine guns were greased down and polished. Navy ships were ready to begin long-distance bombardments, and air reconnaissance planes were sitting on the runway.

The day of invasion had come. Though Patton had only thirty-four thousand troops, he was confident of victory. He had planned a three-pronged lightening-speed convergence on the city of Casablanca, and no one, he believed, would be able to stop him. As he stood in the hotel lobby giving a final briefing to tank commanders, the lobby phone rang and a young lieutenant answered it.

"Sir," he said to Patton, "It's a British field commander in Algeria. He says he needs to urgently speak with you."

Patton trotted over to the phone. "Go ahead," he said into the receiver. "When? How can you be sure? How many surrendered? Who was there? No, of course not! Thank you, but we'll stand by for confirmation."

He turned and stared blankly at his tank officers who had been listening intently. There was an expression of both relief and defeat on his face. The invasion was not to take place. Vichy French forces had already surrendered to the British in Algeria. Hence, French units in Morocco were to follow suit and surrender to the Americans.

"Gentlemen, we are on standby now for this invasion," he said. "There should be a call in any moment from the confirming a surrender. Where's our interpreter?" he asked hurriedly.

"He's waiting outside with a tank squad sir," said the lieutenant.
"Well, where's that French gal who was going to interpret for us?"

"She's back in one of the bedrooms, sir."

"Well, go get her. Bring her here now. We might need her for a phone call."

"Yes, sir," responded the lieutenant, already on his way down the lobby.

After three minutes, the telephone rang again and the lieutenant came running with Sophia to the lobby.

"This is General Patton," he said, speaking into the receiver. "What? Now say that again slowly. Listen, just wait one minute." He waved Sophia over to the phone.

"This is the French High Command in Algeria," he whispered to her, "I want you to interpret for me every word they say. Now go."

Sophia began in French. *"Allo? Oui. Oui Messieur. Oui Messieur, un instant, s'il vous plait."*

Turning to Patton, she spoke with tears welling up in her eyes. "He said he is from the high command, and that they want to make a formal surrender to you, and that they are taking their forces out of Casablanca."

"All right, tell him I need for them to come to the Miramar Hotel and meet me here. We'll arrange for an escort."

Sophia lifted the phone and reported everything he said. Still wiping tears from her eyes, she then smiled and thanked the voice on the phone for the call, adding that it was an answer to prayer.

28

CASABLANCA SPARED

A dozen or so bottles of chilled wine had been left on a buffet in the grand ballroom before three officers of the French High Command arrived. They were impressed with Patton and the apparent readiness of his troops. They were also relieved that they didn't have to contend with him in combat. Though one of them spoke English fluently, Sophia was asked to make herself readily available lest an immediate need for an interpreter arise in the meeting. She waited in the corridor.

The four men spoke respectfully of France and the US, chuckled at the audacity of the Nazi army, and drank $40.00 worth of wine. Patton ventured to mention how Hitler failed to learn from Napoleon's mistake in attempting to invade Russia during winter.

Though the comparison between Hitler and Napoleon was ill received by one commander, the atmosphere of the meeting remained both chivalrous and social, and that pleased Patton.

There were no written agreements outlining any terms of surrender, only a mere handshake and a toast. The two sides would simply have to trust that each one would stand by his word; the French were not to interfere with the Americans' attempt to drive General Rommel out of North Africa, and the Americans were not to pursue any punitive measures against the French for collusion with the Nazis.

Patton telephoned General Eisenhower to relay the news. He knew that the Supreme Allied Commander would be impressed with his efficiency and hoped that he could be sent on his next assignment as soon as possible. The Nazis were still in Tunisia, and General Rommel had outfoxed the British army on several accounts. As Patton was ordered to wait, he knew it would be best to assume the role of a diplomat in the meantime.

Visiting the Sultan of Morocco and attending local parades therefore became a preoccupation.

"Sir, I want to thank you for the opportunity to serve you and your cause," said Sophia, who was now preparing to return to Casablanca. "But personally, I feel as if I actually did very little for you."

"Sophia, you're a lovely lady, and I wish you all the best. I thank you, and the United States Army thanks you," said Patton. "Now where do you go from here?"

"I need to go back and reconnect with my family. I expect that the British family I was working with will also return soon, since there will be no invasion. For now, all I'm thinking about is attending church tomorrow."

"And didn't you say that it was an Anglican church?"

"Yes, St. John's was the first Anglican church in Casablanca, and I think it's the oldest church still in use."

"Then all the services would be in English, wouldn't they?"

"I believe so. Only the French cathedrals have their services in Latin and French."

"Would St. John's be so gracious as to permit members of the Third Army to attend a service? Some of my boys have been asking about a local place of worship for over a week. They're a long way from home, and it would be good for morale."

"General, St. John's policy is that their doors are to remain opened to anyone. Of course you can come. But if you have many troops, some might have to sit on the floor in the back."

"That's no problem. We'll take a head count tonight of those who want to come, and we'll see you there tomorrow. Give the directions to Lieutenant Johnson in transportation for us."

St. John the Evangelist was a small whitewashed house of worship situated just outside of the city. Completed in 1906, it was adjacent to a small cemetery dedicated to British foreign nationals who died in Morocco in service to their king. And though it was usually frequented by British diplomats and their families, its membership had fallen sharply due to the anticipated invasion. Only a remnant of English-speaking residents remained.

It was customary for the clergyman to greet congregation members just outside the stone arched doorway before the service. However, as Reverend Green was not expecting many visitors this Sunday, he anticipated a quiet, traditional Anglican service. Then, two dusty US Army transport trucks suddenly pulled up in front of the church and stopped. The door flung open and Patton descended.

Reverend Green's eyes grew wide when he saw the American general approach him through the garden doorway.

"You must be Reverend Green," he said, extending his hand. "I'm General George Patton. We were told about your services by a Madam Sophia, so we've come to worship the Lord with you."

"Oh my!" responded the reverend, feeling jolted by Patton's brashness and American bravado. "And how many are you, sir?" he said, attempting to smile.

"We have about thirty God-fearing boys with us, reverend." Just then, Madam Sophia appeared through the garden door.

"Good morning, reverend! I'm sorry I wasn't able to tell you to expect some American visitors this morning. I've been a little rushed lately."

"Friends of yours?" responded the reverend still dumbfounded.

"Madam Sophia has done this city and the US Third Army a great service, reverend," interrupted Patton. "She actually helped save Casablanca from annihilation."

"Well, bring your lads in, sir. Our doors are always opened for worship, though it might be a little tight."

"Don't you worry about that, Reverend. Our boys will adapt." Patton then turned to face the two transport trucks. He raised his arm and waved his hand over his shoulder, signifying to the men to descend in single file. They came jumping out and, in single file, strode through the front door.

"Mornin', Rev," said a tall lance corporal as he shuffled his big boots onto the tile floor.

The small English congregation seated near the front of the church began to notice the noisy group. They whispered, mumbled, and turned around to see their Yankee visitors filling up the aisles. Someone joked about an American invasion in the church. When they had all taken a place, the aisles were filled to near capacity with a majority of US troops in uniform.

The reverend then began to address the British congregation. "Well, I suppose you're wondering to what do we owe this special visit by our American friends in uniform? Brethren, God has sent them here for worship, and I want extend a warm welcome to our brothers and allies here in Morocco."

The congregation smiled, nodded, and verbally expressed their appreciation in hushed tones, still mindful about proper decorum inside the church.

"Gentlemen of the Third Army," the reverend began, "we like to begin our worship with joyful singing. You all have hymnals before you, so please feel free to make a request."

"Song one-hundred and nine," shouted Patton, his voice reverberating off the rafters.

The reverend glanced at the organist, who appeared to be lost. "I'm not sure if we know this one. Perhaps another."

"Don't worry about that, reverend," interrupted Patton. "We practiced this one last week on the ship coming over here." Patton then rose to his feet and, waving his hand, directed his troops to stand at attention. "Now boys," he continued, "one, two, three." And on cue, they all belted out in impressive harmony:

"SOLDIERS OF CHRIST ARISE, AND PUT YOUR ARMOR ON, STRONG IN THE STRENGTH WHICH GOD SUPPLIES THROUGH HIS ETERNAL SON, STRONG IN THE LORD OF HOSTS, AND IN HIS MIGHTY POWER, WHO IN THE STRENGTH OF JESUS TRUSTS IS MORE THAN CONQUEROR…"

The young men continued to sing the old English hymn with all the youthful strength they could muster. The British congregation had never before heard it done so well. Many felt goose bumps all over and rose to their feet in applause when they had finished. Then, Reverend Green discretely put his notes aside as he spontaneously decided to change his sermon message. For an hour and a half he spoke about being more than a conqueror through faith and the whole congregation hung on his every word.

A genuine sense of appreciation for the American allies was fostered that day at St John's. And among Patton's men, a heightened sense of nobility and duty was equally fostered. Friendly acquaintances were formed, and no one wanted to leave the church after the sermon.

Lieutenant Horn wandered away from the small crowd to study one of the stained glass windows. By observing the mosaic style and colors, he was able to estimate that it had probably been made in the early 1900s. The images were simple. Christ was hanging on the cross with visible wounds on his head and in his side. He then felt a sudden surge of panic as he was reminded about the Longinus. He wondered about how accessible it would be and how many Nazi guards had been posted on watch at the church in Nuremberg where he figured it was hidden. Recovering that spear seemed like a death mission.

Patton glanced at his watch, reminding himself of his schedule. "Reverend," he said, "you've blessed our boys immensely this morning. I don't know if you can really understand what it meant for them to be here."

"General, I hope you believe me when I say that we all sincerely hope to see you and your troopers again. How long will you be stationed here?"

"That has yet to be decided, but I think it would be safe to say you can expect to see us for a few more Sundays."

"Well, we know our little church here may feel cramped, but bring as many as you can."

"Thank you. You know reverend, if you were to keep your side door open during the service, we could put more men in the courtyard to hear your sermons."

"Splendid idea!"

"I tell ya what I'll do. I'm going to donate fifty chairs to your church for an overflow. That way we can bring in more of my men, and your regular congregation won't feel too cramped inside."

"We would be most happy to oblige, General. Do let us know how we could be of further assistance to you in any way. You're most welcome at any time."

Patton's men climbed into the army trucks, still waving goodbye to the British residents. It was refreshing for them to be away from the regimented schedule at the military compound and to talk to real civilian women, even if they were older.

The aging British congregation at St. John's would be invigorated with new life from the boys of Patton's Third Army for a considerable time. They came dutifully week after week, filling the capacity of the overflow in the courtyard. It became a home away from home to strangers in a strange land. They learned the discipline of corporate prayer there, and Patton became a regular attendee, further expressing his appreciation by donating a pulpit to the church.

29

PATTON AND MONTGOMERY

The American and British Allied Forces in North Africa had a new mission and a new strategy—to drive General Rommel off the continent and chase him all the way to Berlin. Though Morocco and Algeria now posed no threats against an Allied assault, General Rommel had a stronghold in Tunisia, and British forces there had grown weary of combat. Morale was low, and Patton was sent to assist. A handful of his top squad leaders were assigned with him, along with Lieutenant Horn, who was sent to translate for any captured soldiers. Patton was happy that Horn had accompanied him in the air transport that would meet General Montgomery on the outskirts in Tunisia.

"This mission won't take long at all," said Patton in the plane. "Once we get Rommel surrounded, we can push him north with his back toward the sea. He'll have nowhere to go then, except to Italy or back home to Germany."

"So we are going to fight with the British?" asked Horn. "That's right. Once I whip them into shape, we'll supply a corps to work with them. What I want you to do is get your hands on one of those SS officers. If we can break one of them, we might be able to get information about where their main defense units are in Europe, and you can probably even get him to spill the beans about the location of the spear in Nuremburg."

"Sir, I know where the spear was originally put. The only problem is that I think it was moved to another location in the same city."

"Well, that's what I'm telling you. An SS officer should have the latest news."

The plane began to descend for a landing on a dirt field in Tunisia. They had flown four hours from Morocco to Tunisia with very little change of landscape. It all appeared to be one country.

Upon landing, British troops let out a cheer for General Patton when the plane door opened. General Montgomery was standing next to them. Patton descended the mobile stair case with his squad members, and the two generals met.

"I say, it's jolly good to see you again, George. How is Beatrice?"

"Doing well, thank you. I write her once a week. She's better informed about this war than some or our pinhead politicians in Washington."

(chuckling) "I see. Well, we've got some hot chow for you and your lads. We want you to be able to have a good meal before we have to get down to business."

"I figured you might offer that now. You know, in the States, we handle business before eating."

"Yes, yes, I know that ol' boy. But we find it better for the digestion to eat first. Besides, it may start to go foul if we wait another ten minutes."

(chuckling) "Show me the way, Monty."

The British Tommies and selected members of Patton's Third Army sat down and ate a mixture of military K rations and warm homemade bread from a local village. They ate until they were full. The British even offered small cups of tea after the meal, but none of Patton's men were interested.

"You know, George," Montgomery began, "we heard about what happened in Casablanca. We were sure it was destined to be a bloodbath."

"The Third Army was ready. Our boys were chomping at the bit. It just wasn't meant to be," replied Patton, finishing his plate of food.

"I suppose you're right about that. Some things may simply be destined to turn out one way or another, but your number can be called up at any time, you know."

"I can only agree with you up to a point, Monty. It's true that your number can be called up at any time, but some of us know that we've been destined for great things, and until those things have been achieved, our days will be prolonged."

"George, I've never known you to be an existentialist," said Montgomery, slightly shocked.

"Do ya want to know another thing I'm sure about?" said Patton confidently.

"What's that?"

"Hitler's days are numbered."

Montgomery was encouraged by Patton's self-confidence. He spoke as if he had already seen the end of the war. Though Monty realized that he himself had been telling his troops some of the same things, he knew that he didn't seem to have the level of confidence that Patton had, and perhaps it was for this reason that their morale was low.

"Okay Monty, let's get down to business, what do you say?"

"Right, our maps are drawn up in the large tent," he said, getting up. "We can leave through this way."

Montgomery led Patton and selected men to a large tent covered by a camouflage mesh net. There was a huge map of North Africa lying across three tables, with several clusters of red and white indicator pins stuck at various locations. Patton immediately deduced that the red pins signified concentrations of the Nazi Africa corps.

According to the map, they were dominating the northern part of the country.

"I'm sure you can see our little problem now, can't you?" said Montgomery. "We're here, (he indicated using a pointer stick) just southeast of the enemy. They've been protected by these mountain ranges here, and our left flank has been quite weak."

"What kind of numbers have we got at the northern left flank?" asked Patton point-blank.

"We have a regiment of about two thousand from our Eighth Army here," he said, pointing just west of the enemy's northern stronghold.

"You know what will happen if they can't hold them, don't you?" asked Patton.

"The Nazis will push westward into Algeria and reclaim lost ground there," said Monty.

"You've got it. But if we can fortify this left flank, we can put them in a giant vice and crush 'em."

The plan was brilliant. Patton explained that he could call for the US to send a corps division to be placed in northwest Tunisia to strengthen the left flank with more troops and air power. This would keep the enemy from moving westward, and during the meantime, the southeast unit could drive them northward with ground attacks. As the northwest flank pushed eastward with air power, and the southeast flank pushed northward, Rommel's army would be caught in a giant vice and forced into the Mediterranean Sea.

After much reconfiguration of small details, the two men shook hands and agreed on the plan, and Patton almost immediately implemented new combat drills for desert warfare. The soldiers of Britain's Eighth Army learned new hand-to-hand fighting maneuvers and exercised rigorously in the desert heat. Their objective was to be able to push the Nazi Africa corps northward as soon as possible to create a tight squeeze.

General Eisenhower, who had already arrived in Algeria, received the message of Patton's request for troops and air power. He immediately radioed Washington. Within two days, troops, supplies, and tanks were transported to Algeria and then sent on to northwest Tunisia. The British Royal Navy also delivered shiploads of supplies off the coast.

With every actor in place now, the great performance commenced. British infantry units cut through barbed wire and fought through enemy lines. Tactical air bombers dropped over one thousand tons of explosives, forcing the Nazi army northward. Then, Patton's Second Army Corps, along with Third Army auxiliary forces, launched a successful surprise attack eastward. The enemy was on the run, and multiple units began to surrender as Rommel's army began to deplete its resources. In the end, his Panzer tanks were outnumbered seven to one, and hundreds of German and Italian forces were killed. Consequently, thousands of Nazi prisoners were also captured and taken into custody.

30

AN INQUISITION

Hitler was seething. "Damn! Damn! Damn!" he shrieked, pounding his oak desk with his sweaty fists and stamping his foot. His inner circle of officers had rarely seen him rant this way, though they had heard rumors about his tendency to throw fits, and such displays were becoming more frequent since the stalemate on the Russian front.

"Where did this man come from, this Patton!" he growled. "He was trained at one of their best military schools, West

Point, sir," answered an officer. "He's probably the best that they've got."

"So how could this bumbling cowboy succeed in challenging the Third Reich's best? Where is Rommel? I had told him there was no retreat plan. It was either victory or death! Why is he not here with you now?"

"He was taken to hospital, sir, for stomach problems. But, if I may explain sir, there was really nothing left for him to do. He was able to hold out until Patton had entered the battle, but then he ran out of resources, and the British and Americans were beginning to break through."

"It was victory or death! Did you hear me—victory or death!" he screamed. "Now the whole campaign is finished. The Allies are sure to try to attack Sicily and then Italy. And that cowboy Patton will most assuredly try to come to our mainland. We need to send more troops into Italy now to drive them back," he began to think pensively.

"But sir, unless we start reassigning divisions from the Russian front, we won't have a large enough force to make an impact."

"We have plenty of resources, starting with the youth! We're going to lower our age restrictions for military service. I want all the registered Hitler youth club chapters to be notified to send in their membership lists, now! And get Rommel in here before this afternoon."

The powdery dusty roads of Tunisia were crowded with a convoy of dusty, defeated Nazi soldiers. There were thousands of them shuffling forward like cattle under the orders of their American and British captors. Many Allied soldiers thought they were being treated far better than they deserved to be and knew that the Nazis didn't treat their prisoners with half the respect that they were being shown.

Though Lieutenant Horn was able to sit down in a processing tent, he was one of the busiest men at this time. Patton had ordered that all SS officers undergo intense interrogation, and Horn was one of the few interpreters assigned to the job. It was hot and dry outside. And many of the prisoners couldn't speak because of near dehydration.

"It's no use," said Horn after questioning an SS officer. "He's too tired to talk. He's nearly delusional."

"No, I think he's bluffing," said a commanding colonel assisting the interrogations. "These folks are stubborn. They'll do anything to play ignorant. You can't tell me that out of all the officers we've questioned today, only two have a slight idea about Nazi controlled airfields in Sicily. I don't buy that."

"Colonel, if I may, I need to explain something," said Horn desperately. "The Nazi chain of command doesn't work like ours. Often when they say that they don't know anything, they really don't know anything. And they aren't trained to think like we are. They simply wait for their orders from high command, from Hitler himself, and follow them."

"These are officers, lieutenant. Surely they have some idea about the strategies made at high command."

"No, sir, they don't. If they do, it's usually because they've personally heard something by accident."

"So how do you know all these things, Lieutenant?"

"Colonel, I'm able to work as a translator because German was my first language. I know that my accent is fading, but I was born in Germany. I studied there at university, and I had friends who had joined the Luftwaffe."

Just then, an SS officer was led in to take a seat. His haggard face was almost completely covered in dried mud, which made his glaring white eyes appear very ominous. He stared at Lieutenant Horn, who was finishing his conversation with the colonel, and suddenly attempted to say something, but then he immediately stopped himself.

Horn studied his face. Their eyes met for a moment before the prisoner inclined his head and lowered his eyes to the dirt floor.

"Wie is Ihr Name?"

"What is your name?" asked Horn.

The officer said nothing.

Horn asked again, *"Wie is Ihr Name?"* to which there was still no reply.

"Welch Ihre Reine ist? "What is your rank?" asked Horn. *"Ich ben ein Oberst."*

"I am a colonel," responded the prisoner, with pride in his voice.

"Wo sind Luftwaffe Flugplatz in Sizilien?"

"Where are the Luftwaffe airfields in Sicily?" asked Horn.

The colonel then looked directly at him. Sternly he said, *"Sie werden ni im stande sein un aufzuhoren, Walter."*

"You will never be able to stop us, Walter."

Lieutenant Horn was shocked. It was not so much that the prisoner knew his first name when there was no nametag on his shirt, but it was the familiar way in which he pronounced it that caught his attention. Horn stood up and slowly removed the prisoner's cap, revealing his bright blond hair. He put his hand under the prisoner's chin and lifted his face to better study it. Then he was certain. His heart sank when he realized that it was his former neighbor and friend.

"*Verrater,*"

"Traitor,"

"*Verrater,*"

"Traitor," the prisoner yelled.

Two military police guards ran into the tent. They had started to restrain the prisoner when Horn stopped them. "It's okay, it's okay. He can't do anything. He's unarmed. Let him sit down please," said Horn. The two MPs slowly loosened their grip of his arms and guided him down, back to his seat. He was breathing heavily, and his eyes revealed a deep hatred for Horn.

"Gentlemen," said Horn, "this man was a good friend—like family. We studied at university together before I fled the country years ago. And now..." he stopped as tears began to well up in his eyes. He sniffled, swallowed, and continued, "and now he hates me."

Horn slumped into his seat and stared at the colonel. His mind raced back to warm memories of birthday parties, family picnics, and jumping in the Rhine together. His friend had always been popular with girls because of his sociable personality. Now there was no trace of it. The events streaming through his mind seemed as if they had occurred just yesterday. Horn remained silent for five minutes, and then attempted to make a civil conversation.

"Frederick, Frederick, listen to me. I know what you must be thinking now. But despite what is happening all around us, we are still connected, Frederick. Frederick, talk to me."

"If we were in Germany, I would turn you in to the police.

They would hang you," said the colonel.

"Frederick, you are a prisoner of war now. You belong to a defeated army, but I would never have you hanged for the choices of loyalty you've made. I just want to ask you to help us so that we can end this war."

"There is nothing I can do to help you," he said. "I don't know about any airfields in Sicily."

"That's not what I want to ask you, Frederick. You were with me at university, and we had many discussions together. I want to know where I can find the Longinus."

Frederick scoffed. "I see your American friends have made a mystic out of you. What good can that do you? That's not going to end any war. If the Americans ever try to invade the mainland, they'll be slaughtered by our Panzer divisions. No ancient relic will change that!"

"Frederick," said Horn softly, "it was stolen by the Nazi party, all I want to do is put it back."

"They will torture you for being a traitor. Then they will publicly execute you. If you even set foot in Nuremberg they'll...."

"Where in Nuremberg, Frederick? Where in Nuremberg are they hiding it?"

Frederick knew there was no use hiding the information and submitted. "Okay, since you want to know, it's in a vault under the medieval castle, as you should have already known. But it doesn't matter. None of that matters because the Americans will never reach it. You've made a big mistake, my friend. They may have beaten the Africa Corps, but they will be wiped out if they try to invade the mainland."

Frederick was given a canteen of water and escorted from the tent. The friendship they had once enjoyed belonged to a different era, and Horn knew that it was highly unlikely that they would ever be the same. He waited for the next prisoner.

31

THE SUSPENSION

Newsreels of the Casablanca conference made an enormous impression on the American public. For the first time, President Roosevelt, Prime Minister Winston Churchill, and General de Gaulle all met at the Anfa Hotel to discuss the unconditional surrender of Germany. They also purposed to officially invite the free French to agree with the plan to invade Sicily and then Italy before attacking mainland Europe.

"Well, it's clear, is it not?" said de Gaulle. "Your generals, Patton and Montgomery, worked very well together in Tunisia. I would think that they should also be able to continue a successful campaign in Sicily."

"Indeed," said Churchill, "their co-labor in this undertaking has been exceptional. I couldn't imagine any other combination better suited for this hour."

"Good, gentlemen," said Roosevelt, "let us now therefore be in agreement that on whatever course this path takes us, we will win through to victory."

The three heads of state, representing free Western civilization, shook hands and smiled into the newsreel cameras. It was the dawning of a new day. It was the beginning of new relationships. It was the spark of a new hope—and the invasion of Sicily was now official.

In July, under the cover of darkness, a British patrol ship carried a top-secret container near the coastline of Sicily. Inside the container was the unidentified corpse of a British soldier. No one knew from where he had come when he was alive, but though there were no tags of true identification on the body, his role in Operation Mincemeat was crucial.

This was the name of the operation designed to hoodwink Nazi and Italian military intelligence. It was war trickery at its best. The body had been provided with false identification in its clothes pockets. It was also attached, by the arm, to a briefcase loaded with false documents indicating that the Allied forces had chosen not to invade Sicily.

Then, the body was dumped off Sicily's coast in hopes that enemy intelligence would pick it up, once washed ashore, and believe him to be a drowned military agent working with Allied intelligence.

General Rommel was sitting down across from Hitler in his office. The light was dimmed because Hitler had been suffering from migraines. He had lost much sleep over the failure in North Africa and conveyed his dissatisfaction ever so poignantly to his stellar general. Though Rommel knew that he was truly not to blame, he did not defend himself. Instead, he spoke optimistically about how finding the secret documents attached to the floating corpse afforded them now an advantage to prepare for a US invasion elsewhere.

"If they are trying to get to the mainland," he said, "they could possibly try Greece or perhaps the island of Sardinia. But Sicily looks like it will be safe."

"Be sure that those beaches are wired for the possibility of an attack," said Hitler, "and don't waste your time with enlisted prisoners when they come. I'm only interested in captured officers, particularly Patton."

By early September, it was evident that Operation Mincemeat was a success. Many German divisions of ground defense units were reassigned to Greece and the island of Sardinia, where the falsified documents intimated the landings would take place. It was estimated that thousands of British and American lives were saved because of this clever operation. And now, with the success of Operation Mincemeat completed, Operation Husky, the attack of Sicily, could begin.

Twenty-five hundred Allied warships cruised through Sicilian waters to draw near to the coastline. They had to follow narrow sea lanes as the Nazis had left many floatable mines in the region. Then the Allied ships took their positions and broke the silence by bombarding the shoreline with heavy guns to begin the invasion. They pounded the region with high explosives for hours to eliminate any enemy ground forces left on watch. Though they lost six ships through minimal enemy resistance, they overpowered the ground forces and decided to invade. Montgomery and his Eighth Army landed on the east coast of the island, and Patton and his newly assigned Seventh Army task force landed on the south coast. The Third Army was to remain in Tunisia.

Despite the sandbars and high waves making it difficult for the landing craft, nothing could stop them. The Nazi high command scrambled to send ground defense units from the northern part of the island, which was miles away. They were surprised the invasion did not take place in Greece and made every effort to get to the city of Gela as quickly as possible to help Italian ground forces. But it was to no avail. US warplanes swooped down and strafed all enemy convoys before their arrival. Before long, the British and American armies were marching in antlike files to the north toward the capital, Palermo.

The advancing British and American forces were supposed to meet at a midway point on the island. However, there was a sudden change of plans as Montgomery's army was confronted by dug-in German troops. Unable to advance further, he requested that high command allow him to use a different route, which had been promised to the Americans. It was a fast-track route to the northern city of Messina (an enemy stronghold), which would thus assure the conquest of Sicily. When Patton was told of Monty's request, he felt slighted. To him, this change in strategy would relegate his army to doing a 'mop up' job after the British, leaving no glory of conquest for his Seventh Army.

It therefore became a frustrating race to the finish, in which Patton pushed furiously.

"This is a war," he argued. "We shouldn't have to wait for them now. Whichever side gets their first should get the glory." He decided to personally urge his troops to fight onward. He visited them in their tents for casual pep talks and sometimes rode alongside of them in his official jeep to talk with squad leaders marching their troops at ease. In early August, he stopped by an army hospital outside the city of Nicosia and chatted with injured soldiers. He was impressed with their stories of bravery, but then he met Private Charles Kuhl. When Patton had walked into the hospital, everyone jumped to attention except him. Kuhl remained slouched in his chair. He had been diagnosed with battle fatigue, though it would be discovered later that he had actually contracted malaria and did not realize this.

Patton looked down in disappointment at the man. "Well, what's the matter soldier? Where were you hurt?"

Kuhl was silent and shrugged his shoulders. "I'm not wounded, sir," he said. "It's my nerves. I guess I just can't take it."

Patton was flabbergasted in disbelief and erupted. "Your nerves!" he said bitterly. "You're nothing but a yellow coward!" And he took his gloves and slapped him several times across his face. Then he grabbed him by his collar, dragged him outside of the tent, and kicked his backside, yelling, "You're going back to the front lines, you gutless coward!"

Later, Patton wrote in his journal that it had made his blood boil to see cowards babied in such a way, and that the man should have been tried for cowardice and shot. However, Patton didn't realize the seriousness of what he had done. The incident would change his life, his career, and his pursuit of the Longinus.

"The people in the press don't know the first thing about soldiering," said Patton in defense. "That private was better off being slapped because it sobered him up."

Eisenhower now was growing angry. He had been trying to convey to Patton the graveness of his mistake, but he would not receive the rebuke.

"Millions of Americans feel they are sacrificing their husbands, sons, and sweethearts over here fighting tyranny. And when they hear that one of our boys is being slapped around just for having battle fatigue that makes us look no better than the Nazis. Now look George, you're going to make a public apology for that incident, understand?" Eisenhower then paused before continuing. "And I'm afraid I'll have to suspend you from duty for a little while."

Patton couldn't believe his ears. "Suspend me from duty? At this crucial time in this war?"

"Yes, I'm afraid I have to. Public criticism has become too great over this. I have no other choice."

"How long?" asked Patton with resignation.

"I don't know yet. But you'll be able to rest a while before your next orders. You will not be going to Italy. I'm sorry."

Though Eisenhower knew that Patton needed to learn more self-control, he also knew that his raw talents still made him imperative in this war. They needed his natural aggressiveness on the battlefield. Moreover, his psychological effect on the enemy was undeniable. Eisenhower was careful therefore not to crush his spirit. Patton would be treated well during his suspension.

"Don't think of it as a suspension, George. We simply have to show our public that we addressed the incident. You're one of our best! But the other thing is this, we need you to lie low for a while to put the Nazis off their guard. We know that Hitler's afraid of you, George. He's anticipating that you're going to lead an invasion of the mainland somewhere. And this is going to create an advantage for us. The British command is working on a plan called Operation Fortitude. They'll be able to tell us more about its development very soon."

Patton said nothing.

"You just get some rest and let us keep the enemy guessing for a while. And you have my word that you'll get new orders before the war is through."

They shook hands and Patton was driven to US officers' quarters in Northern Sicily by jeep. The officers' quarters consisted of private villas in secured areas outside the city. Though the complete capture of the island had not yet fully taken place, he decided to take a walk.

He thought about the slapping incident, still marveling at how exaggerated the public response had become. He also began to think about his own destiny. Was his career supposed to end this way, and what about the Longinus? What would become of that?

As he meandered around the dry hills in northern Sicily, a German artillery shell suddenly exploded a few feet away. He had been the singular target of a cannon attack but came through unscathed. He thus thought to himself, *"This confirms it; my destiny has yet to be fulfilled."*

32

OPERATION FORTITUDE

Lieutenant Horn and most of the Third Army regiment were sent to England to wait for redeployment orders.

They considered it as a vacation away from hostilities and began to look forward to eating fish and chips in British pubs and meeting British lassies. The war was reaching a climax in Europe. Italy was falling to the Allies, and Mussolini was being pursued by a mob. Hence they suspected that their next orders would probably be their last.

The social life in London had come to a standstill. Thousands of people had moved to the northern part of the country to avoid the Nazi night bombings. Those who chose to remain lived mostly around bomb shelters. People slept in the underground subway stations at night and hurried about their days, keeping away from the town's main center.

From week to week soldiers of the Third Army had to report to their assigned duty stations, just outside the city, for briefings. If they remained on good behavior, they were given a weekend pass to travel within a small radius. This allowed them to sightsee or attend a big band grand ballroom dance event. Several Hollywood celebrities would stop over on their way to appear at the USO shows: Marlene Dietrich, Bing Crosby, Benny Goodman, and the Andrew Sisters were a main draw for both British and Americans alike. Though the British women could not dance the jitterbug as well as American women, most of the soldiers found their reserved proper social graces attractive, and this made them fun to be around.

Spring was approaching, which usually meant fewer rainy days around England, which usually meant more time outdoors, which usually meant better chances to meet nice ladies at Piccadilly Circus or a local pub. For the Third Army however, it now meant an important briefing on a new war strategy. All weekend passes were cancelled, and military police guards were posted around the station as the soldiers were ordered to march single-file to their meeting hall.

Lieutenant Horn was seated in the midsection of the hall and caught a glimpse of top-brass officers near the front row. He was pleased to see General Patton mingling with British officers. Though he appeared to have gained a few pounds, he seemed no less rigorous than when he last saw him. A small group of privates was trying to talk with him.

A British officer took the center platform to make an announcement. According to his insignia, he held a high rank and worked with the Joint Allied Command. He grabbed the microphone:

"Gentlemen, gentlemen, you need to take your seats quickly now. We have a great deal on our agenda, so we need to get started."

All social huddles dispersed as everyone darted to an available seat.

"You've all had temporary cancellations to your leave and weekend passes for great reason. We are entering a new phase in this war, which will require your obedience and attention to details. I would like now to invite General Williams from the Allied Expeditionary Force to brief us."

The British officer took his seat in the front row, and US General Brett Williams took the stand.

"Gentlemen of the Third Army, I trust that you've rested well during these past few weeks. I know that you haven't been able to stray very far from this duty station, but I hope you've been able to get a little sightseeing in. My experience here has been illuminating. Getting acquainted with our British allies in the Expeditionary Force has opened my eyes about how our new strategy is designed to work. We're calling it "Operation Fortitude," and to understand it is to understand our British allies. Men, back in the States we all understand Hollywood cinema, and I've noticed quite a few Dorothy Lamour posters around your workout rooms, so I know that you understand Hollywood cinema."

This prompted laughter in the audience.

"Though we may understand Hollywood," he continued, "I don't think we understand theater the way the British do. Well, I want to suggest to you today that 'Operation Fortitude' will be run like a giant theatrical production, and you are the players. The Nazi high command is expecting the Third Army to invade the mainland at Calais, France, and they're expecting General Patton to lead it. They're waiting for us to launch our warships from Dover and sail across the English Channel. Sounds like a good plan, eh? Well, so we've decided to go along with this. At this time, we've assigned a task force to place dummy tanks, aircraft, and ships all along the coast of Dover. These are real-to-life inflatable decoys, which appear genuine from air surveillance cameras, and we know that they're taking pictures! But here's where you come in. We've designed special uniforms for a fictitious army unit. You men are to wear the uniforms and pose for pictures at certain designated locations along the coast of Dover. You will pose with General Patton, since he is the presumed commander. It may seem trivial, but this little work of theater will allow us to finalize our plans of invasion, which naturally will not take place near Dover. Your unit commanders will brief you on any real invasions in due time, but I must add, stay ready. You may be called up for the real show at any time!" It was as if they were recruited for a casting call in a major production. Three privates wheeled in carts filled with new fake uniforms. Everything appeared to be authentic except the pentagonal red patch on the sleeve with the capital 'I' in the middle, signifying that they were a part of the nonexistent First Army group. There was every size for every rank up to a chief master sergeant.

The men were led, single file, to the carts to pick out their sizes of uniforms. For their remaining days in England, they were supposed to wear it at all times, which included around town and at their duty stations. There was more than enough for everyone, and once suited up, they headed out.

Twelve US transport trucks, filled with soldiers wearing the new uniforms, drove to the Dover embankment of the English Channel. With the chalky white cliffs standing like a stone wall in the background, the region was picturesque. It had been arranged as a port city with decoy gunboats in the bay, phony tanks placed along the shoreline, and even fake aircraft fighter planes placed inland. When the men clamored out of the trucks, they tried not to amuse themselves too much as they bustled around in a charade of contrived activities. General Patton stood by silently appearing to supervise, and an army photographer snapped pictures.

Exactly twenty-six miles and two feet east from where Patton was standing was the port of Calais, France. As his crew was laboring to arrange a seaport of fabricated attack vehicles, General Rommel and a crew of nine hundred military engineers were constructing a highly complex and deadly network of combat booby traps in anticipation of their arrival. There were miles of land mines placed beneath the sand, and hundreds of steel constructed anti-tank obstacles placed along the shore. It was a death trap of bombs, barricades, and barbed wire.

"No, no, no. The Americans are sure to embark at this region here," said Rommel to a junior officer. "This is the shallowest point of the water's edge, so it will be the easiest place for their landing crafts."

"Sir, are you expecting Patton to land with his troops?"

"I'm not sure what to expect of that man. But I know that he's coming. We need to be sure all the major beaches have been prepared, not only here, but in Normandy, too."

"How many do they think will come?" asked the junior officer.

"We don't know," said Rommel, "but they will probably come with the British and some Canadian units. And when they come, it will be our last test. It'll be the test of our destiny."

Rommel's team labored two days at the port in Calais, France. There were several accidents involving exploding mines, which killed five top engineers. Still, the work continued until completion. Then, an infantry captain brought Rommel a map.

"Sir, I believe we've covered every point on this map," he said, running his finger over the penciled-in landmarks. "For every ten feet, they'll be an explosive device waiting for them. I wouldn't want to be sent to invade a beach like this!"

General Rommel took the map and smirked. It seemed impossible that any army would be able to advance through such traps, and yet he knew that eventually they would, despite the high costs.

"Captain," he said, "a remnant of the enemy may make it through, but even if they do, it'll be their longest day."

A cat and mouse game continued for several months. Nazi reconnaissance aircraft took photos of the dummy war machines at the Dover beaches, then American and British intelligence units would sneak there at night and reposition their props to create an impression of troop mobilization. Every two weeks they would add more fake props to simulate the build-up of an invasion force. They would continue in this even after the true invasion took place.

It was early June, and General Eisenhower had been appointed Supreme Allied Commander of Europe. Lieutenant Horn had been promoted to captain. And plans for the largest amphibious invasion ever had been finalized. The Allies had broadened their base of support to include Canada and the Free French, while thousands of landing craft would be used to deliver troops to the shores of Normandy. The invasion would begin with overnight parachute and glider landings, massive air attacks, as well as naval bombardments. It would culminate in the land invasions of five beaches code named Juno, Gold, Omaha, Utah, and Sword.

Patton was becoming restless. He was tired of masquerading for a fictitious army. However, Operation Fortitude continued to work as many of the best German defensive units remained in Calais, France, awaiting an invasion. His orders therefore were to remain in Britain and avoid any public appearances. But though he was denied a role in the true invasion, Eisenhower wanted him to prep the US invasion forces before "D-day" in a private appearance. Since it would be their last briefing as a division, and Patton continued to consider them his men, he seized the opportunity. The same meeting hall where they had all chuckled in gathering the phony uniforms for make-believe photographs was now dead silent. The Third Army had become painfully aware of mortality.

Patton was still for a moment, and then walked slowly toward the platform to deliver his encouragement. The men were frozen, standing at attention. To many he now seemed bigger than life as he confidently sauntered to the middle of the stage like a big league baseball hero at bat, readying himself to slam a home run. He inhaled. Then he spoke.

"Be seated. Men, this stuff that some sources sling around about America wanting out of this war, not wanting to fight, is a load of hooey. Americans love to fight, traditionally. All real Americans love the sting and clash of battle. You are here today for three reasons. First, to defend your homes and your loved ones. Second, you are here for your own self-respect, because you would not want to be anywhere else. Third, you are here because you are real men and all real men like to fight. When you, here, every one of you, were kids, you all admired the champion marble player, the fastest runner, the toughest boxer, the big league ball players, and the All-American football players. Americans love a winner. Americans will not tolerate a loser! Americans despise cowards. Americans play to win all of the time. I wouldn't give a hoot for a man who lost and laughed. That's why Americans have never lost nor will ever lose a war; for the very idea of losing is hateful to an American. Now, you are not all going to die. Only two percent of you right here today would die in a major battle. So death must not be feared. Death, in time, comes to all men. Yes, every man is scared in his first battle. If he says he's not, he's a liar. Some men are cowards, but they fight the same as the brave men, or they get the heck slammed out of them watching men fight who are just as scared as they are. The real hero is the man who fights even though he is scared. Some men get over their fright in a minute under fire. For some, it takes an hour. For some, it takes days. But a real man will never let his fear of death overpower his honor, his sense of duty to his country, and his innate manhood.

"A man must be alert at all times if he expects to stay alive.

If you're not alert, sometime, a German is going to sneak up behind you and beat you to death. There are four hundred neatly marked graves somewhere in Sicily, all because one man went to sleep on the job. But they are German graves, because we caught the b----s asleep.

"My men don't surrender, and I don't want to hear of any soldier under my command being captured unless he has been hit. Even if you are hit, you can still fight back. Don't forget, you men don't know that I'm here. No mention of that fact is to be made in any letters. The world is not supposed to know what happened to me. I'm not supposed to be commanding this army. Let the first fools to find out be the Germans. Someday, I want to see them rise up and howl, 'oh no,' it's the Third Army again and that, Patton.

"Sure, we want to go home. We want this war over with. The quicker they are whipped, the quicker we can go home. The shortest way home is through Berlin and Tokyo. And when we get to Berlin, I am personally going to shoot that paper hanging Hitler, just like I'd shoot a snake!

"War is a bloody, killing business. You've got to spill their blood, or they will spill yours. So *you* rip them up the belly. Shoot them in the guts. When shells are hitting all around you and you wipe the dirt off your face and realize that instead of dirt it's the blood and guts of what once was your best friend beside you, you'll know what to do!

"Now, I don't want to get any messages saying, 'I am holding my position.' We are not holding anything. Let the Germans do that. We are advancing constantly, and we are not interested in holding onto anything, except the enemy's jugular. Our basic plan of operation is to advance and to keep on advancing regardless of whether we have to go over, under, or through the enemy. We are going to go through him like dung through a goose. From time to time there will be some complaints that we are pushing our people too hard. I don't care about such complaints. I believe in the old and sound rule that an ounce of sweat will save a gallon of blood. The harder *we* push, the more Germans we will kill. The more Germans we kill, the fewer of our men will be killed. Pushing means fewer casualties. I want you all to remember that. There is one great thing that you men will all be able to say after this war is over and you're home once again. You may be thankful that twenty years from now when you are sitting by the fireplace with your grandson on your knee and he asks you what you did in the great World War II, you *won't* have to say, 'Well, your granddaddy shoveled manure in Louisiana.' No, sir, you can look him straight in the eye and say, 'Son, your granddaddy rode with the Great Third Army and that son-of-a-gun named Georgie Patton! That is all!"

33

THE CRESCENDO

It would be the largest invasion armada in world history. On a full moonlit night, roughly five thousand warships and amphibious transports moved stealthily across the English Channel for Normandy, France. What was once Operation Overlord was now D-day, and once publicized, churches all across the western Allied nations would call for their members to pray and fast.

It would begin on June 6, at roughly 6:30 a.m., not six o'clock, as certain commanders were aware of ominous numerology involving the number six in triple digits. As the numbers 666 were understood to represent a cursed satanic symbol, commanders would hold back any bombardments until at least half past the hour. For the record, commencement would begin on the sixth month, the sixth day, and thirty minutes past the sixth hour. The complete invasion fleet required warships from eight different navies. Out of the 2,468 major landing vessels, three hundred or so were American. Of the twenty-three cruisers that were to cover the landings, about seventeen were from the Royal Navy. The Allied forces had formed a 'do or die' alliance, unlike the fragile bonds between the Germans and Italians. This brotherhood would cement their resolve to capture the five beachheads. However, at this time, only a few servicemen were sure where they were going.

"It can't be another dry run," said a Third Army staff sergeant. "Look at all of those ships on our port side! I tell ya, it's the real thing!"

"Brother, I've heard that so many times I don't know what to think anymore," said a chief master sergeant. "But if it's the real thing, let's hope that we catch the Germans asleep."

"It's the real thing, Sergeant," said Captain Horn, who happened to overhear their conversation, "but I don't know if they'll be sleeping. You remember what 'Ol' Blood and Guts' said about catching them asleep in Sicily, don't you?"

"Yes, sir."

"Well, I'm sure they've learned their lesson."

"Yes, sir," responded the chief master sergeant.

A Nazi pillbox overlooking a beach on Normandy was armed and ready for action. Four soldiers were on a routine night watch and had already consumed a half-gallon of coffee to remain awake. There were conflicting reports of enemy aircraft in the area, but all they had heard was the crashing of waves along the shoreline and the drizzle of rain atop their cement pillbox. They were anticipating their replacements to arrive within forty-five minutes.

"Any ships that try to get through these mine infested waters wouldn't stand a chance. The explosions would wake the whole division up, and they'd all be here in ten minutes," said a corporal.

"So what's your point?" asked his superior.

"So why do we still need these night watch rotations? Everyone knows they're going to hit Calais, anyway."

"We still can't be too sure about that," said his superior. "Maybe they'll split the invasion between here and Calais. And when the tide is low out there, the enemy would be able to see those floating mines and maneuver around them. You could sail right up to the beach without making a sound."

The third lookout guard picked up his binoculars to make a routine check of the shoreline as dawn was just beginning to break and visibility was improving. He fixed his focus on maximum range and thought he could see silhouettes behind the fog. They appeared as large grayish blocks, which would disappear and reappear from behind the dense mist.

"What do you see?" asked the corporal.

"I can't make anything out, sir, the fog is, oh no!"

"What, what is it?"

"It's them! They're coming! Sir, they're coming. There must be thousands of them. There are ships as far as the eye can see. This can't be possible!"

The corporal ran over and grabbed his binoculars. Then he yelled, "Alert the command post, quickly."

As one of the guards jumped across the cement floor to reach the phone, there was a tremendous explosion thirty feet away, which knocked them off their feet. Then the shelling increased. The bombardments continued one after the other, rocking their outpost and spraying sand hundreds of feet high. An alarm was sounded, and Nazi soldiers scrambled all along the embankment to take their positions behind their big guns.

"There can't be that many," gasped the corporal, still in unbelief. We'll never be able to hold them off. We wouldn't have enough ammunition. Get the command post to contact the Fuhrer. He needs to send at least ten Panzer divisions down here.

"That can't happen, Corporal," said their superior. "We are under strict orders to not disturb him as he sleeps."

"What!"

The Allied landing craft, attached to the sides of the mother ships, were now filled to their capacity of thirty men and ready to be lowered into the water. The mother ship cruisers were ten miles from the shoreline, and everyone could hear the distant return of enemy fire.

It would have normally taken roughly thirty minutes to reach the shore once they were detached in the sea. However, today the water was extremely choppy, setting them off schedule. The Higgins landing craft heaved from side to side with every wave, causing most of the men to become seasick. They had to use their helmets to catch their own vomit before pouring it over the side. Then they washed out their helmets using the seawater settled on the floor of the vessel. They were wet, shivering from the cold, frightened, and seasick. And now they could hear the rapid tapping of machine gun rounds against their vessel.

"We have twenty-five seconds to landing, sir," said the pilot of the vessel to the squad leader in command.

Nerves were frayed. The craft eventually ran into shallow sand bars, prompting the draw bridge door to be lowered. Then a hail of German MG 42 caliber machine gun rounds showered the craft, fatally mowing down the first group even before they could jump out.

"Let's go! Climb over them. Move! Move!" shouted a first sergeant in the group. The rest of the men jumped out and clamored their way to shore. Bombs exploded beside them. Bullets popped in the water all around them, and by now, land mines were being tripped on the beach as men from other craft were making their embarkation.

The Allied landing forces had to scramble up to 400 yards against bombs and a spray of MG 34 and 42 caliber machine gun fire, which crisscrossed up and down the beaches. For the Nazi gunmen on the cliffs, shooting the first wave of invaders was like shooting fish in a barrel. But still, they kept coming.

In Berlin, General Rommel and a secret gathering of high ranking SS officers made sober calculations. They concluded, after reviewing the Russian advancement in the east along with the Allied landings in Normandy, that their defeat would be inevitable. However, surrendering would be impossible without first eliminating Hitler. Therefore, they plotted and schemed.

"We know that if we don't eliminate him, he will bring us all to ruin—this is sure!" said Rommel.

"This is a very risky business," said another officer. "I am in agreement with you, but do you realize how many attempts have been made on his life, and have failed. Maybe he does have some kind of special power coming from someplace."

"Whatever power he has will have to be overcome by our diligence. We have no other choice now. He's sending old men and boys to the front lines to die for the Fatherland. What type of society will we have left when the Allies finally break through and massacre them?" said another officer.

"Listen, it's already been decided," interrupted Rommel. "I once thought that such an act would incite a civil war, but I now realize that it could save Germany. Lieutenant Colonel Claus von Stauffenberg is our key player. He's the one to do the job."

Lieutenant Colonel Stauffenberg had been appointed chief of staff in central Berlin. He thus was able to attend Hitler's military conferences and work close enough to him to be able to initiate a plan of assassination.

Their plot was fully prepared by the month of July, and it was simple. Stauffenberg was to attend Hitler's conferences carrying a bomb in his briefcase. According to the plan, he was to place the briefcase in Hitler's conference room after activating a timer, nonchalantly excuse himself from the gathering, wait for the explosion, then return to Berlin by airplane and join the other plotters. After the assassination, the Reserve Army would take control of Germany, and head Nazi leaders would be arrested.

On the day of the conference, more than twenty high-ranking officers filled the room. As the proceedings began, Stauffenberg excused himself to use the bathroom in an adjoining office.

While there, he used pliers to crush the tip of a pencil detonator that had been inserted into a block of plastic explosives. The detonator was a copper tube that contained acid that would take roughly ten minutes to eat through to a wire. Once the wire was eaten through, a chain reaction would trigger a firing pin and set off the bomb.

Stauffenberg was summonsed to quickly return to the meeting, so he reentered the room and placed his briefcase under the table next to Hitler. Within five minutes the phone rang.

"Hello?" an officer answered.

"Yes, I need to talk with Colonel Stauffenberg. Is he attending the meeting?"

"Just a minute," he responded.

The officer beaconed to Stauffenberg with his arm. When he arrived he was handed the receiver.

"This is Colonel Stauffenberg."

"Is everything in order, Colonel?" the voice whispered. "Yes, yes right away. I'm leaving now," responded Stauffenberg with a rehearsed air of graveness. He then hung up, explaining that he couldn't stay for the remainder of the meeting and would have to be briefed later. He left immediately. After nearly four minutes, an older colonel, standing next to Hitler, used his foot to slide the briefcase aside, unwittingly pushing it just behind the leg of the conference table. Then the bomb detonated with an enormous explosion, blowing off the leg of the colonel next to Hitler. Three officers and a stenographer were killed. The room was demolished, but those who had been standing in front of the conference table leg were shielded from the blast. Hitler suffered only minor arm injuries and a perforated eardrum.

34

PATTON'S RETURN

He was back, and the situation needed his skill, brashness, and insight. The final waves of Allied invaders had advanced beyond the beaches and were deep into Normandy when they were halted and hemmed in by the bushy hedgerows. There was a maze of hedgerows throughout the plains. Spotting the enemy or running them down was nearly impossible in the tanks until a clever sergeant made use of the metal barriers that the Nazis had placed along the beaches. He created the "rhino tank," which was an ordinary tank with sharpened metal forks welded to its front. The forks enabled it to cut through hedgerows with little difficulty. The spontaneous invention was estimated to have saved ten hundred lives, and Patton was ecstatic about the adaptability of his men. It reminded him of how Charles Martel of France galloped into battle leaping over obstacles with the Longinus in hand during the early 700s. The enemy now was on the run, but they would need his leadership to drive them completely out of Normandy.

Patton continued to lead the Third Army from the south as British, French, Canadian, and Polish units advanced from the west. They sped through villages in their tanks, aided by superior air power, and drove the Fifth Panzer tank division eastward. In two weeks, the Third Army advanced farther and faster than any army in the history of war. A German field marshal asked Hitler for permission to fall back in order to regroup. However, Hitler insisted that there be no retreat. Though they were losing ground, he believed in their superiority and trusted they would drive the Allies back toward the sea. He was beginning to lose touch with reality and believed that his field marshals were conspiring to negotiate a surrender with the Allies.

The Nazis made a last stand at the city of Falaise, but the Allies surrounded them, squeezing ninety thousand troops into a pocket and forcing them to retreat. Fifteen thousand were killed, and the Panzer division lost 94 percent of its armor. Taking heavy casualties, Falaise was liberated from the enemy, and the final phase of the battle for Normandy was complete.

General Eisenhower and Patton both wanted to continue the momentum and rush into Germany. However the question of liberating Paris now loomed over Eisenhower's head. The people of Paris had waited four years to be liberated, and now heard that the Americans were coming in their direction. Exiled citizens, who were hiding in the outskirts, made their way into the city to prepare to fight alongside the Allies. The Free French resistance militia was gathering ammunition, and parts of the German armies were slowly beginning to evacuate the city.

Hitler had sent strict orders to leave Paris in ruins. The Eiffel Tower was to be blown up and used as an entanglement to block advancing Allies. The Arc de Triomphe was to be blown up as well. However, his commanders found little time to arrange such plans.

General Charles de Gaulle was commanding the Free French forces and called Eisenhower to ask him to divert his forces to Paris. He also warned him that if the Allies didn't liberate the city, he would do it on his own.

"We are too close now to turn away," said de Gaulle. "There are still Nazi terrorists there, and my army would be able to do the job on its own, but we would like for you to help us."

"Okay, listen, you take your forces into the city and engage the enemy. I will divert a portion of my forces to help you, but most of them are going to Germany with Patton. We can't afford to get bogged down in liberating this city and committing units to stay and police the place. It's too early for that," said Eisenhower.

American army units fought alongside French resistance from house to house in firefights. In time, the German commander of Paris was taken prisoner without resistance and he signed a formal surrender agreement. Despite the continuation of sporadic fighting on the outskirts of Paris, General de Gaulle entered his city in a triumphal procession. French women showered their liberators with hugs and kisses. Victory dances were held in the streets and public squares. Paris was free after four years.

Captain Horn and his small team of interpreters had been kept away from the frontlines. Though they wanted to fight, they were constantly reminded of their mission, which was to interrogate captured Germans for vital strategic information and relay messages to Allied intelligence in London; the US Army could not afford to have them injured. They had to follow in the footsteps of Allied forces throughout major battles and talk with captured or dying German soldiers, many of whom were too young to offer any substantive information, though some were sincere in their apologies about the war and their conquests. Some others were still hateful toward the Allies and maintained their "super race" attitude, even in the face of a humiliating defeat. Others had lost their minds from battle fatigue, but no one offered strategic help for the Allies to invade Germany and bring the war to a quick end.

They entered the outskirts of Paris with high expectations of questioning key prisoners. Paris had been a Nazi-controlled city for years, where official pipelines of German intelligence were established by Hitler himself. He had visited there with a personal entourage of officers. There was moreover an underground network of French resistance that could still prove to be helpful.

Horn and five men parked their jeeps in a region called Montrouge, just outside of the city, where they heard the distant sounds of bells tolling. They descended their vehicles.

"Will you listen to that?" said Horn.

"It's beautiful. Back at home, this is what Christmas morning sounds like," said his assistant.

The bells of Notre Dame Cathedral and several churches in nearby parishes were tolling continually. Car horns were honking, and crowds of people, young and old, were running toward the city. Yet, at the same time, one could hear the crack of gunfire. They were not celebratory shots, but rapid fire.

"They haven't cleaned out all their wasp nets yet," said Horn.

"They're still enemy soldiers here making a last stand."

All of the men then checked their weapons to be certain they were fully loaded.

"Why do they do that?" asked a young lieutenant on the team. "Don't they know it's a lost cause—might as well give up and wait in Paris 'til the war ends."

"They're fanatics," replied Horn. "They don't know what it means to surrender. These are the types that Hitler wanted, and these are the types that we need to question and break down. These kind are usually the most informative when they break." The five men climbed into their jeeps and began to drive down side streets in first gear. It felt different to drive over cobblestone roads after traveling hundreds of miles through dirt roads. They watched the tops of buildings for any suspicious signs of snipers, though they could tell that all signs of belligerence had ceased on this side of town.

As they approached a hilltop, they could see Paris in the distance. The Eiffel Tower loomed high, as beautiful as ever, and the great boulevard, the Champs-Élysées, was swollen to capacity with festive gatherings.

"What do you say we stick around for a while and take a break, Captain?"

"We have a rendezvous, Corporal. There's a major prisoner holding facility not far from the town center, and we need to get there now. Sorry, no time for champagne and romance for us."

They proceeded into the city, stopping periodically to wave at small crowds that waved and threw roses at them. Captain Horn ordered the driver to proceed at five miles per hour, saying he wanted to be sure not to hit anyone. Everyone suspected however that he also wanted to linger a while in heroic glory amid the cheering crowds.

When they reached the address of the prisoner holding facility, they were surprised at its actual location. The US military police had sectioned the area off with a barricade, but the facility was underneath the Arc de Triomphe where the Nazis had made prisoner torture cells for the French resistance. Evidently, not very many local people knew of its existence.

When a US military police guard saw Horn and his team, he called them over.

"Are you the team of interpreters from the Third Army?" he asked.

"Yes, I'm Captain Horn."

"Bring your men this way."

The men descended through what had appeared to be a subway entrance just feet away from the Arc de Triomphe. There was an overwhelming smell of sulfur in the thick air.

"What was this place, sergeant?" asked Horn as he descended.

"Believe it or not, the Nazis used these underground chambers 1to torture people. There are human remains all around here. We thought there'd be no better place to hold them for questioning." Sixteen bedraggled looking German soldiers were standing at attention when Horn's team descended. The team observed them closely; they appeared to be young and all but one bore a low-ranking insignia on his coat sleeve. A long processing table had been prepared for questioning with notepads, pencils, and cups of water.

"Okay, boys, you know what we're after," he said to his team. "I want you to pair up and talk to one soldier at a time. We need to get any information about troop formations in Germany, production plants, and anything else we might need to tell intelligence." The team members sat down at the tables, and the guards escorted the prisoners one by one to be questioned. Horn directed a guard to escort the higher-ranking soldier to sit in front of him.

"What's your name, soldier?" asked Horn.

"Fritz."

"Fritz what?"

"Fritz Henkel"

"Fritz, I'm Captain Horn, and the reason why I speak German so well is because I'm German too. But I left Germany because of that idiot you call the Fuhrer."

"Yes, I noticed that your accent was perfect—not like the others."

"Fritz, I'm sure you know that this war is finished, don't you?"

"Yes, sir. I do."

"Good. Then you can help us bring it to closure so we can all go home and rebuild our lives, right?"

"Yes, sir."

"Good. What was your job in the military, Fritz?"

"I was an assistant for Hitler's architectural bureau."

"Architectural bureau? Why would Hitler be interested in the architecture of Paris?"

"Well, Hitler really didn't run the bureau, sir, it was Albert Speer. He was sent here after the invasion."

"I know of this man. He was Hitler's chief architect, wasn't he?"

"Yes, sir, he was sent here to get ideas for Berlin. Hitler told him that he wanted Berlin to be better than Paris. I think he said he wanted it to be another wonder of the world or something. So they started a small office here after the invasion."

"What did you do in the office?"

"Anything that Speer wanted, sir. But then he was called back into Germany to be a part of war production, so I was allowed to stay here and wait for his return."

"So you should know where the main cities of munitions production are?"

"Yes, sir, Hamburg and Dresden, sir. Those are the main ones, and there is something going on in Nuremburg, but I'm not sure what it is."

"There's a production plant in Nuremburg? I would never have thought that."

"No, sir, I don't think that it's a munitions production site. Speer was called to design a type of stadium there, and he also worked on a project for underground air conditioning. I think it was for storage."

"For storing bombs, perhaps?"

"No, no, not bombs. It was a place to store things. They put some soldiers on detail to carry things into this building, and they had to walk one hundred feet underground to put them there. I think they were stolen jewels and artifacts from Belgium."

"And perhaps an ancient spear from Austria?"

"I don't know about. Well, there were things from Austria, now that you mention it. And it's funny, because I remember hearing jokes about how Speer had the spear. I never thought anything of it."

Captain Horn stared at the prisoner. No other questions came to his mind.

"May I go now, sir?" he asked. "Yes, yes you may. Thank you."

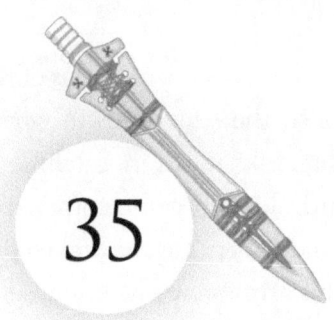

35

THE LAST ATTEMPT

Paranoiac impulses began to plague his mind, and he felt that even the walls of his vast office were beginning to close in on him. There would be no more time for the propaganda of goose-stepping parades. The war on two fronts, Russia and Britain, was more than enough to rob him of sleep, rest, and concentration, but now the war was on three fronts—Russia, Britain and Germany's front door, the Siegfried line. Patton had advanced from northern France to the border of Germany and was anxious for a new battle to finally get close enough to personally shoot Hitler and take the Longinus.

American and British infantry units that had advanced into northern Europe were bogged down by the snow. They settled in Flatzbourhof, Luxembourg, near the Ardennes forest, to rest and regroup as there was little German resistance there. Many had arrived by the Belgium port of Antwerp, which became a major supply line for the Allies. Hence, Hitler's last realistic attempt to defeat the Allies was formed. If he could drive a wedge between the Allies in Luxembourg and Belgium, that would allow him to capture the port of Antwerp and keep further Allied supplies from entering Europe—then he could restrategize a plan for the Eastern Front.

He decided to send twenty divisions of King Tiger tanks to Belgium in order to ambush the Americans in what would become the Battle of the Bulge. The tanks rolled in, catching the American 101 airborne division off guard. They became cornered in a city named Bastogne, and seven thousand Americans were taken prisoner just south of the city.

Patton and his army were one hundred miles away when an urgent call came through his field radio operated by a unit captain.

"Sir," said the captain, "it's from the command post. You're summonsed for an important meeting in Verdun."

"Captain, tell them that I am in a firefight right now, and we're about to head into Germany."

"Yes, sir." The captain responded as instructed and communicated the message. Then the reply came.

"Sir," the captain reported, "General Eisenhower himself says to be over here by tomorrow morning."

Frustrated, Patton called his troops to fall back and regroup. Though he was ready to invade Germany, he knew better than to initiate this invasion without approval. He suspected that Eisenhower would probably order him now to take a slightly different plan of action. He traveled to Verdun.

General Eisenhower, General Patton, General Bradley, General Jacob Devers, Major General Sir Kenneth Strong, and Deputy Supreme Commander Arthur Tedder attended the meeting along with a host of staff members. Eisenhower led the meeting, describing it as an opportunity rather than a quagmire and needed creative input.

"The one-hundred-and-first division doesn't have much time at all," he said. "More snow is forecast for the coming weeks, and they'll be running short on supplies." He then turned to Patton and asked, "George, how long would it take you to send three divisions up there to launch a counterattack?"

"Well, I've already worked out a plan for a counterattack. I had already anticipated that this type of scenario might happen. I could be there in two days."

Some generals chuckled, others laughed, but Eisenhower was shocked. "Don't be fatuous, George. If you go that early you won't have all the divisions ready, and you'll have to go piecemeal. You're one hundred and forty miles away."

"General, I can deliver three full divisions to that hostile area by December twenty-first, just watch me!"

"Nonetheless," interrupted Eisenhower, "I'm ordering you to attack on December twenty-second, and you will stay in close communications with the British command."

"I hear you. Don't worry about us," he reassured. "We'll be there on the twenty-second as expected."

When the meeting was over, Patton strode outdoors and found a field telephone. He picked it up to make a call. When he contacted his command, he simply uttered the words, "play ball," which was a code phrase meaning that they were to mobilize three divisions according to his plan. Two infantry divisions and one armored division mobilized for the rescue mission.

He became the perfect maestro. He determined which routes would be best, calculated the amount of fuel they all would need, and knew the minimum number of miles they had to cover in a day. He was energized. He decided to dedicate the mission to his ultimate objective by ordering the tank divisions to organize in the form of a giant spear, with several lead tanks aligning themselves to form the shape of a spear tip as they rolled. A single file of tanks followed.

They journeyed through the arduous forest area for a day. Then their worst fears began to crystallize; plummeting temperatures brought them to a standstill. It was the worst weather to hit the area in twenty years. Heavy rains produced ice and visibility became nearly impossible. Guns froze. Snow banks prevented forward motion, and tanks slid.

"We're on a timetable," Patton said to his division leaders. "We've got to find a way to get to Bastogne by the twenty-second of December, and I don't care how cold it gets! Now I want you men to start thinking. Let's get some ideas going."

"Sir, we could use the flame torches to melt some of that ice out there. Maybe that'll help us get some time back," said one captain.

"That's good, Ted, but I don't think we'll be able to melt that ice long enough to get all our tanks through before the roads freezes up again. Then we'd have to face the problem of being separated."

"The only thing I can think of is prayer," said a major. "If God controls everything, why can't we simply go to Him and ask Him to stop this bad weather?"

Patton was silent. He looked at the major and was impressed with the boldness of such a request. He then started to nod his head affirmatively.

"Tell Chaplain O'Neill to get over here," he said.

Colonel O'Neill was in the process of meeting with army members waiting in their vehicles for orders to head out. He was praying for those who were currently suffering over trench foot disease and took personal requests for loved ones back home. When he was summonsed to see Patton, he worried that the general had been taken ill. He hurried to their makeshift tent.

"Colonel O'Neill reports as ordered, sir," he said upon entering with a salute.

"Colonel, if this weather doesn't break, it may cost many lives for the men in the one-hundred-and-first. I want you to compose a battle prayer for us. Then I want you to distribute this prayer to our troops so that we can all pray in the same mind. Do you understand?"

"Yes, sir. I understand."

Patton then turned his back to him and suddenly became solemn. The colonel had never seen him this way before. His tough, impressive six foot two body now softened in demeanor, becoming less noticeable than the heart that it enshrined.

"Colonel?" the commander said, turning around. "I'm a firm believer in prayer, and I believe that we don't pray enough. Those who pray do more for the world than those who fight. Urge all of your men to pray, not alone in church, but everywhere. We need to pray while driving and pray while fighting. Pray alone and pray with others. Pray by night and pray by day. Pray for the cessation of these immoderate rains, for good weather for battle. Pray for victory, pray for our army, and pray for peace. And remember this, Nazi tyranny will be defeated by the might of the Third Army and Allied forces, but evil will be put back in place and defeated through prayer. Okay, now that I've given you a little direction on this matter, go work on that prayer so we can come before God corporately."

The chaplain departed and secluded himself for roughly forty-five minutes. He composed what he was sure to be an acceptable prayer for his general. It was brief but solemn:

"Almighty and most merciful Father, we humbly beseech Thee, of Thy great goodness, to restrain these immoderate rains, with which we have to contend. Grant us fair weather for battle. Graciously hearken to us soldiers who call upon Thee that, armed with Thy power, we may advance from victory to victory and crush the oppression and wickedness of our enemies, and establish Thy justice among men and nations. Amen."

The prayer was distributed as a Christmas prayer. And when the weather cleared soon after, Colonel O'Neill was immediately awarded a Bronze Star by Patton himself. They would continue to pray throughout their days in battle, and their prayers would carry them all the way to the end until wickedness was crushed. Pretty powder-blue skies, mild temperatures, and perfect visibility were set before them. Despite their wet combat jackets and soggy socks, all the men were encouraged and anxious to get to Bastogne.

TheyadvanceduntiltheyweremetbyaGermancounterattack, which bogged them down, and consequently, set them back. Yet still they persevered and overcame. By December 23rd, Patton's conscience was heavy. He had promised to arrive on the 22nd, but could not make good on his word. Soldiers in the 101st were doing all they could to survive and fight off the advancing enemy in Bastogne. Major William

Westmorland had expected to be in Berlin by this time and reluctantly called upon the wounded in his squad to take firing positions.

"Okay, boys," he said, "the bad weather gave us a little break for a while 'cause the enemy couldn't see us. But they're advancing again through those forests out there. We've got to hold them until help gets here. We still control the skies, and I expect air support will be on its way soon, but until then, keep firing. Shoot at anything that moves out there."

'Westy' Westmorland was an artillery officer from South Carolina. He had the reputation of showing care for his men even when he needed them to respond to urgent situations. However, now it was becoming increasingly difficult to lead them. He heard rumors that some of them wanted to surrender. He had been told about the enemy's offer to allow the division to surrender and was glad his commanding general, who was also pinned down, rejected it, but now they had to accept that this might be a fight to the death.

"Corporal Miller," said Westmorland, "I want you to sneak into the periphery and see if you can spot any signs of US tanks. Sending out a full squad would be too conspicuous, so you go alone and keep your head low. Report back here in two hours."

"Yes, sir," he responded.

The awaited miracle was beginning to break through. Though planes had been aloft since Christmas Eve, when Patton radioed that their "Christmas present" was en route, the P-47 fighter-bombers could now be heard drawing near. They were policing the skies mile by mile, in search for ground skirmishes while tank divisions pushed forward.

The tanks pushed and overcame ambushes by continually firing at the forests, never allowing the enemy to raise his head. And on Christmas Day, in an open clearing, they saw a lone soldier dressed in an American corporal's uniform. They took caution in observing him as there had been reports of English-speaking Nazi soldiers masquerading in the uniforms of fallen Americans.

The tank division leader raised the top of the turret to speak directly to him.

"I am from the US Fourth Armored Division," said the lieutenant, "Tell me who you are, or I will open fire."

The soldier responded, "I'm Corporal Miller from the One-hundred-and-first airborne. Thank God you're here."

36

IN THE FATHERLAND

A fter the Battle of the Bulge, the Nazis would have to fight for the Fatherland on the Fatherland, the strongest of strongholds. It was the very heart of Nazism, where Patton knew the dagger had to be thrust ever so ruthlessly. He expected heavy fighting would accompany the crossing of the Rhine.

As the Third Army pushed eastward, Patton grew ecstatic because they were marching in the historic footsteps of Caesar's Roman legions when they went to battle against the Huns. Only two things now were on his mind, conquering Berlin like Caesar, and seizing the spear.

They cut through German hills and valleys aided by maps that had been drawn by US aerial reconnaissance teams. They could see the great river from a distance. They looked desperately for a bridge to cross. They had already passed one that had been destroyed by the retreating Nazis.

Another bridge now came into view. Supply trucks were traveling over it, and hundreds of Nazi soldiers were marching, double time, to the eastern shore. The Third Army tank division crept up on them, and once within firing range, decided to attack. With their tanks firing, the division chased the retreating Germans over the bridge and onto the eastern shore.

They were only two miles away from the bridge before the enemy began to return fire from 88 millimeter guns, which were hidden along the shoreline. A massive barrage of defensive cannon fire would continue sporadically until the next day, thundering shells all along the riverbank. Then their guns suddenly fell silent.

Most tank operators identified this type of silence as an interval for reloading a cannon or allowing it to cool down. Infantrymen from Third Army units thus came out of their foxholes and began to walk toward an open clearing in the field. The lookout captain was focusing his binoculars at maximum range when he saw the bridge suddenly explode into the sky. It crumbled as a house of cards into the Rhine—no vehicle would be able to use it to cross into Germany. However, the momentum for the Allies resumed.

"All right, all right, we know what to do, men. I want twenty-four soldiers to cross this river in assault boats," said Patton to combat-support group leaders. "Let's get them going."

Twenty-four men were chosen to row across the river in small assault boats. Their mission was to paddle to the opposite bank and help construct a floatable pontoon bridge with the engineering unit. It would be the first time since the Napoleonic wars that an army used assault boats to cross the Rhine.

After the bridge was completed, the armored divisions began to roll onto the eastern bank. It was the story newsreels were waiting for; after four years of harassing and murdering their neighbors, Germany would now have to struggle to defend her own soil. As trucks rolled cautiously over the ten-foot wide bridge, military photographers that had been dispatched into the area snapped photos. Then newsreel photographers filmed the tanks creeping, one by one, to safety on the other side.

Patton directed his jeep driver to slowly take him across. When they arrived at the center of the bridge however, he made him stop.

"Is something wrong, sir," asked the driver.

"No, nothing's wrong. Just wait here," said Patton.

He then carefully stepped out of the jeep to approach the edge of the bridge. It appeared to his on looking commanders that he was preparing to dive in. But then they couldn't believe what they were seeing. He shocked everyone by unzipping his trousers and urinating into the Rhine. He then climbed back into the jeep, and when they arrived at the opposite side, he dramatically leapt to the ground and arose with his fists full of soil, shouting, "Thus, Frederick the Great."

The newsreel journalists later learned that he was referring to Frederick the Great of Prussia, who had a victorious moment in the 1700s; he claimed to have taken a nation with two hands after falling upon the land and grasping the soil in his fists. Patton was both ready to make and relive history.

History was also in the making on Germany's Eastern Front. Winter was melting into spring, and the hungry Red Bear was awakening from apparent hibernation. Four hundred thousand Soviet troops set out to charge into the heart of Germany with tanks, heavy artillery units, munitions trucks, and bright red flags bearing the hammer and sickle. German troops were forced to fall back. For every mile of conquered ground, the Russians waved their red flags proudly. Undoubtedly, the tide was turning. Soviet heroes and heroines were being made. There were rumors that Josef Stalin was demanding that Hitler's body be brought to him in Russia.

Ironically, the newsreels were presenting a mixed-message, suggesting that the Soviets did not only want to defeat the Third Reich, but claim new land for communist ideology. This both strengthened the German resolve to resist them and disturbed US politicians and high-ranking officers. There was mistrust growing against them.

Nonetheless, desperation was beginning to grow in Berlin as the Allies were beginning to increase bombing raids on industrial and now residential sectors. Any time the bomber pilots spotted a town that appeared to have a main highway, they unloaded bombs on it. Food stocks were plummeting, and people were beginning to spend more time in their cellars.

"My Fuhrer," said a Nazi field marshal during an emergency meeting, "the Russians have reached the city of Karlshorst, in the east. The only thing that was left for us to do was retreat. Most of the men fought to the very end, but we've lost that city."

Hitler's nervousness was producing delirium. Still wearing his now grimy official light green uniform, he appeared to be drowning, grasping at any remote possibility of a counterattack. His top generals were attempting to pay him their last respects by not making mention of any peace treaty with the Allies, but they knew they needed to force him to accept reality.

"General Steiner should be on his way to Berlin," said Hitler in an attempt to reassure himself. "You won't have to worry about Patton over there. Steiner should be able to drive the enemy back."

"But my Fuhrer," said another field marshal hesitatingly, "General Steiner doesn't have enough men now. He failed to make his assault. He was completely overrun."

Hitler screamed. "That can't be true! I gave him direct orders! I gave them to him myself! How can anyone dare to disobey my orders? You've been lying to me, all of you. You're all traitors and cowards. You tried to trap me, and you tried to kill me, but that couldn't work, and now you are trying to lie to me. Well, that won't work, either."

His generals glanced at each other to see who would dare to speak first. They were all filled with shame, sadness, and regret. The Fuhrer, who was once the larger-than-life symbol of an auspicious thousand-year Reich, was reduced to a humble, groveling, defeated shell of a man.

General Eisenhower had returned to France and was screening every update of the war's progress. He had spoken at length with Winston Churchill concerning a political plan for post-war Europe, and Patton's push toward Berlin. He was holding a secret discussion with a selected group of generals.

"It won't be long now, but what happens when Berlin falls? You think the Ruskies are just going to pack up and go home? Let me tell you brother, they're going to be there to stay. We will have defeated

Nazism only to replace it with communism—and they ain't much better!"

Eisenhower was pensive. He had already heard about the growing anxiety over the Soviets advancing in Germany and shared his thoughts with the president and joint chiefs of staff. Now he would share his intimate thoughts with his generals.

"I spoke with Patton yesterday," he said, "and I had to remind him that we are not at war with the Russians. We are not going to muddle things up right at the end of this war. Patton suggests that we not only push to Berlin, but once Berlin falls, he wants to drive the Russians back to Moscow and take that city too! Gentlemen, victory is too close. Communism is not our immediate threat. I don't want to hear of any field commander showing aggression or any disrespect to our Russian allies, no matter how many red flags they put up. When they hoist a flag, you just be sure to hoist the Stars and Stripes alongside of it and smile. I have decided to reassign Patton to keep him away from Berlin for the moment, and I may have to reassign some of you."

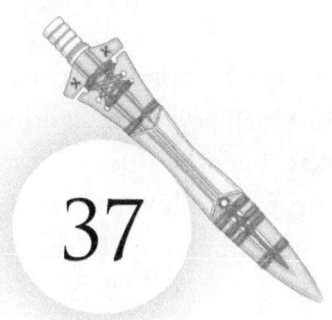

37

CAMPS AND CASTLES

Private Tommy Jakes was assigned to the 761 tank division called the black panthers. They were an African American tank unit that fought under Patton's command at the Battle of the Bulge and were now in central Germany, ready to invade Berlin with him. Jakes was always a joyful tank gunner. He was always sure to spit shine his ammunition shells before using them in combat. And he loved to whistle. He was singing and whistling a popular tune. "They'll be a hot time in the town of Berlin, when-the –Yanks-go-marching-in…I wanna be there, boy…and spread some jooooy…when we take ol' Berlin…"

Jakes was still singing and whistling as he worked on his tank, until he was interrupted by a combat buddy.

"Man, you can change that tune 'cause we ain't goin' to Berlin," he said.

"Are you crazy? What d'ya mean, we ain't goin' to Berlin? There's nowhere else to go! Once we take them out, were going home. Like the boss general said, 'the shortest way home is through Berlin.'"

"I'm telling you, we ain't going to Berlin."

Jakes put down his glad rag. "So you're telling me we've done all this fighin', we're now only three hours away from Berlin, and we're gonna go home?"

"No, Charlie said he overheard Ike telling the 'Old Man' that we'd be diverted to Austria. They're still fighting over there."

"Austria? Okay, but why turn away now when we're so close? It doesn't make sense. Especially when you know how the 'Old Man' feels about taking Berlin all by himself. They're keeping him from taking the prize."

Eisenhower and General Bradley were now talking with Patton at their camp in the city of Erfurt, roughly one hundred and forty-six miles from Berlin. Just as Patton was strategically poised to make a killer attack on the city, he was told of his reassignment to combat duty in Austria and Czechoslovakia. He knew that the glory of conquering Hitler's city would now go to the British and the Russians, and tears filled his eyes. He didn't argue. He didn't even speak for several minutes. Then he pulled himself together, reminding himself that he would eventually get there, and that nothing could change his destiny. He just wouldn't get their first.

The three generals ended their meeting and directed a combat unit to take them on a tour of the area. Eisenhower always insisted that, after combat, a task force needed to survey the region to be sure the wounded were cared for. Patton, Eisenhower, and Bradley were escorted by three armored vehicles and sixty infantrymen on a spontaneous tour of Erfurt's decimated townships. One such township was Ohrdruf.

While driving, they approached a clearing that appeared to be a type of parade ground. The trees had been cleared, and there were small huts along the side of a vast dirt field. As they drew closer, however, it became apparent that it was something more like a camp with barbed wire fencing. When they entered, they were immediately repulsed. The stench was horrific, and they recoiled in shock at the vomitus sight of roughly two hundred emaciated bodies strewn across the dirt. This was different from a battle scene. They had become accustomed to seeing the remains of fallen soldiers after heavy combat. Sometimes there were only body parts left, and sometimes hardly any body parts were discernible. But this was different; it was a living nightmare.

"Could it have been a clinic for the diseased?" asked a captain to General Bradley. "Look at those corpses! And why would they leave them in the dirt like that?"

A corporal approached Eisenhower.

"Sir, I think you should see this," he said. He then led him over to the center of the camp where a large iron grid structure had been laid. There was a huge pit covered by an iron grid over heaps of partially charred human bodies. The Nazis had executed their Jewish labor prisoners and attempted to incinerate them only hours ago.

Eisenhower was dumbfounded. "Boys," he said, turning to his men, "now you know why we're fighting this war."

"I don't know why the local authorities didn't do anything about this," said a captain.

"They probably didn't know," mumbled a lieutenant. "They couldn't have known about something like this without stopping it." Patton interrupted, "Well, they're going to know now." He then turned to Eisenhower and Bradley, suggesting that the local village residents be rounded up and made to walk through the camp. They were in unanimous agreement that it should be a punitive tour. They used military trucks to pick up the local town people from the town square. When they arrived, they walked them through some of the most horrific sites of the camp. Even the mayor and his wife were compelled to come, and most left feeling confused, incredulous, and guilty.

As the three generals departed the camp, they struggled to find the appropriate words to describe in their military journals what they had witnessed. The saddening sites of inhumanity would be etched in their conscience for the remainder of their lives. They all departed in silence.

It was April 30th, 1945. Patton's Third Army had been divided into units and support groups for battles at different fronts. Some accompanied him into Austria, others were sent to accompany Major Westmorland with the 101st division in Berlin, and others had to report to duty in Nuremberg, where the last pocket of resistance was holding out.

Nuremberg would be the city of the last great offensive during the war in Europe. It was the shrine of the Nazi party. All of the anti-Semitic laws were written and recorded there. Though Berlin was known to be the heart of Germany, Nuremburg was known to be its soul, and Hitler himself called it the most German of all German cities.

As a communication center, it was a connecting link between Munich and Berlin. As a transportation center, a superhighway called the autobahn allowed easy transportation of military hardware to be dispatched throughout Germany. In the heyday of the Third Reich, Nuremberg was the location of massive political rallies and book burnings. Now, parts of the city were still burning from Allied bombings, and much of it lay in ruins.

Thousands of Nazi soldiers retreated to Nuremberg from neighboring cities to hide in the massive amounts of rubble and carnage. Their general morale was low, but because of their fanatical love for the Fuhrer, resistance was strong. They were assembling now more as a militia than an organized force.

Captain Horn and two junior interpreters were directing a jeep driver through parts of the city using a handmade map. Interrogating prisoners however was not his priority now. He was attempting to locate an ancient church.

"It was here, driver. It had to be here," said the captain, referring to the map. He looked up but could only see rubble. Whole sectors of the city had been demolished, making it nearly impossible to find absolute locations.

"I thought the Geneva Convention made it against international law to bomb churches?" said the driver.

"It does," said the captain, "but how well do you think night bombers can see church steeples."

"Captain, look over there," said an aide pointing in the opposite direction. "Doesn't that look like a steeple?"

It was a burned-out building. Only the four walls remained, with a semblance of a steeple at one end.

"Let's go," said the captain.

They walked over to the skeletal structure of the church, which lay among ashes and broken glass. They walked over the concrete foundation, breaking bits of stained glass as they went.

"Captain, what are we looking for?"

"A relic."

"A relic of what?"

"Just tell me if you find anything that looks like an ancient relic or a box."

They all walked up and down on the concrete foundation, scouring the floor. They picked up charred remains of hymnals, melted candles, and tiles.

"Wait a minute," said the captain, "the prisoner said that it was placed underground, hundreds of feet underground. Look to see if there's a trap door here. Feel along the floor with your boots for a trap door."

They paced up and down the length of St. Katherine's church, dragging their feet to feel any separation in the concrete. Nothing.

As the jeep driver had patrolled parts of the city prior to Horn's arrival, he knew of another landmark location that remained intact. Allied bombs had not completely destroyed it, and it was on the other side of the Pegnitz River.

"Captain, there's the 'Castle of Nuremberg' in the middle of the city, and relics are known to be stored there. It's an old walled city with a dry moat, and there isn't any fighting going on now because the Allies drove the enemy out of there."

"Okay, let's go there," he said.

They sped through the town with the thundering sounds of artillery in the distance. Though mountains of ash and rubble had been neatly pushed to the sides of the streets, it nonetheless appeared to be as deserted as a distant planet. Several stone churches had been razed and gutted by night bombers, which accentuated the medieval castle's looming profile against the skyline.

"This gives me the creeps," said an aide. "Look at that castle. Who lives there, the hunchback?"

"It's the stuff Hollywood films are made of," said the driver, looking for a place to park his jeep. "You know I remember someone telling me that for hundreds of years, it was the headquarters of the Holy Roman Empire."

"Well, let's be careful in there," said the captain. "It looks strong, but that bomb damage could cause the walls to fall in."

The four men descended from the jeep, checked to see that their pistols were fully loaded, and made their way to the hilly front of the fortress. They hiked up through the dusty incline, avoiding fallen bricks and stones before reaching an opening in the side.

"Be careful, come through this way," directed the captain.

The castle had a high vaulted ceiling and Roman archways. It had the feel of both an enormous church and an enormous bathroom at a ritzy hotel.

"Hello? Anybody here?" said the captain's aide as they all stepped inside. There was no response. The men fanned out as if on field patrol. They crept through the cold barren room, kicking up the chalklike dust that was all over.

"Hey, I found something," yelled the jeep driver.

The men scrambled toward his echoing voice. He was looking down what appeared to be an internal well. The hole at the surface was six feet in diameter.

"If there's no water down there, this would be the perfect storage place," said the captain looking inside. "Someone, give me a rock."

His aide handed him a shattered piece of clay, and he dropped it into the hole. Seconds passed into what felt like minutes before they heard a splash.

"Now that's deep!" said the captain. "Look, the prisoner said that there were underground air conditioned rooms and vaults here, and judging by the depth of that well, there may be rooms over one-hundred feet deep. We've got to find a staircase."

They went from one room to the next looking for a stairwell. As the centuries-old castle had been built in stages, there were adjoining rooms of different architectural design. One could see the contrast in stone masonry by comparing the different types and shapes of brick that had been broken by the bomb blasts.

"Here, I found a stairwell over here, Captain," said an aide. A small doorway had been cut into the tower structure with a spiraling staircase. Each of the men stepped through and carefully began their descent. They circled around three times as they walked downward, now noticing the sudden drop in temperature.

"Why is it getting so cold?" asked the driver, still walking down slowly.

"Probably because we're below ground level," said the aide. "No, do you hear that?" asked the captain. "A motor is running. It's coming from that door down there."

They cautiously continued their descent before arriving at a level where they found a doorway. Dim light was spilling through the cracks, so Captain Horn took hold of his pistol and slowly pushed the door open, speaking in German. There was no answer. A small light bulb was suspended overhead with a cord that ran along the ceiling into the ceiling of an adjoining room. They could all hear now the loud hum of an air-conditioning unit.

"It's so cool down here you could probably store meat," said his aide. "What could they have possibly been doing down here."

"I'll tell you what they were doing," said the captain, "they had to keep the temperature down and control humidity to protect the kind of things we're looking for. We're getting close, but I don't see any storage sections around here," he said as he panned the walls with his eyes.

The ceiling light was bright enough to illuminate only the center of the small room. When the captain's aide stepped into the corner, he couldn't see where he was going and bumped into the wall, making it give way.

"Hey, the wall moved over here," he said as his voice resonated from within the shadows. "But I can't see anything."

"Stay right there," said the captain. He then spoke to his aide, saying, "Get down on your hands and knees so I can stand on your back. I'm going to tilt that light bulb up there so he can see what he's doing."

The jeep driver knelt on his hands and knees to allow the captain to climb on. Then he raised himself just enough to allow him to reach the ceiling light bulb and tilt it in his aide's direction. With enough light, the aide touched the wall again and a five-foot piece of it wobbled and fell toward him with a thud, leaving a small opening.

"There's something in there, Captain," he said.

"Well, go in there. I'll keep the light on you."

He stepped in halfway. The back part of his body was still visible, and it was clear that he was bending down to lift something. When he emerged from the shadows, he was carrying a slender one-foot box, extremely light but well enclosed. Captain Horn stepped down and they all surrounded the box.

"Step back," he said. He then began to pull the box apart slowly, strip by strip. A glowing light flashed from within it as he methodically striped pieces away. They knew that this must have been what he came for, and it now would be theirs. The captain hesitated before removing the largest piece of wood. He bent the very tip upwards and quickly pried it off, sending a shimmering spearhead bouncing into the air, just before their eyes.

It landed back in the box, and the men gasped in awe, and at that very moment, in a bunker back in Berlin, Adolf Hitler put a gun to his head and desperately shot himself.

38

THE LONGINUS

It had finally ended in Europe. It was not a cease-fire, but an unconditional surrender. Church bells rang into the heavens.

Celebratory gunfire could be heard all around. Grown men and soldiers shed momentary tears of joy, and women cried over the loss of their loved ones, the return of their men, and the suffering of other women. Hitler was as dead as Napoleon, but so were fifty-five million people throughout Europe. The stench of decaying corpses would fill the air throughout the continent for months, and shallow graves could not be dug fast enough. But it was over. Finally, it was over. Evil had met its destiny in an act of moral righteousness that had been expedited by persistent prayers since the Battle of the Bulge. Though it would take decades to return the continent to some semblance of order and international cooperation, it was over. Finally, it was over. And celebrations would not cease for months.

Patton was still in Austria when his field radio indicated another incoming call. Eisenhower had just contacted him, requesting that he oversee an occupying military force in Berlin, to which he agreed. His staff answered the field telephone.

"This is the Third Army field division artillery battalion, go ahead."

"This is Captain Walter Horn from Third Army in Nuremberg, and I need to speak with General Patton, ASAP."

"Yes, sir," he said.

The aide walked over to Patton and handed him the receiver. "This is Patton, go ahead."

"Sir, this is Captain Horn. I had to contact you to let you know I've got it. We located the item in Nuremberg at the suspected location."

"Good. Didn't think we'd hear from you in a while! Listen, I'm going to arrange for you to have it loaded on a C-47 cargo plane and sent right here to Austria."

"Sir, we found a host of other things, too."

"That's all right. Just put everything on the plane, and it'll arrive at our base camp here."

"Yes, sir."

He was still living in anticipation. Though the war in Europe was over, he knew his own destiny would not be complete until he took possession of the spear before going to Berlin. He felt there was unfinished business to tend to, and that the momentum of the Allied victory in Europe could now reach further heights. He worried about Russia and its global influence. Communism was no better than Nazism in his mind. Any institution that not only failed to acknowledge God in heaven, but defined Him out of existence, was as uncivilized as the deifying of Hitler. However, he would soon be able to take hold of the solution for such willful, dark imaginings and leave his mark on humanity. Europe had been saved once more by keeping the spear from a tyrant, first with Napoleon, now with Hitler. But questions remained. Patton knew that his decided plans for the Longinus were crucial, not only for world peace but for a new world order, and the war in Asia represented the last theater where the powers of righteousness needed to eradicate dictatorial rule.

As with Europe, there were two conflicts still plaguing Asia; militant Japanese imperialism, which showed no signs of letting up, and the threat of communism beginning to take root in China.

Friendly Chinese allies, such as Chiang Kai-shek, were not only battling the Japanese but had to fight communist antagonists in their own country. If Chiang Kai-shek could possess the spear, however, Asia could be secured. He could use it to both beat the Japanese army and protect against the forces of spiritual darkness in China, the type of darkness that denies the existence of God in political platforms. Though Europe now would probably be able to stamp out any resurgence of dictatorial rule and restrain the spread of communism, Asia was another case.

General George C Marshal was an Army chief of staff who was very interested in the Asian theater. He had arrived in Austria, at the captured air base, to meet with Eisenhower and now was discussing effective battle strategies with Patton.

"We need to understand more about the way those people think, George," said Marshall. "The Japanese military is not like the German military. Sure, they're disciplined and imperialistic, but they're more fanatical. The kamikazes are becoming a huge problem."

"So you don't think MacArthur is up to the challenge?" asked Patton.

"No, Douglas is doing a fine job down there. But to spare American lives, we're going to have to do something big. Those soldiers will die for their emperor. He's like a god to them. Our military has never had to deal with fanaticism like this before."

"Listen," said Patton, "do you really want to know how to fight a militant, religiously fanatical enemy?"

"Go ahead, I'm listening," said Marshal.

"With the power behind true religion, that's how."

"George, it's a little late to start sending in missionaries now."

"That's not what I'm talking about," he said. "Can I speak to you privately for a moment?"

"Sure."

The two walked outside in the open air. They stood opposite each other as Marshal took out a cigarette.

"I've got something I want to give MacArthur, and I believe it will be fruitful in helping to end the war in Asia."

"Is this classified, George? Does the war department know about this?"

"No! Those bureaucrats would be the first to foul things up."

"Well, then you can't send it to him. You know the regulations."

"What if I simply send it as a gift, as a personal gift to him?"

"Gifts and war souvenirs are treated differently, you know that. But any weapons of war cannot be counted as gifts. Just what are you getting at?"

"I would simply like to send my friend, General MacArthur, a personal gift that he can share with our allies in China, that's all," he said defensively.

"George, you know the regulations. If you're sending any weapons, you'd better talk with high command. You could be court-martialed otherwise."

In the middle of their conversation a duel-engine C-47 cargo plane began to descend onto the landing strip. Patton momentarily excused himself from the discussion, saying that he had to oversee its delivery.

For ground crew members on duty, there was nothing special about the landing of another cargo plane. When the propellers ceased turning, a side door was lowered, and two ground crew personnel approached the unfolding staircase.

"What'ya got?" yelled a crewmember to the co-pilot standing in the doorway.

"Oh, it looks like a load of furniture. There's a couple of boxes and picture frames wrapped up. This stuff's coming from the base at Nuremberg. Just send up four men."

"Got it," responded the ground crew sergeant on duty.

Four army supply workers were sent to collect the items and carry them into the aircraft hangar at the base. The large pieces were handled by two soldiers, one on each end. They were told to be very careful. The two men descended the plane with a large box, and two others descended with two large works of art, but one soldier went back and singularly brought two boxes. One was large and thin, and the other was small and wide.

Patton was waiting in the hangar, supervising the delivery and checking each box. When the ground crew member walked in with the two boxes, he stopped him. He knew the smaller box contained the spearhead, and the larger one contained the staff. He then carefully observed the cargo and found his name written on the brown wrapping paper signed by Captain Horn.

"You can put that down right here, private," he said.

"Yes, sir," responded the private in compliance.

Before the landing crew was able to walk back to the plane, sign a manifest, and depart down the runway, Patton slipped to the back of the hangar with the two packages. No one could see him as half of the facility was filled with parked military jeeps and boxes of field equipment. When he unwrapped the smaller box, he was awestruck by the aura of the spear. It was identical to the image he had studied in the manuscripts of Roman history back at Fort Meade. Then he put his hand underneath a jeep and slid out a package he had hidden. It was the duplicate spear. He was impressed at its uncanny resemblance as he laid them both side by side. The boys of the welding crew in B Company had followed his detailed instructions to the letter. Even the gold plated midsection appeared Romanesque. No one would know the difference between the real and counterfeit spear without carbon dating the metal in a laboratory. He thus repackaged the counterfeit spear with the wrappings of the original, and carried the boxes back to the loading zone where the other items had been laid.

Generals Eisenhower and Marshal were walking into the hangar with an entourage of selected military press members who were allowed to cover the story of stolen relics.

They only took pictures of the packages and were told to wait until the following day if they wanted to return to see the unveiling.

"George," said Eisenhower, "they finally got here, and it looks like there hasn't been any damage. I know how you feel about this shipment, but, as I said before, all things must go back to the museums from where they were stolen."

Patton silently nodded before Marshal interrupted.

"I was thinking about the gift you wanted to send MacArthur," he said with an air of confidentiality. "You know, I'm going to be stopping over at a remote base in Pyongyang Korea. The Chinese and Koreans have driven the Japanese out of that area, so we're going to have a three-day conference about a big development in munitions. If you want to, you can send me that gift, and I'll be sure MacArthur gets it."

"With the war still going over there, isn't it a little early for personal gifts?" asked Eisenhower.

"Oh, I don't mind," said Marshal. "And I think it'll be an encouragement to him anyway."

"All right, George, fine," said Eisenhower, "but we need you to report to duty in Berlin in two days.

"I'll be there," said Patton.

Patton and Marshal departed toward the officers' dining tent, leaving Eisenhower to talk with base security officers about the relics in the hangar. The two continued their discussion.

"They'll be a plane flying outta here after tomorrow to deliver field supplies to MacArthur's units in Asia. It'll stop in Cairo first and then continue to Pyongyang Korea. Put your package on that plane with the cargo, and Doug will have it in two days."

"Thank you, I'll have it addressed to him," said Patton. "Will you be flying out in the same plane?"

"No, I won't be going with any cargo. But it'll catch up with me. In fact, I'll wait for it if I arrive before it does."

The following day, Marshal departed on a circuitous route to Asia. He reassuringly shook hands with Patton, thanking him for sharing his insights on effective battle strategies that could be applied on the sandy terrains in Asia. Patton thanked him for being resourceful.

Trucks, jeeps, and field equipment were moved from the hangar to the cargo plane bound for Korea. Patton was sure to repackage the Longinus in excessive wrappings addressed to General MacArthur from 'Georgie' with a note inside. He thought no one would dare to open it if he knew it was a personal gift.

39

LONGINUS LOST

The following chain of events would ignite a series of reactions that would be felt well into the twenty-first century. When General Marshal arrived at his destination in Korea, he was told the terrible news. The cargo plane containing the field equipment and supplies—and Patton's gift—went down in a storm. Its last radio signal was identified while flying between the Chinese and Korean border. Japanese aircraft could have shot it down. Nothing had been recovered. Then, surprisingly, months later, two horrific bombs were dropped, one on Hiroshima and the other on Nagasaki, causing the Japanese emperor to admit defeat. He signed an unconditional surrender to the United States, officiated by MacArthur. However, by December, a roving group of Chinese nationals secretly spotted the wreckage of an American C-47 cargo plane along the Changbai Mountain Ranges between Korea and China. They took possession of every item that was left intact, including the packaged Longinus, and two seconds later, at 11:45 Greenwich meantime, in Germany, Patton had a freak car accident as his vehicle hit a swerving truck at an uncontrolled intersection. He died and was buried with his men in Luxembourg.

www.ingramcontent.com/pod-product-compliance
Lightning Source LLC
LaVergne TN
LVHW041754060526
838201LV00046B/994